MAKING IT WITH MUSIC

"Sweet Michael

How sweet it is

Thank You

Kenny Rogers

Making It With Music

KENNY ROGERS' GUIDE

TO THE MUSIC BUSINESS

By Kenny Rogers and Len Epand

1817

HARPER & ROW, PUBLISHERS
NEW YORK, HAGERSTOWN, SAN FRANCISCO, LONDON

For all our friends at various stages
of making it with music

Photo credits appear on page 219.

MAKING IT WITH MUSIC: KENNY ROGERS' GUIDE TO THE MUSIC BUSINESS. Copyright © 1978 by Len Epand and Kenny Rogers. All rights reserved. Printed in the United States of America. No part of this book may be used or reproduced in any manner whatsoever without written permission except in the case of brief quotations embodied in critical articles and reviews. For information address Harper & Row, Publishers, Inc., 10 East 53rd Street, New York, N.Y. 10022. Published simultaneously in Canada by Fitzhenry & Whiteside Limited, Toronto.

FIRST EDITION

Designed by Sidney Feinberg

Library of Congress Cataloging in Publication Data

Rogers, Kenny.
Making it with music.
   1. Music as a profession. 2. Music—Economic aspects. I. Epand, Len, joint author. II. Title.
ML3795.R66   658'.91'784   78–2164
ISBN 0–06–013598–0   78 79 80 81 82 10 9 8 7 6 5 4 3 2 1
ISBN 0–06–465091–X pbk.   78 79 80 81 82 10 9 8 7 6 5 4 3 2 1

Contents

Acknowledgments

If it's a cliché to say that this work wouldn't have been possible without the contributions of many, so be it. It's true. *Making It with Music* wouldn't have a foundation had Kenny not been given an understanding of music by Bobby Doyle and an understanding of the business of music by Kirby Stone, people with whom he respectively played and toured clubs in the early sixties. It wouldn't have gotten under way had Ken Kragen not pursued the idea and Michael O'Daniel not helped put us together, and had Peter Skolnik, our agent, and Harper & Row's Irv Levey not believed in the project.

And it wouldn't be as informed without the legal advice of attorneys Lanny Waggoner, Robert Freedman, and Dr. Ekke Schnabel, senior vice president of Polydor and Phonogram Records; the music publishing expertise of Chappell Music's Randy Talmadge; the views on performing rights of Intersong Music's Rick Riccobono (formerly of Broadcast Music, Inc.) and Screen Gems-EMI Music's Tad Maloney (previously with the American Society of Composers, Authors, and Publishers); and the remembrance of things past by former First Edition members Mike Settle and Kin Vassy.

Making It with Music furthermore wouldn't be as substantive without the record promotion philosophies of Dr. Gerald Jaffe, Polydor Records' promotion director, and Bill Brill, Ariola Records' singles promotion director; and without the artists and repertoire advice of Cliff Bernstein, A & R consultant for Polygram Inc; the marketing expertise of Sterling Devers, director of training for Polygram Distribution; and the library of *Billboard* magazine editor Alan Penchansky.

The book would also be lesser without the generosity of Geraldine Houston, who lent memorabilia from her younger brother's nascent career; the brainstorm of Polydor's publicity director Bob Sarlin, whose twisted little amendment to the title made all the difference in the world; and the overall support of author Suzanne Gordon.

Making It with Music may have reached print had Khloella Beaty and Kathy Honaker not transcribed and Judy Kidder not typed and proofread beyond any reasonable expectation, but it would have taken another miracle. In any case, the book wouldn't now appear in a form that satisfies us had not our editor, Jeanne Flagg, taken such care fine-tuning the manuscript.

At bottom, however, *Making It with Music* wouldn't have reached fruition without the contributions of two—Marianne Gordon Rogers and Joan Gilbertson Epand. They kept us at it and sane when the demands of writing and managing additional careers—Kenny a recording artist and Len a journalist and record company executive—seemed about to render us mad. Also sharing some responsibility for our effort are our parents, Edward Floyd Rogers and Lucille Rogers and Harold and Jacqueline Epand. They made us with music.

To those mentioned, and others we may have inadvertently overlooked whose help was just as indispensable, we offer our most sincere thanks.

KENNY ROGERS AND LEN EPAND

Introduction

> The weeks passed and nothing happened. They continued playing their local dates on Merseyside, but all the time expecting Decca to whisk them to the bigtime. Then . . . after a lot of pestering, Brian [Epstein] heard from Dick Rowe, Mike Smith's boss at Decca, that they had decided not to record the Beatles. "He told me [recalled Epstein] they didn't like the sound. Groups of guitars were on the way out. I told him I was completely confident that these boys were going to be bigger than Elvis Presley."
>
> HUNTER DAVIES, *The Beatles**

It's easy to look back at the Beatles and accept their existence and careers as given. Like other pop heroes of the era—the Beach Boys, Cream, the Rolling Stones, the Who—they came onto the scene fully blown, and for as long as they lasted, and longer, they held our imaginations. Yet it must be remembered that when the Beatles began recording they were only serviceably capable as musicians and singers. As a group they were magical, and far greater than the sum of their parts. (Their inconsistencies as solo artists after the group disbanded in 1969 seem to bear this out.) Through their late teens, however, they paid the proverbial dues heavily. They practiced constantly, borrowed techniques and tricks that would improve the act, and performed wherever they could earn a few coins—even though that meant working fifteen hours a day in roughhouse West German cabarets or in Liverpool's dank Cavern Club. They loved it.

But that still would not have been enough. In large measure they benefited from the firm, business-minded management provided by an intrigued record-store owner named Brian Epstein. To broaden their appeal to audiences and employers, Epstein refined their appearance, their rough working-class manners, and their undisciplined onstage performance. He knew how to generate and exploit publicity, and he used his contacts in the record industry, no matter how meager, to make his boys heard. The Beatles succeeded, in short, as much

---

*Dell, 1968, pp. 149–50.

through determination, persistence, and business savvy as through talent.

But what about those countless specific problems the Beatles encountered and solved to function as an entity in the music business? What steps can aspiring musicians take to improve the odds of achieving their goals?

Who should be in your group and what kind of sound do you want? What instruments and equipment should you buy? How do you choose or write material and arrange sets and staging for maximum effect? What is the most efficient way to rehearse and, once an act is together, how do you go about contracting band jobs? As important, how can you deal with club owners, managers, booking agents, and, later, music publishers and record companies without being taken advantage of? How do you best go about getting signed to a record contract and recorded? And, once a record is out, how do you promote it? Finally, having achieved success, how do you stay successful and not succumb to being just another broke flash-in-the-pan?

This is what was on Kenny Rogers' mind when we first met to talk about collaborating on a book. Rogers, as the former leader/singer/bassist of Kenny Rogers and the First Edition, one of the era's more successful—and lasting—pop groups, said that wherever he travels, young musicians approach him and talk about starting groups or ask how they might enlarge their group's stature beyond local club-party-dance confines. One day, after answering another series of questions, he told someone he'd send him a copy of his book. He was joking, but his manager, Ken Kragen, overheard him and thought that a book based on Kenny's experience might not be a bad idea. Later they discussed it. They got serious. Kragen called me.

The project was right up my alley. A music critic and feature writer, I was also an ex-professional rock musician. Like so many of my ilk, I had been captivated in 1964 by the dreams of rock stardom projected by the Beatles *et al.* on "The Ed Sullivan Show." The rest of the sixties found me fighting with my parents about haircuts and playing lead guitar with rock bands; in high school there was the Rayne and at the University of Wisconsin in Madison there were Portia and the Soul Kids, the Tayles, John Doe. None of my groups ever got signed to a record label, although a couple did come close, but it was enough to know the sorts of things amateur and professional pop musicians need and want to know and be attuned to the stories, knowledge, and wisdom Kenny would impart to me in more than thirty hours of interviews. The idea made even more sense for me as I became the West Coast publicity manager for Polydor Inc., in 1976 and then director of publicity, West Coast, in 1978. I could infuse the book with direct knowledge of the record business and make it as practical, authoritative, and lasting a reference work as possible by speaking with top specialists in the field: attorneys, booking agents, managers, music publishers, producers, and record promotion, artists and repertoire (A & R),* and marketing executives.

Kenny Rogers' career remains the book's unifying factor, however, and so all is told from his perspective. And well it should be. Kenneth Ray Rogers has experienced enough facets and levels of the music world for a dozen people. He has gone from bottom to top, from folk to jazz to rock to country/pop, from sideman to star of a hit group to owner of a record label (Jolly Rogers, now defunct), from has-been in 1975 to comeback sensation in the late seventies as a solo singer with chart-topping hit singles and albums. This easygoing, person-able, athletic, and youthful man, born in 1938, has been in professional music since 1956, when he enjoyed some local fame with a four-man vocal group of his Houston high-school friends called the Scholars. They put out several singles that made the Houston Top 10 ("Poor Little Doggie," "Spin the Wheel"), recording with Cue Records, a local minor-league label. After graduating, the Scholars disbanded and Rogers recorded a million-selling hit called "That Crazy Feeling" (produced by his brother Lelan on their own Kenlee Records label and distributed by Carlton Records), a hit that even got him an appearance on Dick Clark's "American Bandstand." Unfortunately, it was a lesson in how *not* to be a professional: Unprepared, Kenny didn't have an act together and so could not play concerts to profit from it. The experience wised him up.

Subsequently, Kenny displayed an extraordinarily strong sense for and grasp of the *business* of music. Hence the First Edition, with no sacrifice to its proven artistic integrity, became a model of a well-run business enterprise. That it did was largely because Rogers is unfailingly realistic, a trait that seems to be an essential component of making it in the fantastic, egoistic world of pop music. Those who have succeeded almost always are those who have been able to manipulate the business machinery into helping them achieve their goal.

It has been many years since the First Edition's first smash—Mickey New-bury's "Just Dropped In (To See What Condition My Condition Was In)." That was in 1967, but by most standards Kenny had already carved out a modest chunk of success. He met Bobby Doyle, a blind pianist, at a local Houston recording session in 1959, and played bass and sang with Doyle's pop-jazz Trio for six and a half years. Though the Trio's artiness restricted its popularity, people in the business dug them—they had one album released on Columbia Records, *In a Most Unusual Way,* and such stars as Tony Bennett and Johnny

---

*This is the record company department that finds, develops, and sees through the recording of the company's artists.

Rivers occasionally sat in. The Trio toured with another jazz group, the Kirby Stone Four, which was managed by the same people who handled the large, nine-member folk group, the New Christy Minstrels. This connection led Rogers into joining the Minstrels in 1966 when they needed a bassist who sang high parts. The Christies promised less income than his Trio work, but Kenny made a pragmatic career decision to accept the offer. Of the two ladders to success, the monetary and the professional, the professional offered him a qualitative leap into at least the fringe area of stardom.

Rogers' days of touring with the venerable Christy Minstrels lasted only a year and a half. The split came when he and three other members—Mike Settle, Terry Williams, and Thelma Camacho—worked up eight songs by Settle which would have brought up to date the group that in the happening days of the late sixties was still relying on the folk standards it had made famous ("Green Green" and "This Land Is Your Land"). They sang those for the Christies' owners, but they were rejected; the owners were afraid to tamper with the Christy Minstrels' established image. The four left to become the First Edition, and those eight songs became their first album. They were concerned with longevity and felt that the way to achieve it was to be responsive to changing times—something Kenny remains unafraid of being.

The First Edition's second single, "Just Dropped In," was a pseudo-psychedelic rocker that went straight to the top of the Top 40. It was calculated to bring what was basically a country/folk/rock band to the attention of the huge rock audience. Rogers had learned the trick from Bobby Darin's similar use of such nonsense rock and roll numbers as "Splish Splash" in 1956. Darin established himself by performing songs geared to contemporary popular tastes. Once accepted, he then gradually bent the market toward what he really wanted to do, a sort of pseudo-jazz exemplified by "Mack the Knife." The First Edition was no more psychedelic than Bobby Darin was a rock and roller; most of the seven hits that followed "Just Dropped In" clung to an alternately aggressive and melodic country-tinged folk-rock idiom: "But You Know I Love You," "Ruby," "Tell It All, Brother," "Heed the Call," "Reuben James," "Someone Who Cares," and "Something's Burning."

Despite all the musical concerns, the First Edition had to flex the heaviest show-biz connections they could muster to break in. One connection led to a contract with Warner Brothers/Reprise Records. Another led to a spot on prime-time network television. Mike Settle's attorney, Lee Colton, also represented the Smothers Brothers. For weeks and weeks Colton exhorted the Smothers' then co-manager, Ken Kragen, to hear the gestating band at Ledbetters, a folk club in Los Angeles. Kragen was extremely busy at the time, co-producing the original "Smothers Brothers Comedy Hour," but he finally acquiesced. Excited by what he witnessed, Kragen then brought down his partner, Ken Fritz, Tommy Smothers, and the chief writer of the ". . . Comedy Hour," Mason Williams. As Kragen tells it, it helped that Williams fell in love with Thelma Camacho, but all were sufficiently overwhelmed. Subsequently, Tommy Smothers came to the First Edition's rehearsals to help with their between-song "patter," and Kragen signed them to a management contract. (Now a vice president in Jerry Weintraub's Management III, Kragen remains with Rogers today.) In January 1968 the hitherto unknown First Edition guested on the highly rated ". . . Comedy Hour." They went on to appear on seventy network shows in the next three years—a show almost every two weeks, more television than any other act in the business had done.

The band toured regularly, of course, but by 1971 their record sales began tapering off. To stay vital, they took the suggestion of their agent at International Creative Management, Herman Rush, and of Ken Kragen, for another way to feature the group, a way that would also show the depth of the various members' talents: They began "Rollin'," their own weekly TV musical-variety series, which was produced by Winters/Rosen Productions in Toronto, Canada. One of the first shows of its type, it gave performing spots to then unknown groups, including Cheech and Chong, Helen Reddy, Tony Orlando and Dawn, Bill Withers, and Jim Croce, and exposure to others not commonly seen on TV, such as Kris Kristofferson, B. J. Thomas, Bo Diddley, and B. B. King. It was a success—it was carried on 192 stations throughout the United States and Canada—but after two years Rogers stopped "Rollin'." This vehicle, too, had exhausted itself. From there, Kenny Rogers and the First Edition entered the state-fair circuit. In their first year, by virtue of the broad popularity their TV work had generated, they succeeded in netting more than $500,000. And that was more dough than they'd brought home from fairs in any of their previous eight years!

Longevity, Rogers found, is a matter of pyramiding. You work one area for awhile but at the same time lay the groundwork to go elsewhere. This gives you an alternative when you've worn yourself out in one kind of pursuit.

A year after their state-fair bonanza, however, the inescapable fact began to get to the members: The First Edition was becoming yesterday's paper. The TV show was over, the singles had stopped hitting, individual interests were diverging. Ennui and bickering set in. Things perked up briefly during a 1974 tour of New Zealand where they were still regarded as superstars (the tour was filmed and yielded an hour-long television special in 1975), but the trend proved irreversible and in January 1976 the First Edition officially disbanded.

One of the group's last editions included co-owners Rogers, bassist and lead singer, and Terry Williams, lead guitar; salaried members Mickey Jones, drums, who joined six months after the group's inception; singer Mary Arnold, who replaced her roommate, Thelma Camacho, when Camacho left; and lead guitarist Jimmy Hassell and keyboardist Gene Lorenzo, both formerly with the Kirby Stone Four. The story of the original rhythm guitarist/songwriter/partner Mike Settle seems particularly telling in relation to the dynamics of pop-group personnel. Having been on the road for many years, Mike quit in 1970 because his marriage was being strained to the limit in the absence of a home life. Well, after a year of life at home he got a divorce. Some time later Rogers took Settle to New Zealand to open the First Edition's shows because it struck him as sad to see his old friend, especially such a talented one, scuffling again. (Settle had penned much of the group's material, including "But You Know I Love You." Subsequently, he has had some success writing songs for Glen Campbell, B. W. Stevenson, and others.)

Success and failure, fortune and misfortune, continue to travel together in the music business. But pop music has matured immensely and the business itself keeps on booming. According to figures gathered by the Record Industry Association of America (RIAA), when the Beatles first appeared on the scene in 1964, the industry grossed approximately $800 million a year. Thirteen years later, in 1977, more than $3 billion was earned on record sales alone, and the RIAA certified 183 albums gold (sales of 500,000-plus units) and 68 platinum (1 million-plus units). Back in 1958 only one album, Gordon MacRae's *Oklahoma*, sold enough to qualify for gold! The business of concerts similarly has skyrocketed to a yearly $700 million business. And many industry leaders believe the music business will continue to match these gains. Whether it does or not, its outlook certainly remains big, and the business always will need fresh talent.

Why, for the love of playing music, should you be concerned with the record business? Simply, the business is a vehicle to the widest possible appreciation and sharing of music while offering potentially enormous financial rewards as well. Recording is an art form in itself, an opportunity to present a song in ways not possible in a personal appearance. Then, too, with a record, your song can pour into people's cars and homes and places of business—radios are ubiquitous—and even become part of the national consciousness. And the more you're known, the more people will pay to see you in public appearances. Rock concert television shows are important, but appearing on them usually follows success with records.

It is with the idolization of famous, talented people who with their charisma and glamour become bigger than life that stardom is made. But only a handful of bands or solo artists ever reach that nebulous peak, so Kenny and I feel that it is foolish to embark on a music career with stardom as your singular goal. In most cases, those at the top are there because they have a most rare talent and exceptional originality. And there are just a few so-called supergroups—those you read about in *Rolling Stone* magazine—that are so popular that every record hits high in the charts, every fifty-city concert tour sells out, and every activity makes news, while the members live in royal opulence with an entourage that takes care of all their needs and satisfies their most petty whims. For every group of that magnitude—say, Aerosmith, the Beach Boys, the Bee Gees, Alice Cooper, Chicago, Bob Dylan, Elton John, Crosby, Stills and Nash, the Eagles, Fleetwood Mac, Paul McCartney and Wings, the Rolling Stones, the Who, Yes and Led Zeppelin—there are hundreds of groups on the fringes of stardom who look successful onstage but who are living below the poverty level to build a base for big-time success. They're constantly out on exhausting record promotional tours, opening shows for crowds anxious to hear the main act, and seeing little more of the world than airports and miserable hotel rooms and dressing rooms.

But for all of those groups gambling that such hard work and sacrifice will soon pay off grandly, there are thousands enjoying the gratifying response derived from playing in local clubs and shows. This is the bread and butter for groups: the places people go to daily for relaxation, entertainment, or celebration—bars, nightclubs, supper clubs, fairs, parties, weddings, bar mitzvahs, hotels, and resort lodges from Hawaii and Las Vegas to the Catskills and Miami Beach, and the dances held frequently at colleges and high schools. Here is where a fair living can be made playing familiar and danceable material to stimulate the sale of drinks and insure a good time. But here, too, is where a new act, which may have larger career potential, can be developed, tested, and exposed. And virtually every accomplished musician or group can relate a story or two of such modest beginnings.

The business of music is unavoidable once your thoughts turn from amateur to professional. Thus, no matter which part of the spectrum you're eyeing, gearing for it is essential. It may seem crass to deal with such a magical and honest mode of human expression as music in terms of organization, contracts, image making, and salesmanship; it may seem that planning is anathema to the spontaneity and sheer energy of music. In fact, however, the guidance of this book should free you from the mundane problems hampering your group's functioning to allow you to deal more directly with music and take it so much higher.

Such a realistic business consciousness is Kenny Rogers' most important secret to success. But there's an even more important element that gives life to the whole endeavor. It's the attitude that playing music is, first and foremost, fun. Maintaining this attitude is essential, because the odds against making it are astronomical. You can be *determined* to make it, but if stardom becomes an overriding obsession you're bound to lose touch with what music, at bottom, is really all about: to entertain and be entertained.

One last thing. When Kenny and I began the project early in 1976, Kenny was plotting his solo career. Despite the fact that the First Edition's corpse was barely cold, to much of the world Kenny Rogers was a name from the past. Six years had passed since their last hit. When I informed friends that we were working on a book together, some flashed me dubious looks and politely suggested I would have a more promising co-author if I collaborated with a currently successful name, like Jimmy Page or Glenn Frey. I countered that Rogers was not only as qualified as anyone but that he was bound to be on top again soon. I sensed this from the methodical way he approached his solo career and from the genuine talent he exhibited in performing new songs for me with his acoustic guitar in his living room. His distinctive voice and style were as captivating as ever. No way, I thought, could he fade into a cutout-bin relic.

Rogers, newly signed with United Artists Records, was even more confident. Like Babe Ruth pointing to the place in the stands where he would swat his next home run, he told me that in a year he would have a song that would first top the country charts and then cross over onto the pop charts and peak in the Top 10. "If I don't," he half jokingly vowed, "tell the readers to disregard everything I say."

Incredibly, "Lucille," his second single from his second solo album, picked a fine time to wind up number five in *Billboard* magazine's Hot 100: It came to pass in June 1977—the very month of his prophecy.

LEN EPAND

Getting Started

1

Well I was sixteen
And sick of school
I didn't know what I wanted to do
I bought a guitar
I got the fever
That's rock 'n' roll.*

ERIC CARMEN,
"That's Rock 'n' Roll"

You design a great building and it's years before it's finally completed, and people say, "That's a beautiful building." But when you go onstage, you do one song and the applause starts. You get that immediate response and it's every night—or as often as you need it. So it wasn't the money that attracted me to the music business. It was, I guess, the glamour, the instant gratification—not to mention the fact that in *my* high school the musicians and singers and football players got all the girls. The impetus to actually start my first group, though, was supplied by one of the annual school talent shows. A friend and I heard a group that was terrible, and we felt that, as average at music as we were, we could put something together that was at least as good, and in any event it would be fun to try.

The Scholars was a meager effort. In the mid-fifties, when rock and roll was being nursed over the pop radio airwaves by such vocal groups as the Coasters, Drifters, Four Aces, and Four Lads, I persuaded two friends who sang with me in the church choir to join. I played a good flattop acoustical guitar. Bought with money I earned as a busboy, it was quite an advance over my first instrument, an all-steel Dobro, which must have weighed forty pounds, that my uncle gave me when I was fourteen. The others in the band held down drums and piano, while one tapped a tambourine and sang. Better at singing than playing instruments, we copied the vocal groups and eventually, when Elvis Presley and Chuck Berry made it *de rigueur*, added an electric guitarist.

The first professional job I ever worked in my life was with the Scholars. We drove 170 miles from Houston to San Antonio to perform at an Air Force base officers' club. The five of us rode for three hours with our makeshift gear in one 1956 Chevrolet. We performed two twenty-minute shows, made $13 each, and turned around to drive back. We drove 340 miles to make $13 each. Obviously, it wasn't really the money that attracted us to music. But the Air Force loved us and it really bolstered our egos. Having no idea we were raw amateurs, they treated us as professionals. And that's when we started taking ourselves seriously. We decided we were capable of entertaining, that, yes, we were entertainers.

Over the next two years we played school dances and talent contests and local youth clubs. And we recorded some singles for Cue, a very small local record label. The high point had to be when Lelan, my older brother, got us a deal to record a few songs for Imperial Records (a major label since absorbed by United Artists Records). Lelan worked for a distributor that handled Imperial and knew one of the company's executives. Imperial paid our way to Los Angeles, put us up at the Hollywood Roosevelt Hotel, and supplied us with some of the town's best musicians in the studio. For all practical purposes, the sessions were worthless. We recorded, among others, a dumb Afro/Cuban-tinged song called "Kangewah" by Louella Parsons, who had a syndicated radio show. We did the song thinking that because it was hers, she'd plug us and we'd become stars overnight. Of course that fantasy evaporated after the record came out and went nowhere, but coming to L.A. was the thrill of a lifetime for a kid from Houston. It didn't matter that we returned broke, having spent our $150 each union scale on the trip.

The band fell apart shortly thereafter, however. One of the Scholars decided—or his dad decided for him—to get scholarly and attend college, to apply himself to a "real" profession. It was all right, actually, because having improved musically and taken up the upright bass (at the time there was more demand for a bad bassist than a bad guitarist), I was offered a position with the Bobby Doyle Trio. Eighteen years later, of the other Scholars, one is MC'ing a children's TV show in Palm Springs, California, one is an attorney, another is an official of Houston's water company, and the last is an Arthur Murray School of Dance instructor. We still see each other once in awhile.

**Come,
Gather Now,
Musicians**
It's fair to assume that most musicians' first rock-group experiences were primitive. Their groups started with neighborhood friends who emulated the popular groups of the day, and only a small percentage of the musicians remained in the business long enough to make it a career.

Of primary concern—whether you are forming a band at an early level or are advanced to the point of methodically gathering an organization to assault the national pop charts—is the group's composition: its personnel (who should be in the group), its instrumentation (what combination of instruments and voices will create the right sound), and its equipment (what is needed and how much money—or how little—should be spent for it).

Obviously, the type of music and work to be done dictates the answers to these questions. But a certain minimal personnel and instrumentation is fundamental to playing most forms of pop, rock and roll, blues, jazz, soul, country, and reggae. Needed are a drummer, to provide a beat, keep reliable time, and create sonic and percussive textures; a bass guitarist, to supply the tonal bottom and sheer physical power and also contribute to keeping time; an electric guitarist, for rhythmic chording in a broad tonal/textural midrange and for upper-register lead melodies, which can vary from the warmly lyrical to the searing space-age maniacal; and, lastly, a keyboardist (piano or organ), to combine the guitar's rhythmic and lead functions in their tonal fields.

Taken together, these instruments—drums, bass guitar, electric guitar, and keyboard—yield a primary depth that, complete and flexible, is enough in itself for most groups. Yet, more and more, bands are exploring still broader fields of sound by adding not more members, but related instruments. Some pianists, for example, equip themselves with clavinet, electric piano, organ, harpsichord, synthesizer, and mellotron. Though these require some adaptation, the basic know-how is transferable. Drummers can handle, besides the standard drum kit, conga, Indian tabla, tympani, bells, gong, maracas, claves, and chimes and perhaps a mallet instrument such as vibraharp or marimba. And a guitarist can move easily from a standard six-string guitar to a twelve-string, feed the sound through a variety of foot pedals—echoplex, vibrato, echo, wah wah, phaser, fuzztone, and synthesizer—or switch from electrified to amplified acoustical guitar. The more sonic variations an individual brings to the group, the more he is an asset.

This concept extends further if the musicians double on other instruments; if, for instance, the guitarist occasionally plays a keyboard instrument in conjunction with the keyboardist on another, or if the keyboardist also plays guitar to perform complementary leads with the guitarist, or if one or more musicians can switch to horns, woodwinds, or strings when called for by a song.

Finding musicians adept on several instruments is difficult enough without expecting them to come to the band with such a costly collection. Though they may not be virtuosos or lavishly equipped, your best bets are people you know, those whom you respect both musically and, just as important, personally.

Personal compatibility cannot be overstressed. In forming a group, if musicianship is secondary to anything, it's this. For no matter how talented a musician or singer is, if his or her temperament is eccentric to the point where working together is an unenjoyable struggle, the discord will surface in the music and eventually destroy the band. It is preferable to have, say, five average musicians who constructively contribute to the group and subordinate themselves a bit to satisfy the group's larger needs, than four musicians at the same ability level plus one intimidating "superstar" who fights to run things. If someone persists in playing the star, it is probably better for all concerned that he leave to start his own group. Get three, four, or five musicians who are willing to help each other improve, who genuinely want to work and enjoy it and share similar expectations, and you'll grow together and stand a far greater chance of succeeding. Don't expect that inner conflicts can be concealed onstage, where they can do the most harm. Excitement and fun are irresistibly contagious—when the group is having a good time, it's hard for the audience *not* to. If you're worried, tense, or openly bickering among yourselves, people will focus on that instead of the music and turn off.

Although the members of your band need not be inseparable, you should get along socially and have similar concerns. This is important because you are going to live with these people on the road. The First Edition, for instance, played golf tournaments and football games in which hundreds of dollars amicably changed hands. In fact, one football game left our manager with a pulled hamstring and one guitarist with a broken arm. Though $700 was bet, we made a medical decision to quit before the whole band ended up hospitalized. Of course we had our own lives to lead. But when we weren't together for a time, I looked forward to getting back together with my friends to work. It's this extra something that made our group so durable.

Ideally, group members should be close in age, because musical and outside interests are apt to be similar, reducing conflict further. If someone in a

The group that dribbles to-
gether plays together longer?
(Left to right) Manager Ken
Kragen, road manager Keith
Bugos, yours truly, guitarist
Jimmy Hassell, and drummer
Mickey Jones.

The First Edition broke out of the staid New Christy Minstrels folk group. *(Left to right)*
Terry Williams, Bobby Buchanan, Mike Settle, Kim Carnes, Michael McGinnis, Kyoko
Ito, Mark Holly, Peter Morse, and Kenny Rogers. (Thelma Camacho had also been a
Minstrel; she joined some time after this photo was taken.)

predominantly teenage band is, say, in his mid-twenties, he may be interested in a sound and style fashionable when *he* was a teenager. And he will probably have a lot more responsibility, perhaps a wife and child to support. Not working for three weeks doesn't matter much to those who are still living at home and being supported by their parents, or to those who have no one to answer to, but it is critical to the family man. Nevertheless, if someone fits the criteria, age itself shouldn't be a deterrent. When Mike Settle began forming the First Edition, it was doubtful for a while that I would be allowed in it. My age (in 1967 I was 28) and appearance (from the jazz circuit, I was wearing mohair suits and diamond stickpins and cuff links) were decidedly too mature for the group's intended image. The only reason I got into the group, really, was because I sang parts well, played bass, and was available for rehearsals. Once surrounded by folk and rock people, though, naturally wanting to feel comfortable, I put on blue jeans and let my hair grow long. People can change to a certain extent.

Finding musicians close to home offers another built-in element of compatibility, a shared frame of reference. Put simply, it is convenient, and this is important for conducting rehearsals regularly. If you are in school, for example, don't advertise for members in the newspaper of the school across town—unless your group is so accomplished that trekking a distance to rehearsal several times a week would be considered worthwhile by those who see the ad. Besides the school paper, advertise on bulletin boards at neighborhood grocery stores, record and musical instrument stores, hangouts, and the musicians union hall.

Other musician-finding means are available, but these are progressively less localized. You can try advertising in local newspapers' classified sections. Beyond that are the American Federation of Musicians' monthly paper, and the many record trade magazines, such as *Billboard, Cash Box,* and *Record World.* In some cities, computerized musician contact centers operate. For a reasonable fee, you can type an ad into a machine and periodically receive in the mail a listing of musicians with similar inclinations and interests.

Another way, somewhat sneaky but legitimate just the same, is to hear other groups and discreetly approach the members who interest you. Of course, your band must promise to be an improvement over theirs. This method, like the one of finding friends, has the advantage of demonstrating to you a potential member's capabilities and style without the need for exhaustive auditions. When the First Edition faced replacing its original lady singer, Thelma Camacho, we advertised in the music trade papers. It was a mini disaster. Though the ad read "contemporary rock group," hundreds of girls of *all* kinds showed up at the recording studio where we were holding the auditions. One was a 250-pound Hawaiian lady equipped with a ukelele who was sure she was perfect for the group and insisted upon playing the "Hawaiian Wedding Song." Ironically, we ended up hiring the original girl's roommate, Mary Arnold. It was phenomenal. We had spent weeks looking and the right person had been around all along; Mary had been to our rehearsals from the beginning and knew all of our material. After one rehearsal, she performed with us that night in concert.*

Incidentally, if you're a male group and considering adding a female singer, consider some pros and cons before making the move. At the risk of sounding like a sexist, I'll venture that while many women can provide a higher singing range than you may possess, add a visual classiness and attractiveness you may lack, and cause you to be more conscious about your appearance and manners, the addition often promotes a romance between the woman and one of the band members, a romance that ends up causing persistent tensions and problems if it doesn't work out. And then there's the practical matter of always needing at least two dressing rooms (assuming the woman minds dressing with the men) and an additional hotel room on the road. Although pop music thankfully is becoming as much a woman's profession as a man's (note the Joy of Cooking, Heart, Fleetwood Mac, the Runaways, etc.), be sure the women (or, in the opposite case, men) you bring into the band fit in logistically as well as musically.

However you get the word out, there are enough musicians looking for work in this business so that you soon should be showered with responses. When someone does call who sounds promising over the phone, arrange a preliminary audition. Have him prepare to play on a trial basis for a week or two. A musician might be dazzling in a single audition, whereas in a week or more of woodshedding he'll prove erratic. And it takes at least that long to learn if he's compatible, and if he makes it to rehearsals and jobs consistently on time.

Musical Style   Personality and sex aside, the decision should be based on how well the musician fits the style and type of group you are to have. Is the group a funk band, a rock band, a blues band, a pop-rock band, a jazz-rock band, a heavy-metal band, a new-wave band, or a country-rock band? Whatever the case, the music should cohere fairly consistently to that style so that the group has a definite identity by which it is known and sold. Some bar bands that play music of many styles can only be known as Top-40 bands, playing the hits everyone knows. But no matter how well they cover the hits, they never advance in the business. They remain nonentities. Sticking to a style

---

*By the same token, you may reject a winner. One of those we turned down was Karen Carpenter!

is preferable, but it will present some problems because some members inevitably have other interests. If, for example, you find a great guitarist who's more into country than, say, English rock, he could still fit in if you concede to him a country number somewhere in the show, though the main diet probably will frustrate him after awhile. Lead guitarist Terry Williams and I each owned 50 percent of the First Edition after Settle and Camacho left. Though Terry, who is ten years younger than I, liked hard rock as opposed to the progressive country-rock I preferred, he stayed with the group for so long (he finally sold his First Edition interest in 1975 to pursue his ambition) not just because our group was very successful, but because his musical taste was accommodated in the show and he shared my love of entertaining, which was the group's chosen reason for existence.

A style in mind, also consider in what direction the group will go—what *type* of group it'll be. If it's to be a "concert" group that plays song after song, many originals, and leaves stage presence to be solely embodied in the music, then your primary concern is with musicianship and creativity. If, on the other hand, it's to be a "show" group that is to entertain, try to secure, say, a drummer who is willing to toss in one-liners, look as though he's having a good time, and keep a straight beat rather than one who is the most avant-garde expert on hand. In such a case, musical talent can be sacrificed to a degree for other valuable stage abilities. Actually, it's harder in many ways to be a good show group than any other kind. You must be in control of so many more levels of activity.

A third type of band is the "dance" band, which, not surprisingly, focuses on performing danceable hit songs. For these groups, the musicians should be adept at copying parts from records and not be too creative. At least one member, usually the guitarist or keyboardist, must be truly proficient at figuring out and teaching songs to the band, because dance bands must constantly update their sets to accommodate the audience's and (hence) management's requests.

I remember sitting down with the First Edition and asking ourselves if we wanted to be esthetic and progressive and set the world on fire musically or simply to entertain as a show group. We settled on the latter because we recognized our strong points were as personalities and as a group of singers who just happened to play instruments.

After these major points, think about what the musicians should be able to provide in terms of technical expertise. Music is a form of expression. We can express ourselves intellectually or emotionally. Some musicians are so schooled they can sight-read any piece of music put before them, but when asked to improvise something in four bars, they either think you mean "drink all over town" or they fall apart. I would rather have in my group someone with a feeling for their instrument than someone who knows everything about that instrument and music theory. I've been in recording sessions in which someone might go for a note and not quite make it, but the feeling was so good we didn't interrupt the take. This is not to say a sloppy performance is acceptable, just that the ideal is when a musician combines the two elements. Most to the point was the late, great Louis Armstrong's response to a question about his reading trumpet parts. "Not enough," he said, "to hurt my playing any." Still, I'm sure Armstrong would have agreed that the more a musician understands about music, the better his chances are for coming up with new ideas and more beautiful ways of playing. And the more advantages he gives himself, the better his chances are of succeeding in this intensely competitive field.

One of rock (and country, folk, and blues) music's attractions is that it requires little formal training. Many self-taught singers/songwriters/instrumentalists have had long, lucrative careers, while some musicians with years of formal classical training sell insurance policies to survive. Although this might make a case for state-supported arts, I merely want to point out that, while I do not belittle knowledge and make a virtue out of ignorance, as an unschooled musician myself, I do not heavily stress it. To work successfully with a group, what you do need to know is some rudimentary theory, music symbols, and terminology. This is essential so that in rehearsing songs with the other musicians you can communicate clearly and read a "lead sheet," a notation of a song's melody and lyrics with the key, time, and chord symbols. Much of this knowledge will accumulate as you play with better and better musicians. But at first learn the basic terms—key, tacit, coda, repeat, fade, retard, bridge, twelve-bar blues progression, modulation, time signatures, chord structure, harmony, turnarounds, etc.—which any fundamental music book covers.

Songs can be learned from sheet music, but the most common—and, since sheet music often is oversimplified, more accurate—method is that of listening to records. Passage by passage, try duplicating the music on your instrument until it sounds right. This also serves to train your ear, which you'll know is most perfectly developed when you can play what you want to by merely thinking of it (something that only a master can do). As far as putting the band together, the members should start roughly at the same level of ability. If there are major discrepancies, conflicts will crop up as the slower members persistently inhibit the faster ones. The ideal situation is one in which the members, each superior at his particular specialty, can learn from each other.

The First Edition, having been a melding of different talents, developed

such a no-compete situation; that is, we competed on quality, not style. Mike
Settle, later replaced by Kin Vassy and then Jimmy Hassell, sang songs that
required a hard-rock voice, for example, while I was suited to the soft ballads,
and Terry Williams, having a supple, melodic voice, covered the softer rock
numbers. Consequently, animosity rarely grew. If we wanted to do a song
calling for a searing lead vocal, Terry and I couldn't have done it if we wanted
to, so we were quick to say, "Hey, Mike, you really have to do this in the show."
And if a pretty ballad came in, everyone realized it would be silly for anyone
but me to do it. A productive rapport built, a feeling that we were all helping
each other.

Although this kind of fine tuning usually doesn't come into play until later
stages in a group's evolution—it's difficult enough to locate workable, equipped
talent—the point should be included as another criterion in selecting personnel. A final personnel problem to anticipate occurs when, among a group of
musicians, no one sings well enough to handle vocals. I don't advise bringing
in someone just to sing unless he's truly exceptional. And if you do find a singer,
make him learn an instrument, even if it's only harmonica or tambourine.
Everyone must work to full advantage, because when money is divided, each
is going to get his share. Make sure it's earned. Chances are you won't stumble
into the ideal members right away. But after a while of searching and auditioning, put the group together, good, bad, or mediocre. Compare it to the process
of selecting stereo components. You can't listen to records with only a turntable,
amplifier, or speaker system. All three are needed. So even if you can't afford
the expensive equipment, start with the lower priced components. At least,
with the hope of making improvements later, you'll have music.

Equipping   Speaking of components, before launching into a discussion of
                 arranging rehearsals, music, and shows, there are a few things
to think about in equipping the band. Unless you plan to perform for no more
than a handful of people in a family room, this can turn into an extreme
matter of thousands and thousands of dollars. Younger musicians commonly
complain that the problem is inescapable—that you have to have money to
buy equipment to get paying performing jobs, and you cannot afford the
equipment until you've *had* the jobs. On the contrary, assuming that parents
or relatives can't advance you the money and that you're determined, you'll
come up with it through summer or part-time work, by mowing lawns, delivering newspapers, baby-sitting, clerking at stores, or, as I did, bussing tables at
restaurants. As for bands with more extravagant requirements, other avenues

of financing, say, of getting advances from speculators, music publishers, record companies, etc., are detailed in a later chapter. For now, it's enough to say everyone should own the equipment he uses. The group shouldn't buy it collectively except, generally, in the case of the public address (P.A.) system, which is employed by the group as a whole for amplifying the vocals. If only the lead vocalist sings, then the P.A. might be considered *his* instrument, expense, and responsibility.

Instruments, amplifiers, microphones, etc., should be bought by those who use them because they will take better care of them, and because one becomes accustomed to his equipment's particular characteristics. If they are bought by someone else, the group or parents, for example, they are more apt to be kicked about and not become an extension of the musician as an instrument ideally should be.

If you believe you are serious about music, begin with a good instrument, not the best money can buy (if you change your mind about music or what instrument you want to play, the investment will prove wasted, discouraging further musical attempts), but one of at least average quality, used or new. A cheap instrument has two disadvantages: It's frustrating because the musician cannot duplicate the sounds other musicians achieve; for example, a cheap guitar's strings usually are so high above the neck that it is a feat of physical masochism to mash them down without a lot of fret noise. Secondly, the trade-in or resale value of a cheap instrument is virtually nil, whereas a reasonably good brand and model instrument in good condition always is in demand and can be sold at close to its original cost. In fact, many older used instruments, made better than newer, more mass-produced models and improved with age, *increase* in value. Just make sure when buying a used instrument, whether from a store or an individual (through a classified ad, etc.), that it comes with some guarantee.

Amplifiers also are an investment. However, these must be selected with the type of room in which you'll most often be working in mind. It doesn't make sense to have a stack of Marshall amps if you are to play at high-school dances and small bars; these are designed for large concert auditoriums. Start with good equipment, but not more or less than is needed. And be aware that sound equipment is not limited to the available brands. You can build your own, customize, or use a combination of components by various manufacturers to suit your individual tastes. I ended up combining a Marshall brain (the electronics and controls) pushing both an Acoustic bottom (speakers and cabinet) and a JBL (James B. Lansing) sound system speaker unit. I liked the edge, the percussiveness that this gave my bass. Some bassists prefer a rounder tone.

Many music stores allow such experimentation. Music stores, incidentally, are great places to decide what instrument to buy, meet other musicians, and pick up tips about technique, the business, and equipment. But be careful. I used to go into a Houston music store almost every day when I was fourteen, trying out instruments and learning from other musicians who were a step or two ahead of me. I would ask one, "Hey, what's that chord you're doing?" He'd show it to me, I'd get a guitar off the rack, and I'd practice it. Then one day I broke a guitar. It cost me $280, which I did not have and had to pay off at $5 a month.

When you hear other bands, notice the types and brands of equipment they use. And, during the breaks or the time after the job, feel free to ask about it. Most musicians happily answer questions as long as you don't make a pest of yourself. And that's how you learn. People have asked me about my bass. (Given to me by Fender when the First Edition started, it's one of the first Fender ever made and was, in fact, my first electric bass.) And people have asked our former lead guitarist, Terry Williams, how he wires together his several amps. If you are at a large rock concert, you probably will not be able to get to the musicians themselves, who are by necessity isolated backstage by security guards. But afterward, once the audience clears out, try talking to the equipment crew while they're tearing down the amplifiers. It's surprising how little many musicians know about the equipment they're playing through, but the road manager and crew know because they set it up for every performance and maintain it. Besides, they have a rough, unglamorous job and the fact that you respect their opinions enough to ask will flatter them. As a rule they are friendly—if you run into someone who isn't, back off and wait for the next group. By the way, even though many popular—and thus influential— groups are sponsored by equipment manufacturers because of their advertising value, you can be fairly sure the musicians would not be using the products if it meant any sacrifice of sound quality.*

In equipping the group, use perspective. I would rather see a band whose musicians had bought $500 amplifiers and spent their other money on a portable lighting system or improved P.A., which make them look and sound better, than see a band with $1,000 amps which their playing doesn't justify and which their listeners don't appreciate (they won't know the amps cost so much, and even if they did, they wouldn't care). If the guitarist, drummer, and organist each save a few hundred dollars, the money can be pooled for things that

_____

*For my post–First Edition backup band, Vocal Point, I made endorsement agreements for the use of Arp Synthesizers, Music Man amplifiers, a Fender Rhodes electric piano, Pearl drums, Ovation acoustic guitars, and Shure microphones.

markedly improve the group—if not a sound system or lights, then a wardrobe, a van for traveling, spare parts, vocal monitors, etc.—things that set you above other groups whose abilities are otherwise similar. Remember that club owners, for one, are selling drinks, not sound. That's your responsibility, along with its related facets, such as lighting. For about $600 two "Christmas trees" with six colored floodlights and spotlights each can be built and placed on each side of the stage. The point is, though you *can* do it strictly on talent, if you give more than people are accustomed to, they'll remember you. When we performed "Abraham, Martin, and John," color slides of Abraham Lincoln, Martin Luther King, Jr., and John F. Kennedy were projected on an electric screen that was dropped down behind us. It was just a small trick that made the song more real. This sort of extra can make the difference between an adequate show and a great show, and attract the club owner's attention.

Rehearsing   With the group essentially gathered and equipped, it's time to launch into rehearsing. The first step is to set up discipline: A rehearsal schedule must be agreed upon and then adhered to. Although the band is, presumably, one of the few activities in your life that you want and *choose* to do (it's not something you're *supposed* to do, pop music not yet being considered as socially "valid" a profession as law, medicine, accounting, or selling insurance), it has to be taken as seriously as a job. If you are still in school, determine that rehearsal will be, say, from 3:30 to 5:30 P.M. Monday, Wednesday, and Thursday, and from 1:00 to 4:00 P.M. Sunday. The weekday sessions allow practice without interfering with family dinner times, schoolwork, other jobs, etc., while the longer Sunday session, less restrictive, permits more time-consuming rehearsing, such as a full run-through of sets. And Fridays and Saturdays are open in case there are band jobs.

This schedule provides adequate work time, as long as members don't abuse it by straggling in late. Tardiness not only is a waste of precious rehearsal time, it's unprofessional and maddeningly rude to those who are on time. As such, the First Edition established a schedule of fines that enforced punctuality evenhandedly. If we agreed to meet at 5:00 and someone who hadn't cleared it in advance showed up at 5:15, he paid a quarter for every minute he was late, or $3.75. After paying a few fines, those amounts became no small incentive for promptness. The money went into a general fund for manuscript paper, wardrobe, spare parts—whatever benefited the group. I remember Bobby Doyle missed an entire three-hour rehearsal of our old Trio, which he himself had arranged the night before. That day he was only thinking about buying a radio.

Well, it ended up costing him $45 more than its price. It's always fun when the leader gets fined.

After knowing when to rehearse, figure out where. This can become a major problem if no one has a garage, basement, or tool shed that is out of earshot of the once-friendly neighbors. Although these places can be sound-proofed to a degree with acoustical tiles, mattresses, drapes, or other heavy materials, it's often less trouble to get a spare, lockable room in a community group's building where, perhaps promising to sweep up after their meetings, you can rehearse without bothering anyone and leave your equipment set up without fear of thefts. If your group is primarily a vocal group, as was the First Edition, you could inoffensively rehearse your parts in a living room with just a guitar or around a piano. When all the parts are together, you can then move to the amplifiers, work out your instrumental parts, and do dress rehearsals, playing and singing at full volume as though on a job.

At the first rehearsals, don't try to overreach, to work out a lot of songs. Just play songs everyone knows and jam; that is, lay out a simple chord progression and get the feel of playing together. Begin by playing rudimentary parts: The drummer plays a straight pattern, the bassist keeps to the root of the chords, the rhythm player (on guitar or keyboards) just chords, and the lead guitarist or keyboardist either improvises or plays a specific melody. Before elaborating on your parts, listen closely to each other to feel out everyone's natural tendencies. Get accustomed to *listening*. If you're oblivious to everyone's playing but your own, you can be great individually, but instead of a group, you're going to be a collection of uncoordinated soloists. Concentrate on enhancing and complementing what the others play.

After a couple of sessions, begin laying the groundwork for an *organization*. As I will stress in the next chapter, each member must have some role outside of his performing one. One such role, indispensable for the most efficient and productive use of rehearsal time, requires the talents of the most capable musician among you. He is to be the group's musical director. The musical director comes to rehearsal with material to be worked on so you won't be discussing what to play instead of playing. He also presents the band with lead sheets written out beforehand so you'll rehearse rather than fish for the chords or words of songs you're not as familiar with as you might have thought. A good lead sheet also indicates where any stops, breaks, solos, modulations, etc., come and is numbered in segments, so whenever you want to go back over a phrase you can say exactly where you mean and see what everyone should be doing at that point. When alterations are made, the lead sheet can be amended so they won't be forgotten.

Having a musical director is not as dictatorial as it may seem. Periodically, the group can hold meetings to determine what material the director should prepare for which sessions. And since the lead sheet is for convenience and provides only the skeleton, things remain quite loose. The musicians and singers still must learn or create their own parts, and everyone must collaborate in giving each song an arrangement.

Early in the game, the members must clearly define their musical roles for the kind of no-compete situation mentioned before. In groups, people often tire of what they do and want to toy around with other instruments or vocal parts. This is healthy, but only up to the point where it does not conflict with someone else's part or leave the group weaker. Here, too, discipline must be established. We brought a rhythm guitarist/singer, Jimmy Hassell, into the First Edition to sing the hard-rock songs. After awhile, wanting to sing a ballad, he complained about his specialization. "All I can tell you is this," I said, trying not to sound as though I was laying down a law, "if a fullback is hired by a football team, his job is to go up the middle. He may get more bruises than anyone else, but that's what he's paid to do. Now, if he doesn't want to do it, he should apply for a job with another team. We need a fullback to run up the middle." Jimmy agreed, but only after extracting from me a promise to abandon such clichéd analogies. The ballads were my job. Yet, inflexibility for its own sake is foolish. If it turned out that I sang enough in the show, that Jimmy could do a good job on a particular ballad, and it wouldn't be at the expense of his regular responsibilities, then fine, he would have been welcome to try one.

How well an organization functions and how long it lasts is directly related to how well it deals with the inevitable disputes. Our group was run largely by majority rule. Though Terry Williams and I admittedly had the overriding veto power after Camacho and Settle departed, we exercised it only when the matter at hand was of lasting importance and involved a great deal of money; we simply had a lot more to lose than everybody else. But the members of a group must feel their opinions matter and they should share in the decision making that affects their roles, life-styles, and careers. Still, there are many times when the end result of a democratically reached decision adversely affects one more than the other. In these cases, in our group, the person having the most to lose by a decision cast the deciding vote. Say, for instance, Jimmy brought a song to rehearsal he wanted to sing. Then, say, as we worked on it, Terry suggested we have a long guitar break, and I objected, pointing out that, in the show, it would be following another number with a big instrumental segment. It would mean too much guitar playing back to back. Now, if we voted to do it and the song did turn out to be too long, it would be unfair to Jimmy since, as the song's singer and focal point, he would suffer for it most. If, on the other hand, Jimmy made the final determination, at least he'd later have no one to blame but himself and could reverse himself without reopening a dispute that's bound to hurt someone's feelings.

Our system worked well because everyone was reasonable. Don't be stubborn! If everybody says, "I think you're playing way too much on this song," then back off a little and don't be personally offended. They're not saying that from jealousy; they're saying it because the group's overall quality is at stake. Alternately, don't hesitate to say so when you feel a figure you can play would better enhance a song than one someone else has been doing. As with taking criticism, all members have to listen open-mindedly and at least try ideas. Otherwise, innovation is stifled. If it comes down to an argument about whose lick is better, bring in the tape recorder, the old reliable touchstone. One hearing of the different versions usually makes the winner readily apparent. Maybe your idea wasn't so great, or you're overruled by the majority. Just look for another spot to embellish. When you find one, however, be sure to let everyone know about it so it doesn't come to them as such a surprise that either everything falls apart in front of several hundred people, or suddenly four other licks are rushing to the hole you hoped to fill. Encourage communication.

Arranging Your Material   Now deeply into rehearsing, knowing how to design—arrange—a song can make all the difference in how effective your music is. If you're not yet playing original material, there's nothing wrong with beginning by copying the arrangements of successful recording acts. It's a great way to learn, playing well-conceived music and showing the most profound respect for artists whom you admire. Not least of all, until you are known for your own music, audiences will *demand* songs they already know. The British groups, including the Beatles and Rolling Stones, started this way, copying note for note the American rock and roll and rhythm and blues records they collected as teenagers in the fifties. The object, though, is to gradually adapt those artists' work into your own *style*. Style is a matter of having some common denominator in your sound and approach that is identifiable, like a trademark. It's a distinctiveness that people can either like or dislike but not be indifferent to. If you don't move people to react in some way, good or bad, then you'll remain anonymous, and anonymity is purgatory for a supposed *pop* group. As versatile as the First Edition was, we still maintained something that was unique to us in every song, even if it was just the manner in which we stacked our voices in harmony.

I feel if I cover other people's material, I must either alter or completely ignore their version. Then I've done something creative, making an existing piece my own. For instance, I sing Paul Simon's "Bridge Over Troubled Water" the way I hear it, employing certain recognizable natural tendencies of mine— for instance, the way I fall off a note or use vibrato—that I have developed into stylistic characteristics. I intentionally began wavering my voice when I started singing in high school. It was a device to counter my lack of confidence and the flatness that seemed to occur when I tried to stretch a note out. People didn't care much for it then. "What the hell are you doing?" they asked. "That's terrible." So I quit doing it. But years later, recording "Something's Burning," I again wavered my voice, and when the song became a smash hit, people started telling me, "Boy, I love the way you do that little thing with your voice." Some even thought it was done electronically. So I looked for other places to put it. But I'm careful not to do it so often that it becomes contrived and predictable.

Similarly, when I sing ballads, certain notes in my lower register crack. If it were wrong, if it were not pleasing to the ear, I would have to go for another note or change keys to get away from it. But it happens to be pleasing, and it's an identifiable gimmick. People think, "That's Kenny Rogers." Idiosyncracies like these naturally fall into place in certain vocal and instrumental notes and phrases. Onstage, it may just be some unique physical movement of your head in singing a difficult note. As to whether to use them or not, judge by friends' opinions.

From the start, the subtle personal stamps that the members apply to their playing will be the seed of a group style in the way they combine. Be aware of the emerging style and capitalize on it in arranging songs. Arranging essentially involves matching your voices and instruments to a song's basic elements— melody, harmony, and rhythm. If you play the song as written a few times at a slowed tempo, certain embellishments will suggest themselves—a guitar lick, drum fill, bass pattern, or some vocal harmony. Be innovative but don't be fancy for the sake of fanciness. The best arrangement doesn't call attention to itself; it enhances. Approach the material conceptually. Think of the feeling you're trying to transmit or the place you want to take listeners. And then try to create a musical imagery that communicates it. Often simple background harmonies will paint a landscape and atmosphere behind the song's subject, the instrumental breaks acting as emotional releases and the music flowing as undercurrents, now in turmoil, now calm, now—whatever. Arrangements speak on much more elemental a level than do lyrics, and good ones really bring a song to life.

One common arrangement calls for a quiet start, gradually peaking toward the middle, and starting over to build up to a strong ending. Avoid a formula approach. Sometimes, for example, it's more effective to end quietly or to build linearly from relaxed to intense. In any event, something new should occur about every eight bars—whether it's an added instrument or voice, a change of color, dynamics, or rhythm, or a startlingly different chord voicing. Songs, like poetry, tend toward a few particular forms—verse, verse, chorus (AAB) or verse, chorus, verse (ABA), instrumental break, and a repetition of the first pattern. Occasionally, as in some story songs, a simple string of verses is used.

Vocal arranging is not very different from instrumental arranging. The lead singer carries the melody, while the others add harmony or unison lines where the lyrics and feeling call for a sense of emotional strength or an altered character. Use discretion. The overuse of harmony, even when all of the singers are great, can be gross and offensive, ironically rendering a song a tuneless wash. What harmony you do use depends, obviously, upon the number, quality, and range of the band's singers. If your lead singer is best in the middle range, someone else in falsetto (a register higher than that of the natural voice), and another in bass, great, your vocal combination is flexible enough. Harmonies—figured out by ear or more surely by voicing the notes on a guitar or keyboard—might be arranged so that three voices start in unison to spread out later, or enter dramatically for the chorus or a later verse. Also effective is the laying out of a wordless harmony line, say, of ooh-wahs or a counterpoint, the background singers answering or echoing the lead vocalist's lines. Here, too, you must listen carefully to each other so that the voices blend and the melody isn't buried.

One-three-five, constituting the basic elements of a major chord, is the most used harmony. But too many groups limit themselves to that and it becomes monotonous. It's little more than barbershop-quartet rock and roll. The more you get to know of chord structure, the more interesting harmonic possibilities you will hear. The group that has my highest admiration is one that can move easily from close harmony to unison and to something spread over a couple of octaves, and then sing the more difficult chord intervals (with seconds, suspended fourths, major sevenths, ninths, etc.), and has a singer who can improvise—scat—on occasion. Remember, by the way, if everyone sings in every song in the show, about halfway through there are going to be some very tired voices. Also, if the main singer, the fullback, runs every play (to resurrect my football analogy), he's going to be tired. Reserve your voices so when they are used, they are at full strength.

Live Presentation   Once you've worked out a few songs, start working on your show. The First Edition consciously designed itself to be versatile. We played rock concerts one night, Vegas showrooms the next, state fairs (where we couldn't play as much rock as we liked) the next, and then a dance (which we normally didn't do). Playing for dances, either at schools or beer halls, is the bread and butter of unknown rock bands. As you move up in the business, you try to phase out dances because most of the audience isn't really listening—they're dancing. This is not to imply there's something inferior about music that makes people want to dance; in fact, with discotheques important again, groups recording funky music specifically for dancing do very well. But even these groups don't play dances. They play concerts.

Playing for dances may be regarded as a dues-paying phase, but it is an important educational experience, because dancers furnish excellent clues as to how well your music coheres. If they seem uncomfortable or confused on the floor, there's something wrong with your rhythms. If, conversely, the audience can sing along, clap, dance, and get involved in the music, then you know your arrangements work.

Dance-band "shows" are basically a stream of rhythmic, even tempoed music, whereas concert and show acts, less concerned with providing for the body than for the ears, eyes, mind, and spirit, must make a well-conceived *presentation.* Everything about concert/show groups—the dress, the selection of music, lighting and sound effects, the sequence of songs, the between-song talking, the entrance and exit—all must be prepared and coordinated. It is this, the arrangment of an effective show, that I want to discuss in depth because it is perhaps the subtlest and most critical aspect of the performing craft.

Consider first that the initial impression you make on people is usually the lasting one. Some groups build to an exciting entrance by turning on the darkened stage, the audience only able to see dark figures moving around. This is all right as long as you don't let it degenerate by taking too long, boring the audience. In most cases, though, having arrived early enough to tune up properly before going on, it's more exciting and professional to launch into the first song as soon as the lights brighten and you appear. You don't want to have to overcome a sloppy opening. What the First Edition did was start in the dark, playing a musical vamp (an improvisation or variation on a tune) over which the MC announced us. If people already know your group and paid to see and hear you, this entrance will help build anticipation. If there's no MC, have your drummer announce in the dark, "Ladies and gentlemen, Catweasle," or "Let's have a warm round of applause for Catweasle." As long as the audience can't see that you've asked for the applause yourselves, this should give you some momentum for your first song.

Once introduced, start in with a song of some driving force or sensational impact to involve the audience immediately and transform their interest into excitement. But even though you want people to think, "All *right,* this is going to be great," musically, your opener should be a throwaway. It must be well done but forget about trying to transmit meaningful lyrics here because the audience is just looking the group over. They're looking at each of the members, their clothes, their instruments, and their equipment. So, during the opener, keep the lighting up full. In effect you're saying, "Here we are, take a good look at us. Let's get that out of the way so we can move on and let you hear what we have to say."

Then segue, that is, shift directly, into the second song, which should be bright but different enough from the first to be unrepetitive. Segueing keeps the show moving and makes you more exciting and professional. It's between the second and third numbers that I like to say something to the audience, preferably something humorous, like "Hi, how are you?— We got rid of the guy who came up with 'Hi, how are you?' " Implicitly, this tells people this is going to be more than a run-of-the-mill show. Also hint at something coming, so they'll have that to listen for. It's a good way to move along, and it relaxes people because they'll realize you're in full control, professionally and personally. Try to be a little humorous because humor seems to be the best way to keep people's attention. We did a bit when working a small town. The first thing I said was:

> We're happy to welcome you to our show tonight. But before we go any further, I want to just take a second and tell you that our group has been together now for—what?—eight years! And the day we put the group together we decided right then and there that there were two places in the entire world we wanted to work. One was a little club in Paris, France, which we finally played three and a half months ago [I turn and look at the group as they nod their heads in assent, reinforcing the sense that this is a true story], and the other place, of course, is—[I raise my hand and look around the room] Fargo, North Dakota!

This joke was such an obvious lie, people loved it. It was a way of laughing at their town without belittling it, and, more importantly, it gave them an insight into my sense of humor and the First Edition's style. It also let them know they could expect more than the commonplace song after song.

Incidentally, it's a good idea to look for a person in one of the front rows who appears to be enjoying the show and direct your playing to that person. Not only is it easier to perform when you believe people are enjoying what you're doing—thereby spreading enjoyment—but the personal element will add an important dimension to your performance. In fact, I find it useful to break that almost palpable barrier between performer and audience. In my solo act I usually pick up a tambourine in the first number, play it for a few bars, and then toss it to someone in one of the front rows. Consequently, people watch to see how well that person plays and they become a part of the show, which is also to say, they become mine.

With the fourth song, change the mood. If, for instance, you're primarily a male group with a woman backup singer, this may be a propitious time for her to do a solo; not only because it's a good part of the show, but because you must start answering the audience's questions. Subconsciously, listeners will be wondering if she sings by herself, what kind of voice she has, and so on, instead of focusing fully upon what you're doing. Try it yourself the next time you're at a show. Notice what your mind is really touching on at different times—"Boy, the guitarist is too loud," "I wish the bass player would sing something," "I wonder if they're going to play their hit"—and why: The guitarist overdid it with equipment, a certain musician is being ignored, they haven't communicated with the audience, the lighting isn't good, etc. Whatever they are, those factors are working against you. Your group should anticipate as many of these potential distractions and shortcomings as possible.

Plan your show to be varied and well paced, with something always happening. Mix fast rockers with ballads, vocal numbers with instrumentals. As a rule, you shouldn't do two ballads in a row because things will tend to bog down. Nor should you program a fast song, a ballad, a fast song, a ballad, *ad infinitum.* Perhaps plan a fast number followed by a loud rocker with a heavy beat, then a placid, pretty ballad with solitary piano or acoustical guitar, and then a soulful number.

One way to work out the flow of your sets is to record them in several different sequences and select the best one. But a far simpler, more methodical way is to graph your material and plot out the songs. First assign each song a certain score for volume, tempo, mood, length, and lyrical feeling. On a scale of 1 to 10, the first could be an 8, the second a 7, and the third might come down to a 4. The graph will show you explicitly whether the show's pace builds or declines, stays at an even level, is erratic, or is too energetic or lethargic. With this done and changes made, it then pays to tape the show to see if the theory bears out in practice. If it does, fasten lists of the songs in the final order to an inconspicuous but convenient place on your instruments so when you're on stage you don't have to stop like amateurs after each number to discuss what to play next.

Count on songs lasting about three to five minutes each, that is, if you're playing *song* songs as opposed to lengthy instrumental concept pieces. If you're scheduled to perform forty-five minutes, plan on ten songs, or fewer, depending upon how much talking you do. But keep a reserve of extra material. Prepare for as many contingencies as possible. Perhaps a singer will lose his voice or a piece of equipment essential to a particular song will break down or you will be offered double-time pay for playing an extra set. Sometimes it seems the most shocking traumas occur routinely in the life of a regularly working band.

Back to the show, put soloing numbers somewhere toward the middle, after the initial presentation. After you've "told" the audience "This is us, this is our group," now add, "Here we are as individuals." If someone has a notable strength, let him play it up and assume the spotlight. Not only is this good for the show, it's good for each member's ego and pays off in the long run by defusing internal problems.

Break up the solo segments with your strongest, most exciting song, the one that shows the group at its ensemble best. We put our most raucous song, "Love Woman," here; it was a great tension releaser. But the next song was my solo, which I did alone with a stool and an acoustical guitar. Contrast is effective. People asked, "Why don't you do more of that, the quiet ballad? I love that." But I knew if I did two, they would dilute each other. Sitting in the audience, people would say to themselves, "Oh, that's another one like he did before." Try not to duplicate. And try to place songs where they stand apart from the others.

Having used your most energetic piece for the mid-set peak, bring out your most popular and thrilling number to close. If you've had hits, play the biggest here. The essential thing is to leave the crowd wanting you to come back and do more. If you give them all they want, they'll go home saying you were pretty good. But if you leave them in a standing ovation, they are probably going to tell all their friends you were stupendous and recount the performance in detail, savoring the show. That's the best response you are going to get. Unless you can top that finish, why return for an encore? If you do get such an enthusiastic response, however, it would be rude to ignore it. When this happened with the First Edition, I would go back out by myself, implying that we're not going to perform any more, and say something to this effect:

> This place seats what—two or three thousand people, which, believe me, is not huge compared to some places we've worked. But given the choice, and I know I speak for the rest of the group, we would much rather work for a smaller group of people like yourselves who care, than for a bigger group that doesn't, any day of the week. Thank you very much. Good night.

With that you've acknowledged their response and you've paid them a compliment. Then leave. There are certain obligations you have—you must give people their money's worth in entertainment—but don't throw away your trump card. Carefully guarding this trump also means turning down premature audience requests for your big song. When someone yells out in the first part of my show, "Do 'Ruby, Don't Take Your Love to Town,' " I diplomatically deflect the request with this anecdote:

> OK. Let me give you a little inside show-biz knowledge here. Eight years ago when "Ruby" was a big hit, I came onstage and after the third song someone yelled, "Do 'Ruby.' " I thought, "Boy, I've got 'em now." Well, for my fourth number I did "Ruby." Before the fifth song, however, everybody left. They'd heard what they came to hear. Since that happened, I've adopted the policy that if you want to hear "Ruby," you have to wade through the rest of the crap.

Onstage Patter   Onstage talking is probably the weakest facet of most groups. Because this more than anything else reveals how together, intelligent, and creative the group really is, or isn't, devote serious attention to what you say and *how* you say it. One general rule we had in the First Edition was that anyone in the group could say anything he or she wanted to say at any time, as long as (1) it didn't step on a punch line someone else was building up to, (2) it wasn't offensive to anyone in the audience, and (3) it included the audience. With this last, if you don't include the audience, if you turn to the group and crack some in-joke that makes the whole group laugh while the audience doesn't know what's funny, you may offend them a little, or even alienate them. If you're going to say something, say it over the microphone or loud enough to project to everyone.

If there's someone in the group who speaks well enough, some songs can be introduced to heighten interest. Just be sure that in explaining a song you're not insulting people's intelligence by not giving them credit for being able to understand it themselves. I set the tone for a ballad I wrote for my grandfather this way:

> Sometimes when you're young, older people say things to you that don't mean a great deal, but they take on significance as you get older and you live those experiences. This song's about something my grandfather used to tell me. It's called, "There's an Old Man in Our Town."

The song's bridge is something my grandfather really did say. "Youth," he said, "only happens to you one time and, so I've been told, if you should miss it in your young time, have it when you're old." Having told people my grandfather said this, it's real to them instead of being just a profundity that some anonymous person once said. It's from the source, and maybe they'll recall the mood of times when their grandfathers said meaningful things to them.

Besides taking care not to ramble on and on in talking onstage, I try not to get too terribly serious. If talk becomes overly dramatic, it loses its impact and bores people mightily. So I usually cap everything with a punch line. With "There's an Old Man in Our Town," after having set up this wonderfully warm mood about how close my grandfather and I were and how much I value the things he told me, very often I'll start to play my guitar purposely out of tune, then stop and add, "He did ask that I play in tune, though." Then, having tuned the string, I'll mutter disdainfully, "He was a picky old man. . . . I don't know why the hell I wrote this song." That takes the somberness off while adding a subtle interruption that allows the song to stand on its own. Yet the personal touch and the song's validity remain established.

Whatever you say, stay away from clichés. Such expressions as "Here's a song entitled . . ." or "Now we'd like to do a little number . . ." are deplorable. The First Edition's sense of humor, as well as mine, developed over our years together. Occasionally bored with our show or wanting to alter it, we spent thousands of dollars hiring writers to create new material. Yet we never did use any material we didn't come up with ourselves. Mine is a dry, cynical humor, which is not always right for the audience. When it wasn't, Gene Lorenzo, our keyboardist, tried his slapstick styled humor, doing more if he got results. In any case, audiences appreciate spontaneity and originality.

But not even Lenny Bruce was spontaneous enough to perform a totally original show every night. So you have to plan and rehearse bits that can be made to *look* spontaneous even though they aren't. We did a bit when some young kids with Instamatics seemed to be having difficulty photographing the band because we were too spread out across the stage. If a photographing session didn't come at a crucial juncture, I would integrate it into the program. I'd say, "Would you like to take a picture of the whole group?" Usually they'd yell back, "Yeah." So we'd all make a dash to the front of the stage and get into a corny pose. Then Terry would walk back to the amplifiers, pull out a camera, and also snap a picture—of the audience—flashing a flashbulb. It was so unexpected that audiences loved it. It looked spontaneous, even though we did it almost every night.

The pose bit is about as far as the First Edition went in mixing theatrics and music. Music is the substance, the *raison d'être* of a music group. Although theatrics, special effects (dry-ice smoke, for one), and certain choreographies can enliven and charge a live performance (witness Pete Townshend flailing at and smashing his guitar as a climax) and add a valuable visual facet (as when the Moody Blues appeared onstage standing in an eerie blanket of smoke and blue light as though they had just dropped in from outer space), becoming too deeply associated with the kind of elaborate productions that developed into a minor trend in the seventies—with plot, props, and costuming—is apt to be detrimental in the long run. In music, theatrics is just another fad, popular for a year or so and then boring the next, each act trying to out-effect the other. If Alice Cooper's songwriting and singing were not so substantive, he would have gone the way of Tiny Tim and countless amusing yet ephemeral others.

There are some performance-enhancing activities that are commendable, however. The First Edition was a fairly static act until Jimmy Hassell joined. Jimmy, a very physically expressive person, could not stand still. Dancing with his guitar, he moved from his side, stage left, all the way to stage right, where I stood, and back. It was exciting! As with any bit, movement must be done tastefully, and to be unpretentious it must be an extension of one's true personality. A bizarre person can act bizarrely on stage. Now I'm a laid back, conservative person. From time to time, though, when the show was going exceptionally well, Jimmy would come over to me and dance a step or two, challenging me to match it. And I would do it. Because it was out of character, unplanned, and took place for only an instant—it was cute. Sometimes I would just laugh at him and he would go back to his corner. Like theatrics or gimmicks, an attention-getting activity like this is all right as long as it remains a means, not an end.

As I said earlier, style can be a visual matter, a distinctive action that supports the projection of your personality. As corny as this sounds, I recommend that you practice playing in front of a full-length mirror at home. Look at yourself from time to time, pick out the aspects that you like and discard those you don't. If the guitar, for instance, is held too high and looks awkward, try letting out the strap a little. Be yourself, but knowing what that self *is* is as important. How you see yourself often differs from how others see you. So ask friends to react to what you do onstage and correlate the two images so you can be yourself and yet respond to people's expectations. Once you've developed an image, be consistent. If you normally act sophisticated and suddenly do something off-color or corny, it's distracting. Two songs later people will still be thinking, "Now why did he do that?"

A final point concerning stage presence is about introducing the members of the band to the audience. There's nothing more boring than the empty kind of intros that list, ". . . on drums, Mickey Jones, and on piano. . . ." With that, you're saying in essence, "Please clap for these people, they're insecure." What we did was give the audience a chance to know the members personally by humorously identifying them with an obvious trait of their personality, almost caricaturing them. Taking about eight minutes, this offers a comic relief, a break in what otherwise might be a straight hour of music, and more importantly, firmly implants in people's minds lasting images of the group's members. Toward the end of our shows, Terry Williams introduced everybody in the First Edition. He would start like this:

> One of the drawbacks of being in a group this large is that few people know you by name. It's true, and I'm as guilty as anyone when it comes to remembering names of musicians. Now poor Jimmy over there [whose hair is white], he goes through life being known as the albino on the left who dances like a chicken. [Jimmy demonstrates his dancing for an instant.] He's from a little town called Waxahatchie, Texas, and I'm sure you'll agree with me that he's a very talented person—Jimmy Hassell.

This always won a reaction; people enjoy laughing with someone. With Gene, Terry usually said:

> People from time to time ask me where we got various members of the group. Well, for one, we worked in Chicago about four years ago and a guy dressed in a black shirt and silver tie came up to me after a show and said [imitating Brando's scorched Godfather voice], "Hey, you guys got an Italian in the group?" Gene joined the very next day. I don't know what it was, just timing, I guess, but we've found a couple of pluses to having Gene with us. Number one, he's an excellent keyboard player and, two, we get great discounts on bananas wherever we go. [Serious, then, Terry would say:] From Boston, Massachusetts, Gene Lorenzo.

We didn't play with Mary's image because it's difficult to get a laugh with a woman without detracting from her quality, which may be a chauvinistic way of thinking, but Terry introduced her this way:

> The young lady in the group has been with us five and a half years and she is truly the most beautiful and talented lady to come from Audubon, Iowa—Mary Arnold.

Williams used Mickey's credentials as a drummer to get into him:

> Mickey spent eight and a half years with Trini Lopez; two and a half years with Johnny Rivers; a year and a half with Bob Dylan; and last night with one of the ugliest women I ever met in my entire life. From Dallas, Texas—Mickey Jones.

Of Terry Williams, the real comedian of the First Edition, who used to adopt a sort of Tommy Smothers attitude onstage and appear to hassle me in one way or another, I'd say:

> Terry Williams is the only member of a musical group to be placed there by the Job Corps. He's from Los Angeles, California, he's been my partner for nine years and, more importantly, my friend for the same length of time. And as partners and friends go, he's the very best there is—Terry Williams.

Terry had a great way of mentioning me to make it seem like an afterthought. As though confounded, he would say over the microphone:

> What can I say about this man? He's responsible for our sound, he sang all the hit records, and I'll bet there's not a person in this room who does not know the name—Kenny Hoges.

These are silly lines, but when done well they make people smile and appreciate the group more deeply. Yet, in working out your stage presence, beware of using lines your personality can't pull off. It'll hurt rather than help your show.

Mistakes   One word on mistakes. When you are performing for people and the inevitable mistake occurs, don't stop, announce that you made a mistake, and begin again. Just keep playing. Usually, unless the goof is glaring, people won't notice. The best musician, as Duke Ellington used to say, is one who can work his way out of any mistake or dead end and make it sound beautiful, as if the error were intentional. Learn to cover mistakes and the other sorts of foul-ups. I have spent fifteen years of my professional life learning to do this. In fact, in one show, everything conceivable broke down—guitar strings broke, an amplifier shorted itself out, a mike stand fell off the stage, a guitar strap broke causing a guitar to fall to the stage, and so on. Instead of panicking, we took advantage of the problems and made them part of the show. Ironically, in the paper the next day, the reviewer complained that the show was *too* smooth. But audiences are impressed if you cope with problems rather than fall to pieces. We had punch lines for most of the typical problems. If someone broke a string, for example, at the end of the song the guitarist held up the guilty ax and said:

> While we're stopped, I'd just like to give credit where credit is due. We'd like to thank the Mattel Company for our equipment. It has been swell.

It was corny, but it got us off the hook. Then we played a song that relied on piano, while the road manager changed the string. Being prepared is what makes a group *professional.* If a football player pops a shoulder pad, they don't have time to stop the game and let 30,000 people in the stands and millions watching TV wait for him to get it fixed. They put in a substitute. After it's repaired, then he comes back into the game. You also have to be coordinated. This means that whoever orders the sets should be conscious of the instrument changes involved, if any. The wrong way is to call a song that is begun by the guitarist but which first requires him to change guitars. Having too little time to adjust to the change, he'd make a sloppy transition. The First Edition kept such mechanics well oiled. For instance, it would have taken me three minutes to prepare for my solo spot myself. Instead, we didn't miss a beat. While I removed my bass and walked back to stand it by my amplifier, Terry put his guitar down and picked up the bass to back me. Meanwhile, Mary brought my stool out front, lowered my vocal mike, and set up a mike for my acoustic guitar. Then, when the song was finished and I bowed and thanked the audience, Mary took the stool, guitar, and mike away and reset my vocal mike. Finally, I took my bass back from Terry, and we launched into the next song with no loss of momentum.

Setting Up   About the final thing to be figured out in rehearsal before playing jobs—gigs—is how the group is to set up on stage. (Choosing a name is discussed in Chapter 2 because it's basically a business decision and entails legal work.) The main idea is counterbalance. You want your keyboards on one side of the stage and the lead guitar on the other—otherwise all of the busy melody lines will come from one side of the stage. Be concerned with this, too, in designing songs. If a song has two solos, don't have them emanate from exactly the same place. Have people's eyes looking from one side to the other, not necessarily like watching a tennis match, but enough to keep the action moving. Not only will this keep things from getting monotonous, but it offers more of a balanced aural-visual experience to the audience. Another reason for splitting up the lead instruments is that double leads, in unison or harmony, will seem to envelop the group as though it were a living entity, heightening the power of your ensemble playing.

The foundation instruments—bass, drums, and rhythm guitar or keyboard —should share the center stage toward the rear. The lead singer, or frontman (if you have one), meanwhile, should stand in the foreground.

Almost the hypocrite, I was an exception to this design. Instead of placing

The First Edition's stage setup. *(Left to right)* Me (bass), Terry (lead guitar), Mary (vocals, percussion) and Jimmy (second guitar). On the riser is Mickey (drums) and to his right, Gene Lorenzo (keyboards).

my bass together with the drums, I stood on the far right. My only excuse is that this was what I was accustomed to. One night it happened that I did set up in the middle and I felt so disoriented for the entire concert that my moves and playing must have looked and sounded awkward. So once your stage design proves functional, don't rearrange it abruptly. Despite my misplacement, I still wrote my bass parts to work in conjunction with the drummer's playing. At least that was together.

Instrument amplifiers must be placed at the rear of the stage, behind the drummer, so that the group can hear itself to keep the timing and rhythm tight. The drummer must be as close to the sound source as possible so that he can hear what is being played when it's played, not when it has echoed off the front of the hall. Conversely, the vocal P.A. speakers should be placed in the *front* on opposite sides of the stage. This is to insure that the vocals, which carry less well than electric instruments, have some advantage in being heard. Needless to say, situate the sound system so that the sound emanates from the direction of the source. In other words, don't put your speakers at the rear of the hall. I remember we did that when the Bobby Doyle Trio got its first P.A., thinking they also would serve as monitors, so we could hear, too. It turned out to be very deceiving. People thought there was another band in the house. They kept turning around to see what was back there.

If complex vocal work is a main part of your performance, then you should have vocal monitor speakers—smaller speakers connected to the main vocal amplification in front of or at the sides of the stage facing into the group. (Another monitor should be placed beside the drummer.) Without them, it'll be hard to hear and virtually impossible to balance harmonies or even sing in tune. Monitors also save vocal cords because when singers can't hear themselves, they tend to sing louder and harder and strain their voices.

Another electronic modification to aid your sound and tighten your performance can be made by putting extension speakers of certain instruments on the opposite end of the stage. Since our rhythm guitarist was on our far left, we connected a separate amp (via a Y-cord from Jimmy's guitar) on the right side by Terry and me. Being able to hear his rhythm made a 100 percent improvement in unifying the group's feel.

"I'll know my song well before I start singing," sings Bob Dylan in "A Hard Rain's A-Gonna Fall." His point applies to any human endeavor, but musicians ought to take it literally. Nothing is more disturbing to me as a professional musician—and I'm sure this is equally true for every listener—than to hear someone play a song they haven't learned properly. So rehearse your material until it's second nature. As each song passes the point of recurring mistakes, however, lay off rehearsing it. There's a negative effect in becoming so overly familiar with a piece of music that the challenge of executing it is reduced to boredom.

Virtually all must be planned and rehearsed—the songs, the show, the stage setup, the introductions, the mistake-covering raps, and the alternate songs. Practice methodically and you are bound to progress consistently toward this state of readiness. Once you've gone a certain distance, invite friends to the rehearsal to hear part of the show. It's a great feeling to present to someone a piece of work that you've created from scratch. Their feedback, likely to be favorable, will be great incentive to continue building the show properly. And you'll find that steady accomplishment is exciting and personally satisfying. If, on the other hand, you have been fooling around in rehearsals and after a time have little worth playing for friends or yourselves as a group, a negative attitude will grow that is hard to reverse.

Something I learned not long ago is that you have to know your job expertly to be confident and make it look easy, to perform without the tentative tightness that hampers many bands' energy and flow. I was at the Steel Pier in Atlantic City watching the clown high divers and I thought, "I can do that. All you have to do is get up on the ladder and fall off." One of the divers happened to be a friend of mine, though, and he remarked that you have to be a great diver to be a clown diver or you can kill yourself. You have to know what you're doing so you can hit that water properly. You don't just jump off a board seventy feet high.

And there is more to being expert as a group than having a good sound and a good show, as one soon discovers when dealing with club owners, agents, managers, record companies, and concert promoters. Beyond the gathering of a workable and professional group, there are many business matters to take care of to insure that your big splash isn't a belly flop.

Takin' Care of Business 2

Well a man he came along
And told us it was wrong
To think like the way we are.
We all thought it funny
When he told us about the money
And said something about a rock and roll star.
Yeah, well I said to him
Now you can't understand,
And we don't care if you do,
'Cause we're kinda tight
And we're rockin' here tonight
And we're hopin' it's rockin' for you.*

BOB ANDREWS AND NICK LOWE,
"Happy Doin' What We're Doin'"

I count my experience with the Bobby Doyle Trio as my introduction to the business of music. When you start making the kind of money I was, you start paying attention to what you're doing. Still, you tend to learn the hard way. One of the first regular jobs we had was at a place called the Ski Club, where we earned $300 a week each. Not that this wasn't lucrative enough, but when somebody offered us $350 a week we thought, "Great, that's where we go." We gave our notice. Unfortunately, in about three weeks our new employers folded. It wasn't our fault; the club had been sinking and brought us in, in hopes that we'd keep them afloat. But an act generally cannot pick up and expect to bring a clientele with it. People frequent a club for the club as much as for the band. Out of work for a month before the Ski Club took us back, we learned to have consideration for such particulars as longevity.

Subsequently I diversified my sources of income. Soon I was earning a kingly $750 a week—carrying on three jobs. I worked from 5:00 to 7:30 P.M., playing the cocktail hour at a small bar with Joyce Webb, a singer who played

33

the piano bar as I thumped my acoustic bass. We sang duets of Everly Brothers'
material and the like and attempted some comedy patter. This yielded $150 a
week. At 8:00 P.M. I joined the Trio to play dance music for four forty-five-
minute sets. This paid $450 a week. Then there was the after-hours club. It ran
from 12:30 A.M. to 2:00 A.M. and added another $150 to my wallet.

Such a rigorous schedule didn't bother me at all; it was exhilarating. I knew
the groups I was with were good, and as our success seemed to know no limits,
a feeling of confidence grew.

●

It's fine to rehearse until you've honed a couple of sets and have performed
them for friends at the studio or at parties. But to really test the quality of your
performance you must work away from friends. Friends will either harass you
and not take you seriously, or they'll courteously avoid telling you what they
sensed was wrong. Before you start looking for employment, however, you
must not only have prepared your music, you must have prepared your business
organization and decided how you, the members, will interrelate.

Choosing   First, though, settle upon a name. This turns out to be one of the
a Name   more frustrating experiences in starting a group. A name has to
               be just right. And only the corny or overused names come to mind
easily. To help you, I can only offer a thought process.

A name—and the images it conjures—will form people's first impression of
the band, an impression they'll retain and perhaps judge you by even before
they hear you. With a sinister-sounding moniker, like the Dictators or the Blue
Oyster Cult, you might as well scratch the church socials off your Possible
Employment List. On the other hand, if your name is the 1910 Fruitgum
Company, I wouldn't advise applying at bars frequented by burly Detroit auto-
workers. The name must appeal to the audience you wish to attract. Furthermore, it should suggest the image you wish to project and the style of music you
are working toward. It must correlate with your material, sound, act, wardrobe,
humor. You don't want a vague image. Which isn't to say that you can't build
an image out of zany unpredictability. It's just that it's *too* absurd, say, to
emulate the Osmonds musically while passing yourselves off with the threaten-
ing teen-gang aura of a New York punk-rock group like the Ramones.

Besides image and market, also consider the distinctiveness of the name
and whether or not it can be copyrighted, that is, whether or not you can

acquire a service mark for it from the U.S. Patent and Trademark Office in Washington, D.C.

Finally, consider how long the group will be around. The pop-music scene mutates as frequently as skirt lengths, and successful styles bud and die as fast as you can mutter hula hoop. So, if you're only in it for the short term, find a name that sounds like the name of a group that is currently successful.

For longevity, seek a nontrendy name. The First Edition did this because we knew that we'd eventually want to work Las Vegas nightclubs and show-rooms. Even so, we had a terrible time. We rejected dozens of names similar to those that were hot then, the Strawberry Alarm Clock, Country Joe and the Fish. They were a trifle too psychedelic for Mr. and Mrs. Insurance Salesman who haunt the Vegas casinos. We rejected dozens like Go for Baroque. Then one day when we were driving into Denver, Mike Settle looked at the front pages of the latest book he'd been living with, voracious reader that he is, and noticed "First Edition" on the copyright page. Immediately we knew we had it. It was fresh and unusual without being weird or outrageous. And it hadn't been used by a group before. I might add that for the next three years we wore all black and white outfits, to illustrate the print idea. And our first album opened with the sounds of newspapers rolling through the presses.

If you're thinking of using someone's personal name for, or with, the group's, such as Paul McCartney and Wings, consider this: Is that person the chief personality and talent? It's confusing to the audience if, say, the group's owner puts his name out front and he's not the dominant personality. Also, is that person likely to abuse the privilege? This is important, for if he doesn't own or lead the group now, he's going to after his name has been widely publicized. Remember, Alice Cooper had a career after the demise of Alice Cooper; it was a long time before the band could make an attempt—aborted at that—to re-emerge as the Billion Dollar Babies.

It's interesting how my name came to be part of the group's. It wasn't an attempt to gain the band's leadership. In fact, I never really was the leader until much later. This happy twist of fate sprang from our making a mistake in choosing the song to follow the huge success of "Just Dropped In." Not wanting to follow it with a similar song—again we didn't want to be bagged as a psyche-delic rock and roll band—we gambled. We released several ballads, and they all flopped, making 1968 a total bust for us. Finally we struck gold again with "But You Know I Love You," by Mike Settle, not a screamer like the first, but a rocker nonetheless. When it came to following this, then, we weren't inclined to gamble; we didn't know how many more chances we were going to have. So, when Settle came up with a number much like "But You Know . . ." called

"Once Again She's All Alone," we released that. Then the unexpected occurred: d.j.'s all over the country began playing a song on our third album,
"Ruby, Don't Take Your Love to Town."

The record company called a meeting. They said, "You know, it'd be great
if we could keep 'Once Again . . .,' because it looks like it's doing well, *and* have
'Ruby . . .' released as a single, too. But d.j.'s won't play two singles by one group.
They might, however, play one by the First Edition and one by Kenny Rogers
and the First Edition." So, happy to get all we could after a year of drought,
we released "Ruby . . . ." It quickly overpowered the other song, zooming to
number one while "Once Again . . ." fizzled out around forty. It was strange,
because I sang lead on *both* songs. Anyway, after "Ruby . . . ," our psychological
guessing games with the record business increased. Now, deciding to follow
"Ruby . . ." with "Reuben James," we were concerned about the confusion that
might result from our going back to being the First Edition. Like Diana Ross
leaving the Supremes, we thought people might presume that I had left the
band, even though my voice remained the lead voice. So, "Kenny Rogers and
the . . ." stayed. I must say, though, that I resisted having my name out front
at first. Having worked with the Bobby Doyle Trio, I saw Doyle receive extra
favors that weren't shared by Don Russell and me, even though we were equal
members. I didn't want to risk being resented by the other members for such
special treatment. Yet, adding my name to the group's proved to be a wise
business move from which we made a lot more money than we might have
otherwise. People, we found, identify more with an individual's name than with
a group name. The Beatles was one of the few groups to develop strong individual images. On the other hand, the Eagles is one of the largest groups in the
world, but any of the members could walk down the street and not be recognized by anyone but real fans. Although this is a blessing to an extent, it is
deflating for the ego and a problem for one's career; after the group dissolves,
the individuals will have to start virtually from scratch to establish themselves.
This truth led to such group names as Crosby, Stills, Nash, and Young.

Whatever name you select, at bottom it's hard to say how important it is,
other than that it distinguishes you when you're successful. It may be that its
importance is mostly for you. It gives *you* an identity. Also, don't worry how
weird the name may seem, for success will lend it validity. I'd laugh if someone
told me they were putting together a group called . . . the Beatles. That's a weird
name.

With the brain racking over, it's a good idea to insure that the group's name
cannot be stolen and exploited by another act. This is especially worth doing
after you've worked a lot, become known to employers, and built a following.
First, understand that you can't copyright a name. Copyrighting is for creative

works of length, such as songs, novels, and plays, for which originality or novelty
is essential. What you can do is register the name with your state's secretary of
state. Or, if your work involves interstate or foreign business, you can acquire
a service mark from the U.S. Patent and Trademark Office in Washington, D.C.
A service mark doesn't require proof of a name's originality. The name could
be an everyday word. It only requires that it is significantly identified with your
services and no one else's.

Trademarks, a company's identifying symbol or logo, and service marks,
the company's registered name, are based on a double-edged principle. First,
it would be "unfair competition" for a company to exploit the name and logo
of another company, especially after that company spent time, effort, and
money to make the name of their product or service mean something to the
public. (The words used by a company in their name acquire a "secondary
meaning" to the public; the words *scotch* and *tape*, for instance, have a particular meaning as Scotch tape, a registered trademark of the 3M Co.) The other
reason for the law is from the consumer's standpoint: It's to insure that buyers
get what they're led to think they're getting. Not only must there be a record
by the Beatles in the jacket printed with the Beatles' name, but the Beatles must
be the group with John, George, Paul, and Ringo, because that's what the
Beatles' name stands for, not Harry, Charlie, Frank, and Moe. Even if you own
the name, it doesn't give you the right to defraud the public. The ex-manager
of Fleetwood Mac learned this the hard way when, in 1973, engaged in a
dispute with the band, he assembled some unknowns to tour the United States
as Fleetwood Mac, performing their songs. After riots closed down shows in
cities where he tried it, the manager, who claimed he owned the name, was
hauled into court by the real Mac on charges of unfair competition and fraud.
In the opposite situation, if the group leaves the owner of their name, they can't
take the name without buying it from him. This is why the Jackson 5 became
the Jacksons after leaving Motown; Motown's president, Berry Gordy, owns the
Jackson 5 name.

There are two classes of service marks. The "principal register" is for names
of a particularly unconventional character, such as a new spelling of a word or
a completely new word. If we'd spelled the First Edition *Fyrst Edytion,* for
example, we could have had the benefit of this. The second class, "supplemental
register," is less encompassing. It doesn't guarantee exclusive ownership of the
name. If the Beatles, say, had used the common spelling, Beetles, they would
have had a tough time preventing the importation of exploitive merchandise
like Beetles lunch pails into the United States. They would not have had the
right to approve of the merchandise and demand royalties, a percentage of the
income. In addition to changing the spelling of a word to get principal registra-

tion, you can also use a member's name with the group's name. This is how the original Platters finally stopped the dozens of Platters that followed in the wake of their success. They registered as Buck Ram's Platters.

If you still want to use conventional words for the name, or if you want to use a name that is already known to the public for a particular company (and that company grants you permission), you can protect the name by using it in a distinctively designed logo and trademarking that. You won't own the name, but you'll own the name as it appears in that logo. No one else can use the rock group Chicago's scripted logo, for example. Chicago serves to illustrate another consideration, that is, it's wise to steer away from names that are heavily associated with another business, even if that business is wholly unrelated to music. Chicago, formerly the Chicago Transit Authority, and Tower of Power, formerly Pacific Gas and Electric, had to change their names because of the difficulty they had escaping identification with those companies. The groups couldn't have protected those names as their own in any event, because CTA and PG&E had already been registered.

Obviously, then, there's a lot that goes into selecting a name. You may find even more to think about, however, when you attempt to service mark your name. For no matter how original the name you choose, it's possible that someone else has already thought of it or one that's very similar. Since there is a registered Byrds, for instance, you can't get by as the Birds. The public identification is still there. Do your research early, before you make the name important in one locality and find that someone in another locality already owns its rights.

You can't research the name through the U.S. Patent and Trademark Office itself. They only accept or reject applications—at $35 a throw. You can make the search yourself at the Patent Office's Trademark Examining Operation (at the Longfellow Building, 1741 Rhode Island Ave. N.W., Washington, D.C.), or look through a public volume called the *Index to the Trademark Register*. Or, for a small fee, you can have the Trademark Services Corporation in New York City run the check. Such searches, by the way, may reveal that the name has been used so often that it is freely available as property in the public domain. If you're planning to record, publish songs, and perform on TV, also check with the artist unions—the American Federation of Television and Radio Artists (AFTRA) and the American Federation of Musicians—and with the performance-rights licensing agencies—the American Society of Composers, Authors, and Publishers (ASCAP), Broadcast Music, Inc. (BMI), and Sesac. This is worth doing because when you care to join them, it'll hamper you to have a name that conflicts with another member's.

Even when you're sure that your name has no prior owner, you still can't register it. It's not enough to have thought it up. First you have to work with it awhile to prove to the Trademark Office that you've made a commitment to that name. How do you protect it in the meantime? Incorporating the group carries with it a small degree of protection, in that no other corporation in the same business in the state can use the name. The First Edition incorporated in California as Friendship Productions, Inc., *doing business as* the First Edition. This meant that another group could have called itself the First Edition but could not legally present itself as the First Edition who had our hits. Incidentally, this did happen to us. In 1969 a news story came over the wire that the lead guitarist of the First Edition had been electrocuted while playing in the rain. Since we were out on tour at the time, Terry Williams' mother had no way of knowing that it wasn't her son who had been killed. She suffered horribly until it was revealed that the lead guitarist was with an Irish act that had been impersonating us.

When you finally do submit a name to the U.S. Patent and Trademark Office and it's accepted, you'll then own the rights to that name, or logo, for twenty years, renewable every twenty years indefinitely.

Internal   Your next organizational step should be to devise the group's inter-
Setup   nal setup. Just how the members interact depends on the sort of
               group you have, whether it is a democratic unit, a collection of
hired side musicians backing a leader(s), or a synthetic creation of a behind-the-scenes entrepreneur/Svengali.

The Monkees exemplified the last category. Found and salaried by Don Kirshner, then president of Screen Gems Publishing, now producer of "Rock Concert," none of the four Monkees had any responsibility for the musical and business direction or had a share of the profits. They took orders in exchange for a good salary and stardom. Something not commonly known is that the New Christy Minstrels also fell into this category. Randy Sparks started the group based on a concept originated in the 1880s by Pops Christy, who led the Christy Minstrels. Rather than having one frontman backed by sidemen, Christy found it attractive to have each member of the group take a turn as the frontman. For the New Christy Minstrels, Sparks gathered about him people like Barry McGuire (later famous for "The Eve of Destruction"), Larry Ramos (later of the Association), Gayle Caldwell (now a songwriter), Nick Woods (now deceased), Clarence Treat (now a schoolteacher), Jackie Miller (now married to John Davidson), and Art Podell (now a Mercedes dealer). It was a strong format, and the individual personalities became very important. Ironically, that's what de-stroyed it. Some of the members didn't know how to handle their new power, and friction developed as people pushed for those solo spots. Everyone felt he was the star, the yoke of the Christies' success. When Sparks saw his concept diluting, he sold his controlling shares (for several million dollars) to George Greif and Sid Garris. Suddenly the original members lost their say-so in the group and no longer got their fat bonuses. They left, and Garris and Greif replaced them with salaried employees, employees who sang a B flat when they were told to sing a B flat. I came in as a third generation Christy, when there were nine members, four of whom later became the First Edition.

The hirelings situation is fine for those willing to trade their creative integ-rity for money and status. But my experience in it showed me one major day-to-day drawback: On the road, there was a constant tug-of-war between the members, as no one had decision-making powers. A road manager finally solved our problem.

The second formulation—when the leader/owner is also a working member—is much more common than the first. It's frequently found on the club and concert pop-music circuit when an individual singer/songwriter, in trying to establish himself, doesn't allow anyone to steal the show, or when an established singer/songwriter doesn't care to share the control of his ca-reer and earnings with partners. Even the union's scale minimums require that leaders, as musicians *and* contractors, earn 100 percent more than side-men. The First Edition evolved into this situation as the other founders fell away. Now solo, I employ a backing group called Vocal Point that I found in Nashville.

This is as good a time as any to talk about leverage. Leverage is a term you'll see here often. Either you have it or someone else has it. Having leverage is to have the upper hand in a situation. A group leader will take care to maintain leverage. A sideman, on the other hand, need not be too concerned with it, except insofar as he gauges his value to the leader/employer when it's new contract time. At bottom, a sideman does what he's told and takes his salary, with raises coming as merited. When you're in this position—and everybody is at some time in their career—be sure to give a baker's dozen. The First Edi-tion's drummer, Mickey Jones, embodied this beautifully. On the road, when the six of us arrived at an airport, Mickey would go right to the car rental counter, and by the time I had gathered the luggage and hired a porter, he was driving up and we were ready to go. Mickey wasn't the sort of sideman who said, "I just do my job. You pay me X number of dollars a week and I'll be there, wear the right clothes, and smile onstage. But when I'm off, don't talk to me."

Consequently, even if I had found a better drummer, I still would not have let Mickey go.*

If the group becomes successful and you're a sideman, even if you feel that you're what makes the group, you shouldn't resent the leader. It's like this: If I own a hardware store and hire you, and you, as a very personable individual, build the store into a money-maker, it doesn't necessarily mean you'd be successful as the boss. It does mean that I'm smart to own it and smart for hiring you. A smart man isn't necessarily one who knows all the answers; he's the one who knows where to find them.

A word about leading. From the time I helmed the First Edition until I went solo, I never used the words *employer/employee*. People don't work for me, they work *with* me. With some you have to instill the first attitude—you work for me and don't forget it—or they'll walk all over you. But generally that's uncalled for. For the minute a person starts feeling like an employee, he feels that he has set rules to live up to—and nothing more. It's much wiser to make him feel part of the group. Then he won't mind, say, waking up at 5:00 A.M. to do a charity telethon. He'll feel it's for the group's good and that the applause is also directed at him. Alternately, to one who has had the fact that he's a hired peasant continually rubbed into his face, getting up at 5:00 has all the allure of scrubbing an army latrine. From 1970 to 1975 when Terry and I led the First Edition, we consulted with everyone in most matters and decided issues with votes. We believed if three of five felt a certain deal or direction wasn't good, then there must be something wrong with it. Terry and I still retained overriding control in matters affecting our overall financial condition and musical concept, since we stood to lose or gain the most by them. (If the group by vote made a bad decision and we lost work, or our long-range situation was severely damaged, the sidemen would still receive their salaries.)

The third possible group arrangement is, of course, the collective unit. The Scholars, the Bobby Doyle Trio, and the early First Edition were in this class. Intragroup business was simple: We got a check and split it. We all shared in decision making: Yes, we'll work here; no, we won't work there.

To work well under this democratic approach, you must have the active participation of the members. Everyone must understand the business and put the group's interests before their own. There shouldn't be much difference between the two anyway. The main drawback of collective leadership is the

---

*Mickey would tell you that there are better drummers. But he's good, and we never got a review that didn't praise him. Plus, in the First Edition he was visually flashy, projected personality, and had a theatrical sense of humor, all of which was tempered by a primary concern for how the group performed as a whole.

Even when you can afford road managers, the musicians' participation in manual chores is sometimes needed. There I am at left.

Terry Williams and I, the two owning partners of the First Edition.

A hopeful star in 1955, I was driven to performing as much as possible, often for little or no money. Here I am with the Perry Mates at the University of Houston's yearly fraternity show, "Frontier Fiesta," broadcast on Houston's KXYZ radio station.

occasional confusion in divining what the group's best interest is! Another danger is that some members might get stuck handling a disproportionate share of the group's chores if others shirk their responsibilities.

As most groups originate collectively, we'll focus on this. Structure the band by dividing the offstage labors. Chapter 1 describes the job of the musical director. Now, divide among the other members the nonmusical roles: travel arrangements; equipment maintenance and setup; and business. Assigning these requires honest self-evaluation. ("Joe's really better at that than I am.") You might switch roles occasionally, as long as it doesn't ruin a good formula. It keeps things interesting and makes everyone appreciate each other more.

The business person negotiates for the group, talks to agents and club owners, decides which jobs to take and for how much, executes contracts, and handles the finances. Of course he acts within the guidelines set by the group. And other members should feel free to pursue hot job leads. But the leads should be channeled through the business person to maintain a consistency of approach and direction.

The travel arranger sees to it that everyone knows the time, place, date, and purpose of rehearsals, meetings, orgies, and performances. He books hotels, writes up itineraries for road trips, and draws maps of directions to jobs for everyone. He makes sure there are dependable vehicles to transport the band and equipment. If this isn't enough, he might also be charged with handling the band's wardrobe and making sure clothing is brought to the jobs and cleaned afterward.

The equipment manager checks all the amplifiers and instruments regularly for defects and potential defects—either by himself, if he knows how, or by taking them to a shop. He sees that replacement parts are on hand—fuses, tubes, drumheads, guitar strings, guitar and mike patch cords, and even an entire amplifier. He directs—and participates in—the lugging of equipment from rehearsal studio to van to club to onstage setup and tear-down. When you can afford it, you can hire a road manager to do the foregoing, probably the most repugnant and physically wearing part of playing in a group. In the meantime, do it yourself and save the money for better equipment, transportation, and other essentials, and accept it as good exercise.

This decentralization of power throughout the band has a broadly beneficial effect. More gets done and gets done better. And, most valuably, it reduces ego problems. As long as a person feels useful, he performs at his best. Friction develops when one begins feeling unnecessary. I believe that this is what happened to Thelma Camacho, who for the year that she was with the First Edition had such a tremendous impact on people that I'm still asked what happened to her. She could have been a superstar, if she hadn't been so young (eighteen) and inexperienced with music, particularly the business aspects, when success came. Unfortunately, she began feeling she wasn't doing as much for the band outside of performing as everyone else.*

Everyone should understand from the outset that extra chores won't get them extra pay. Unless, that is, their work is significantly greater than everyone else's. If you want to encourage this, create an incentive system. If someone says they're willing to set up all the equipment for an extra $50 a week, that's fine. The point is that extra pay must be tied to extra work. And everyone should know *why* someone is getting more pay, and that if he or she ceases to earn it, he or she ceases to get it. In general, steer away from uneven salaries. It'll lead to a lot of internal rancor.

The Bobby Doyle Trio divided chores this way: Don Russell set up his drums, and the sound system (I carried my upright bass, and the clubs usually provided a piano for Doyle); Doyle wrote the musical and vocal arrangements; and I did the business. I came to handle the business by circumstance. Don was introverted and Bobby was blind. Not that that made them less capable of talking and negotiating, but it made a difference to others. People felt more comfortable talking to me. We were a co-op band. If we earned $300 a night we each received $100. At one point, though, Doyle said he deserved more money because his name was up front and he wrote the arrangements. Don and I were less than agreeable. We rejected out of hand the suggestion that his name warranted a greater salary; it wasn't a good enough reason. The band was a success because of all our talents. As for his writing the arrangements, I said, "When we start paying you for the arrangements, we should start paying me for booking the jobs. I'm the one who's been hustling these things. I pick up the money and cash and write the checks for you guys. I haven't gotten mad because no one drives across town with me to visit clubs. And I haven't complained because I sit up nights doing the bookkeeping. And Don—we ought to pay him for maintaining and setting up the equipment." We never heard another word from Doyle about this.

---

*Of course there was more to it. She had different ideas about musical direction. She wanted to steer us into an acid-rock stance, which the rest of us perceived as too ephemeral. We were older, more concerned with longevity than trend following, even if it cost us the ultra-hip audience. Eventually, by mutual agreement, Thelma left the group. Thelma, married and a mother, has been living in San Diego.

Getting Band Jobs You've assembled the group, rehearsed enough songs for a couple of hour sets, settled on a name, organized the inner functions, and sprouted some confidence. You're ready to play some band jobs. But you're untried, unknown, and not in demand. Unless some members of the group have connections and credibility previously established, you must gently force your foot in some doors. You can do one (or both) of two things: find a booking agent or approach clubs and school dance committees yourselves. We deal with agents later on. Here's how to do it yourself:

If you're in school, a good way to attract work is to play school talent shows. The Scholars got a lot of work through these—jobs at college fraternity parties and dances and teen-age clubs. Until you're eighteen, it's hard to make a lot of money because you're too young to play where liquor is served. But almost any work you can get is worth taking for the exposure and experience. When you're old enough, the way to break into clubs is by doing some undercover work. One member of your band could get friendly with musicians playing a particular place and suggest sitting in with them one night—actually to learn when their contract expires, if they plan to stay or go, how much they're getting paid, and what band jobs they might know of elsewhere. With that special knowledge, he could go to the club owner and say, "Hey, this band's contract is up in a couple of weeks and they're planning to work elsewhere afterward. I'd really like you to hear our group Catweasle and see what you think." The owner may very well take you up on it and have you onstage for a half hour on a slow night.

When you do these auditions, even though not for money, do your best. But never play a full night. Don't let anyone take advantage of you. A crafty club owner might have you come in saying, "You play Thursday night and if I like you I'll use you later," and then pull the same ploy with another group for Friday night. Soon he'll have his week's entertainment—for free! One set is a sufficient audition. If he wants you for more, negotiate. Offer to play for less than a normal gig. Instead of charging $250 for an evening, say you'll work at a special audition rate of $100.

At this point in your career, even though you're not unionized, at least shoot for union scale. Scale varies by locality and type of job; try phoning the American Federation of Musicians in your area to find out exact rates. They may not tell you unless you're a member. If we assume that scale averages $20 per night per musician (for four forty-five-minute sets with fifteen-minute breaks), as an unknown quantity you may not be able to command even that. The owner or manager might say, "Gee, I can't afford to gamble $100 a night. If you want to come in here and play as a rehearsal, or work an hour less than everybody else, then I'm willing to give you $50."

Now the question is, do you need the money, experience, and exposure enough to accept? This is a crucial question. If you work somewhere at $50 a night, you're in effect determining your worth at $50 a night. You might end up remaining at that level until you get better offers. It's like selling a used car. Some people will tell you that it's worth $1,500. But unless you get that much, it's not worth $1,500. After the union's minimum is surpassed, it's a question of what the market will bear, of supply and demand. If there are more groups than jobs, prices will be low, and vice versa. Who has the leverage? Who needs whom? If you are offered a job when you're already working, you're in a position to negotiate. Answer, "I'm sorry, but we're just not interested. We're making good money here, $200 a night, a thousand a week." Their reaction could surprise you: "Well, we'll give you half again of what you're now earning, $1,500." You might take it. But first go to your current boss and say, "Hey, we were offered $500 more a week to play at Smedley's down the street. Would you be willing to pay us that to keep us?"

There are good reasons for doing this, ethical and pragmatic. First, as a courtesy, you owe your employer the chance to keep you. Second, it can set off a small bidding war that could send your salary higher still.* Your boss at the Cripple Crutch Inn may match the figure. Then you return to Smedley: "Gee, I don't know how to tell you this, but our boss has upped our pay and we have been happy there. We're set up there and we know we're going to do well." If Smedley backs out, at least you've won a raise from your boss. Again, having two people negotiating against each other can only help your position—if you play it. Of course, if you don't have the leverage, you're at the mercy of others and circumstance.

When you do accept a job, even if it is just for $50 a night, do your very best, as though you were getting $1,000. Playing according to the amount of money you're earning is a terrible habit, which could eventually take its toll musically. Also, you never know who's in the audience. There might be other

---

*When Greif and Garris asked me to leave Houston for the New Christy Minstrels for $500, I told them I couldn't join for that; I'd been earning $650 and had no travel expenses, as I was living at home. They came up to $650, still excluding expenses. Then I went to the club I was working, told them what the Christies offered me, and said I'd have to leave. They offered me $700 to stay. The Christies, in turn, matched that. Again I went to the club owner saying I really should go— the Christies represented a career step up. He surprised me by coming up to $750. Here I had upped the Christies' offer 50 percent by playing one off the other, something I was obliged to do. I owed the club the chance to keep me and I owed it to myself to be paid my worth, which is best determined by testing what the market can bear. Of course, I took my shot with the Christies.

club owners. There might be potential investors, agents, or record company representatives. Professionalism means doing your best despite bad pay, sparsely filled halls or clubs, fights with your lover, or fresh dents in your new Corvette. Remember, you're always playing for yourself.

Many of your jobs will come through word of mouth. If you're good, other musicians and groups will know about it. To accelerate the process, frequent places conducive to free playing. Before you go onstage at another group's job to jam or perform your material, however, just be certain you're presenting yourself at full strength. If you're not, don't do it, or don't announce your name. Someone out there who is considering hiring you might decide the question by that performance.

After getting this exposure, about the worst thing that can happen is that an employer will like you and then, when he needs you, not know how to contact you. So, before venturing out of the shed, have some inexpensive, but good, business cards printed. It should have the group's name, Catweasle, and the name, address, and phone number of the leader or the member responsible for bookings. Include some indication of the type of music you play. You can leave the cards with school entertainment committees and club owners and post them at music stores and shopping-center bulletin boards. And give them to people when they compliment you at jobs.

Now, the owner of the Cripple Crutch calls you. Your first reaction before finalizing a deal is to switch on what I call "pencil consciousness." Pencil consciousness simply means forcasting on paper all of the probable costs hidden in the deal. You may find that the job just isn't worth it. Suppose, for example, that you're offered $1,000 to play a week in Denver, Colorado. It sounds fantastic. But it sours on paper. After commissions, you have $750. Transportation, say a van and a car, drinks over $100 of gas driving the 2,000 miles from L.A. to Denver and back to L.A. Now the five of you need three hotel rooms for the six days. An average decent room costs about $12 a day; needing three rooms, that's $216. Then there's food—$10 a day each, or $300. Now you're clearing $134! I haven't even counted union fees, the cost of a new set of guitar strings, etc. So you want to start a band? Don't look at gross dollars. Look at *net* dollars.

If the pencil proves an offer insufficient, get back to your agent or manager or the employer and bargain. "I figured it out," you could say, "and we only make $134 working for $1,000 out there. Now if you can give us $1,500, we'd make $509. That would justify our doing it. Or, give us the thousand dollars plus room and board."

Getting room and board is great in that you don't pay commissions on them. Which is why agencies usually book jobs for gross dollars and don't bargain for rooms unless you insist they do. But beware if the agency calls you back and says that they can't get the rooms but did succeed in upping the salary to $1,300. For, after commissions, you're left with only an additional $225. Are you still losing money on the deal?

A good business sense will gain you the respect of agencies and club owners. They'll *want* to work with you.

Besides talking financial terms, discuss the other details with the club owner. Determine what's expected of you and the club. Do they supply drum risers, a piano, dressing rooms, a sound system, lighting? What times do you start, take breaks, quit? Tell the manager how you intend to dress onstage. (For example, "We wear street clothes because we're a casual group, but our clothes won't be filthy." Or, "We wear fancy western suits.") Speaking of dress, be concerned that you don't *under*dress. Most club owners feel they're getting more for their money if you wear special clothes. And most audiences will find a visually interesting act more attractive; they don't care to be entertained by grocery clerks.

Your concern at this juncture is protection, something too easily overlooked by the inexperienced, especially when they're excited by the prospect of performing publicly for money. But unless you happen to be watched over by a friendly angel, you can count on being ripped off sooner or later. And when you are cheated, with the burden of proof on your shoulders in court, you'll need solid evidence.

At bottom it's a question of something that I learned a long time ago: Any person who's unwilling to sign a piece of paper documenting an agreement shows the need for that paper with his signature. If he's not willing to autograph it, he must not really be prepared to deliver his part of the bargain. Don't be embarrassed about asking for a contract. A good business person will respect your desire for it. It protects him as well as you and cleanly precludes most misunderstandings. Both parties know what they're getting despite healthy imaginations, bad memories, and downright devious intentions.

What could happen? Between the time you're hired and the date, a club owner could find another group that might perform just as well but for less money. And you may not learn about it until after you've turned down other work and driven to the club with your equipment, where you meet the other band unloading their van. This happened to me more than a few times. Once a club owner hired the Trio to take the place of a band that had had disagreements with him and said they were quitting. We drove quite a distance to the club, walked in, and the owner said, "Well, the band decided to stay. They've really done well and they've got a following. I'm really sorry."

"Well, so am I," I said. "But you can pay us to sit over here to listen to the band."

Besides the fact that we didn't care to waste the night completely, we stayed the four hours because we didn't want him to be able to say we were supposed to play later but left.

The musicians union made him pay us. If we hadn't had a written agreement, however, it would have been his word against mine. He could have claimed, "I told them the regular band might be there, but they misunderstood." Although a verbal contract is binding, you must have witnesses to the agreement.

I learned the hard way. When I first started with the Scholars, the following happened: A club owner promised, "I'll give you $15 each from 8:00 to 12:00 P.M. And I'll give you 50 percent of the money I take in at the door in cover charges." What he didn't explain was that the $15 was *against* what accrued at the door, that is, the first $75 didn't apply to our earnings. Which would have been all right, except that that wasn't our understanding. So it was a shock when the owner counted out our money and said, "Now that's $75 I've already paid you." Even though it wasn't unfair, we felt cheated and almost quit. Sometimes 200 to 300 people were in the club at one time, and we'd counted on every dollar to buy some new equipment.

When a contract has been broken, there are three avenues of recourse: Hire a sumo wrestler to beat the offender within an inch of his life, file suit in court, or complain to the musicians union. I don't recommend the first as it's bound to land you in jail. The second, if it's a small-claims case, is expedient and inexpensive. The third requires, of course, that you be a union member.

The Musicians Union

You don't need to join the musicians union—the American Federation of Musicians—until you have to. You'll know when that is. It's when you begin playing union establishments—clubs, hotels, restaurants, concert halls that have contracts with the union. It's when employers ask to see your union cards, and union officials visit your jobs and let you know that you must join or give up working that establishment. Virtually all good, commercial places are closed union shops. And they maintain it that way because the better musicians are usually in the union.

Joining is a matter of applying, passing an undemanding audition (they just want to know that you are, in fact, a musician; they don't care how good you are), and paying a onetime initiation fee and quarterly dues, the amounts of which vary by locality. At Los Angeles Local 47, for instance, where there's a concentration of work and broader union services, initiation costs about $160.

The fee in Local 166 in Madison, Wisconsin, is, on the other hand, less than half that. Dues are, respectively, about $12 and $7 per quarter. The union also makes its money through reinstatement fees, fines assessed for late dues payments and other violations, and work dues. In L.A.'s Local 47, work dues amount to 2 percent of your salary from each nightclub, theater, symphony, and casual job, and 3 percent for motion picture, TV, recording, and commercial jingle work. Employers, meanwhile, pay surcharges, sent directly to the union, of 5 percent per individual to the pension fund and 5 percent to the hospital fund. For records, TV, movies, and jingles, these amounts are 10 percent. Record companies also pay a general royalty on record sales. This amounts to $10 million a year, which the AFM divides among those who had records out that year.

What you get, besides the right to work in union clubs, is a guaranteed minimum pay rate. In L.A., scale for a 4½-hour, 6-night club engagement is $200 per group member and $300 for the leader. You get guaranteed working conditions, 15-minute breaks each hour of those 4½-hour dates, and time and a half pay for overtime. You get meager pension and health plans and a subscription to the AFM's monthly tabloid, *The International Musician.* You also get the very beneficial access to their credit union, an easy source of low-interest loans (they understand the musician's itinerant life-style), and their low-cost medical and life insurance coverages.

Most importantly, the union supplies you with protection. They do this by furnishing standardized contracts,* which, after the blanks have been filled in and the contracts signed, they check and approve. The union then files a copy. In the event of a dispute with your employer, you can bring the matter before a trial board. If found in your favor, the employer can appeal to the local's board of directors. If that fails, the matter goes to the International Executive Board. If the employer is still found to be in violation of the contract, the union can seek a judgment from the Municipal Court. Until the matter is resolved, that employer is placed on a defaulters' list (published in *The International Musician*), so he can't use the services of other AFM members. If he wins, though, you must pay back what you owe him or the union will expel you.

The union's history has been one of a struggle to keep live music a major, large-scale profession, to keep musicians gainfully employed.** Beginning as a

---

*The first page of the American Federation of Musicians contract form is reproduced in Appendix I.

**For an excellent, if somewhat dry and obsolete, history of musicians' labor struggles, read *The Musicians and Petrillo* by Robert D. Leiter (New York: Bookman Associates, 1953; reprinted 1975 by Octagon Books, New York).

social club in the mid-nineteenth century, it evolved as a part of the American Federation of Labor and strived to improve conditions and wages. By the twenties, the union's chief concern was technological employment, threatened by radio's use of recorded music and the advent of sound pictures.

The union struck against record companies in 1942 and 1947 to get them to contribute part of their income to health and welfare funds. In the forties and fifties, it moved to regulate television and wired music, such as Muzak. In the sixties, it sought to confine the use of electronic tape and synthesizer instruments, which could replace whole string and brass sections. In the seventies, a major battle shaped up against discotheques.

Today the union maintains the status quo, with a fairly healthy membership of more than 350,000 in the United States and Canada. If only for the struggle of the past, and as an expression of professional solidarity, the union deserves your support. In fact, the union's strongest suit is probably in its helpfulness to beginning professionals. Whereas the big successful groups can hire their own attorneys to write and enforce their contracts, those who can't afford this still need protection. And it's the less-established acts that need the union-scale guidelines.

Understand, however, that in affiliating with the union you aren't guaranteed work. Throughout its history, the union never attempted to force a musician—whatever his degree of competence—on an employer. The union has only tried to preserve the job itself. Whether or not a musician gets and retains a job depends on his or her talents, racial and sex discrimination notwithstanding. Understand also that many union locals aren't effective enough to enforce contracts and punish offenders. Only too rarely will they go into a club and say, "Give us that money or we're taking you to court." This has long bothered me: The union is often ineffectual, unless the case is on a large scale and the local is a strong one. Then it can cripple to get its way, such as in 1976 when New York's Local 802 called its musicians out on strike against the Philharmonic. Unfortunately, in gaining retribution from dishonest, fly-by-night promoters and flaky club owners, they are less aggressive. Putting a crook on the defaulters' list doesn't prevent him from setting up another bogus operation several hundred miles away under another name and phony credentials.

I have also found the union lacking in decisiveness. One dispute seems particularly illustrative. After the Bobby Doyle Trio's expectations of instant fame as recording stars fell flat (the album we recorded on Columbia sold enough to guarantee instant obscurity), Bobby Doyle became especially disillusioned and uncaring and took to drinking. Although this was only temporary, at the time it was detrimental to his performance onstage. It was particularly aggravating to Don Russell and me because the club we were working, The Act

Three, was our own. Finally we fired him. Doyle protested to the union, and they agreed we were obligated to give him two weeks' notice. So we all went downtown to the union office. Don and I explained we couldn't afford to give Doyle that courtesy. Our intention, we said, was not to deprive someone of work unfairly. But if that person is unwilling to perform his job properly, we certainly shouldn't have to keep that person. The man had been hurting our club's business. Each of us told his side of the story, but the union never did decide the case. The Trio ended like that, with bad feelings. But as the years passed, we again became good friends.

Today, to fire someone without showing cause, the union requires two weeks' notice if the person has been with you for less than six months. After six months, you must give him three weeks', and after twelve months, four weeks'. To fire someone instantly you must be able to show cause, such as drunkenness on the job. The fired individual has available the same appeals procedure as the employer accused of violating a contract.

Aside from the Doyle affair, I've been pretty lucky. Since the day I started in the business full-time I've made more than scale and haven't had to depend too heavily on the union. It was more like dealing with the government, filling out the myriad forms and sending out checks for petty amounts. I get fined all the time for not paying dues on time too. Though they know I've been based in Los Angeles for years, they always send my notices to Houston. By the time they reach me in L.A., I'm overdue, and they add a $2 penalty. The same happens with bills for our performances in other locals' jurisdictions.*

The fines are nominal. But to a scuffling musician, such amounts may mean a few dinners. One union official sent me his business card printed, "Shorty so-and-so. The sonofabitch from the union." He must have remembered how he regarded the union when *he* was a working musician. (Seriously, the union people do serve an important purpose.)

Before you have to deal with this benign bureaucracy, devise your own contract. It should state the facts of the job, the dates, times, place, salary, and what equipment each party is to provide. If the club is to provide a piano, for example, specify that it's to be tuned to the standard A440 pitch, so that it's consistent with your unvariable instruments (electric organ, harmonica, etc.). Also specify that you're to be paid by either cash or a cashier's check. As there are many shaky clubs and concert promoters, this insures that you're really

---

*When playing out of town, just mail a copy of the contract to the local you'll be working in. List the date, club, salary, members' names, and social security numbers. They usually bill you for the 2 percent work dues or send someone to the club to collect it. Some cities, including Chicago, prefer that you bring your union card and pay at the office.

walking away with earnings, not rubberized paper. Indeed, this may be this book's most important advice!

Finally, you might opt to include a paragraph in the contract concerning the employer's advertising obligations. This is especially valuable when your salary includes a percentage of the door. In my early days, clubs only advertised in newspapers. Our only responsibility was to furnish photos for inclusion in the ads. The best advertising that we could do—and this remains true—was word of mouth. We'd tell friends and pack the place. Besides doing that, you can announce at other band jobs your upcoming gigs. (This isn't too wise if at a competing club, but it's valid at dances or parties.) The owner of one club where the Bobby Doyle Trio was regularly booked did an interesting variation on this: He gave me a $400-a-month apartment rent-free in a complex he owned in exchange for our playing for free an hour each Sunday by the pool. In the midst of these gatherings, he'd announce that this is the band that plays over at the club. I got a free apartment; his club got a healthy attendance.

Discuss ways you might help the club advertise. For one, if the club pays for printing posters (and isn't far from home), offer to tack them up on bulletin boards and telephone poles. It shouldn't be beneath you, especially if you're scuffling. In any case, the clubs that are derelict in advertising are those that tend to fail. Strategic advertising is an important, not superfluous, cost of doing business.

Making It to Your Gig   With a job booked, the band's travel coordinator distributes his *detailed* itinerary and travel instructions. I stress detailed because in the beginning it's better to overexplain. You don't want any screw-ups to give you a reputation for lateness or no-shows. This comes from someone who has experienced the most monumental of screw-ups, some of which could have been scripted by the Marx Brothers. For example, around 1968, during the First Edition's first stint on the road, we looked at our itinerary. "Proceed one hundred miles to Athens. Plane departs at 8:15 A.M. You arrive in Atlanta at 9. There, transfer to. . . ." Driving into Athens, Tennessee, we found an airport that looked very much like what I'd imagine the Mule Shoe, Texas, airport looks like. Which is to say it rarely saw anything bigger than a crop duster. With unquestioning faith in our itinerary and a lot of naïveté, we unloaded our ton of amplifiers and drums and sat waiting for our plane. And sat. At about 7:45, Mickey walked over to some crotchety Walter Brennan-type guy to inquire when our plane would arrive. "Hell, ain't no plane comin' in here," the man answered. "Hell. There ain't been a plane in here in three weeks. We got a little private plane, a little Cherokee, comin' in here. But you ain't gonna get all that claptrap on her." We must have looked pretty stunned and disbelieving, because the man challenged us to talk to the pilot over the radio. "Well, talk to him," he said. "It's not your plane. He'll tell you he's not your plane."

We had to laugh when we discovered that we were supposed to have met a plane at Athens—*Georgia*. We ended up chartering four private planes, costing us a budget-busting $800. But we made it to the date. Future itineraries would be quite specific.

The First Edition, when we first started, usually drove. We used two cars, one a station wagon pulling a trailer. We communicated via walkie-talkies, this being before citizens-band radio. As the walkie-talkies were limited in range, we occasionally got separated. In one town, we only reunited because we both happened to need gas and found the one station with the brand whose credit card we used.

Anticipate wrong turns and mishaps on the road, and tell everyone to leave with time to spare. In fact, plan to arrive at the club, hall, or theater early, perhaps a couple of hours before showtime. There are bound to be some technical difficulties. Maybe you'll need a drum platform. Or maybe the sound system, adequate for the last act, is inadequate for yours. Maybe the last group didn't need a spotlight and you do. Maybe a tube or fuse in the lead guitarist's amp has broken. If you arrive at the last minute, there'll be no time to rectify such things. Which is not to mention the time required to set up and tune properly, do a sound check (playing a few numbers to test the balance of voices and instruments and adjust to the room's acoustics and peculiarities), and change clothes. Eventually, when you have a road crew of one or two members in charge of the equipment setup, you, the performers, won't have to arrive so early. But initially it's important that everyone does to see that all's well and show commitment to the job.

Checking Your Sound Sound checks involve some psychology. Seemingly, it'd be best to check with the loudest of your numbers to gauge the upper limit of your volume. In fact, it's preferable *not* to. The First Edition almost blew a few jobs before we learned this. Some state fairs even told us that they wouldn't rehire us without a rider in the contract specifying a maximum decibel level. Some insisted on providing the sound system— complete with a man controlling the master volume. The problem is, many club owners are older and their musical tastes run to Andy Williams or Olivia Newton-John. When the club is filled, they probably won't notice the loudness. But when it's empty, it'll scare them. And remember, the first impression you make is the lasting one. So start with a number of some dynamic variation. You'll appeal to the owners and put their minds at rest about your ability to appeal to their customers.

If something goes wrong when you run through the sound check, you'll have to trouble-shoot, trying various equipment combinations until the defective part is isolated. It's only when you're without spare parts that such problems become crises, especially when the item is indispensable. Having allowed enough time, someone could run downtown to a music store and buy, say, the new mike cord. If the defective equipment is something that the club promised to provide, you'll have to ask the owner to give you the money for it, perhaps offering to pick it up at the store for him. If he refuses, you should still rent, buy, or borrow the equipment if possible. (Just remember to take the equipment when you go.) The paramount thing is to sound good. You don't want to be at an important job on Saturday night with an essential amp kaput and face a steaming club owner who's watching people pour out of his place to rush into the Next Door Club.

Before going onstage to perform, the guitars should be in tune. This should be done during the sound check or with a small amplifier in the dressing rooms. Tunings may change slightly before the show, but the point is to minimize tuning in front of the audience. It's distracting and diffuses your impact. Equally, it's important to do your tuning on *your* time. Many club owners are touchy about that. If scheduled to start at 9:15 P.M. and you need to tune to the organ onstage, go onstage ten minutes early.

One ideal way to tune guitars accurately without having to plug into the amplifiers onstage is to use a strobe tuner. A luxury only for groups that can afford it, a strobe shows you, visually, when a string is precisely in pitch. You plug the instrument into the box and a wheel spins to the left or right depending on whether the note is sharp or flat; it stops in the center when correct. If you must tune onstage, between songs or at the start of a set, and it seems to be taking a long time, have something prepared to prevent the audience from getting bored and to take the stigma off your slowness. I use throwaway lines. I might turn, look at the band, and say, "Thank God I don't play harp. We'd be here all night."

Gauging Your Audience　In playing clubs, learn to analyze your audience as the first set progresses. If the club is a familiar one, you'll know what kind of music works best there. Frequently, however, you won't really know, especially as you travel out of town. Some clubs may not want any ballads; they want all rock and roll. If it's a dancing crowd, they'll probably want solid funk. Other places might expect bland cocktail-lounge music. (Try to avoid bad bookings, but they will happen now and then.) In any case, playing what you've planned when it's plain that it's not going over with the paying customers is wrong. So, early in the show, try to gauge people's feelings and play to them.

Something the First Edition did, and I still do, is open with a pair of loud, attention-grabbing songs, and then ask wryly, "Can everybody hear all right?" I'll go on:

> You know, it's really funny that for some sadistic reason the managers of fairgrounds—where the First Edition played for awhile—sometimes put the older people in the front rows. And after the second number, up here we'd hear someone groan, "Oh, God, Martha. It's going to be a long night."

This lets people know that I know we're loud. After that I'll ask: "How many people here love rock and roll? Let me know." I'll get a wave of applause, as most of the places we work draw young people. I'll add, "Now, in the interest of fair play, how many do *not* like rock and roll?" I'll get a response (usually weak, thank God). That tells me what sort of set to play.

Testing the audience also serves to tell the club owner, school entertainment director, or whoever booked you, that you're doing a certain type of show because it pleases the customers. Once an older fair manager complained to me after a show. "You know," he said, "thirty-eight old people out there got up and walked out."

"Yeah, but you had four thousand people stay," I countered. "If you had Johnny Mann here, and there were thirty-eight teenagers out there, would you ask him to play hard rock just for them?"

"No."

"Then you can't expect me to direct my show to thirty-eight older people. I'll try to do something in future shows here that will appeal to them. But I'm not going to gear my show to thirty-eight people."

Handling Requests, Fights, Etc. Working to please your audience also means fielding song requests. Diplomatically. Try honoring ones that you can play well and make sense in terms of the show's format. One rule is, don't repeat a certain song in the same set. If you do a number and twenty minutes later someone comes back saying, "I know you did it before, but would you do it again," answer no. Tell them you're sorry, but you have other requests and you'll try to do it for them in the third set. Nothing ruins a song more than for the musicians to tire of it. Or for the audience to tire of it. It's better to leave them, and yourselves, wanting to hear (and play) it again.

One of the hardest things for me to overcome when I began in the business was handling requests that we couldn't fulfill. I always felt we were disappointing people until I realized that you can't know every song.

Whether you're playing the right job for your music or not, disruptions and outright brawls will occur in the audience every now and then. Or some jerk with a chip on his shoulder may jump onstage to provoke a fight with you. Whatever, stopping disruptions is the club manager's responsibility. It's up to the club to provide an atmosphere conducive to your performing at your best. It's up to you to perform. Also, you look bad if you intercede in fights. If trouble breaks out, one of the members or the road manager should go to the club owner and say, "Hey, the guy over there in the black shirt is causing trouble. He's always coming up and talking into the microphone." If the owner neglects to do anything, go back to him. "Look, I think you'd better correct this because we cannot perform under these conditions. The next time he grabs the mike, we're just going to have to leave the stage."

Being from Texas, I claim some authority in dealing with bar fights. For one thing, when one erupts, don't stop playing. Club owners prefer that you keep the crowd's attention, rather than stop and draw further attention to the fight. Again, it's not up to you to play Henry Kissinger. I've tried the negotiating approach and almost had the position of my teeth renegotiated.

When I was with the Lively Ones,* one near calamity occurred over a song request that we couldn't fulfill. It was absurd enough to be a skit from "Saturday Night Live."

Set up in a club's small horseshoe area, formerly the section for a piano bar, we were sort of trapped when a drunk approached us at two minutes to midnight, closing time.

"Do 'Happy Birthday' for Linda," he slurred.

Well, Paul Massara, our very short guitarist, was a Jehovah's Witness. And Witnesses don't believe in celebrating any birthdays other than Christ's.

"I'm very sorry, sir," explained Paul, "but I'm a Jehovah's Witness and I don't believe in doing that."

"I don't give a damn who you are. I want to hear 'Happy Birthday.' I paid my money."

---

*The Lively Ones was a group I formed after the Bobby Doyle Trio disbanded.

It became plain that the guy was really going to mop up on Paul. So, being by far the biggest person in the group, I stepped in between them.

"Now wait a second," I said. "Don't make an issue of this. First of all, we get off in two minutes. Second, the man doesn't believe in doing this. There are other places you can go."

"I'm gonna beat that sonofabitch . . ."

"Look, you're going to have to go over me to get to him."

And the next thing I knew, the guy was about to fight me. I looked around. Paul, Paula, and Don had retreated. It was 12 o'clock and they'd gone to the bar. At least with the band gone the issue became defused. I was saved by the bell.

A worse situation than the threat or actuality of physical violence is probably that in which you're booked into the worst possible place for your style of music. If all attempts to please the audience fail, I'd turn the volume down and make the best of it. You might get notes that say, "Don't play that loud garbage. Play 'Help Me Make It Through the Night.' " If the engagement is more than a one-nighter, list them so that the next day you can sit down with the band and learn a few of them. When asked for a song that you can't do, suggest a similar song to the customer—"We don't know that, but we've got one we think you'll like." Or you might say, "We don't know that, but tomorrow night we will." Even though the same people may not be back the next night, at least you'll be on the track toward mollifying this clientele.

Dealing with the Club Owner   To do business with club owners, you must understand them. More than loving capacity crowds, they love capacity crowds of drinkers. If filling the cashbox isn't their first reason for having the club, it surely runs a close second. As such, they not only want a great band that draws endless drinkers, they also want a reliable one that they don't have to be concerned with. A club owner is apt to think about an irresponsible act this way: "Oh my God. I'll really be glad when this week's up so I can get rid of them. I need a band that's easy to work with. I'm worrying about the cash register, about the waitresses and bartenders stealing from me. . . . Here the band is supposed to be on at fifteen minutes after and it's usually twenty-five after before they go on, and they come off five minutes early. I can't concentrate on selling drinks. . . ."

The key is to handle yourselves well on the job. Not only will you be retained, but you'll be able to get raises and more cooperation. The owner will be more willing to help you in other areas, perhaps in making improvements in the stage and lighting or recommending you to his friends and other club owners. If you're playing the club for a lengthy engagement, for example, you might approach the owner about helping you afford a new sound system. Show him that it will improve his business. Say you'll buy it—if he's willing to pay you an extra $50 a week. Then, after working your five weeks, you'll own the thousand-dollar sound system (and have saved $250 on it). If it's lighting that you need, offer to install it yourselves if he pays for the materials. As most club owners don't make a fortune, give them a reason to believe that such expenditures contribute to their success and they'll go along with them. And remember, the music is *your* business. So present yourself as the authority. On the whole, I don't recommend that you take music-related advice from club owners. They like to think they know about performing, but they usually don't. And, if you take their suggestion and it doesn't work, you're still to blame.

Some time after it's plain that you've been doing well and business has been good, the band's business person should approach the owner/manager with that fact. It's your leverage for getting a raise. "I know you're paying us $500 a week, but I also know that we've doubled your business. So, could we either get a raise of $150 or a percentage of the take at the door? If we play well and work hard and draw a lot of people, we should be able to split the extra dough coming in." He may turn down the proposal flat. And he may have reason to. The crowd you draw may be sizable but not as thirsty for booze as another. Considering yourself a professional, you should still perform your best. But when your contract is up, go back to him. Tell him, "Well, OK. If you want the group back, we're going to need an extra $150 (or whatever)."

Anytime you renegotiate a contract—and you feel you have the leverage —try to upgrade your salary, even if only slightly. It's as essential psychologically as it is monetarily. You've got to feel that you're advancing, and the employer has to show he appreciates you or you'll feel abused. By offering you raises, the employer supplies you with extra incentive, which, by extension, yields him greater profits. His volume of customers will increase. Just be sure to get what's coming to you. Stand up for yourself.

As time passes, you'll occasionally have problems collecting your salary. If you believe you won't, then you probably also believe in Santa Claus. There are numerous clubs built on financial quicksand. Even armed with a contract, think about your money if, after a few nights, business has been consistently dead slow. By midweek, perhaps, ask the owner for 25 percent in advance. Invent an excuse—say one of the amps broke and you have to buy a new one. Besides being guaranteed that 25 percent, enough to cover expenses if the owner proves a deadbeat, it's a psychological help toward collecting the full amount. At week's end, chances are the club owner will have forgotten how hard it was to pay you the 25 percent and will be relieved to think that he need only come up with 75 percent, say $750 instead of $1,000. He'll remember you more fondly and perhaps hire you again. The next time, however, you'd better draw some customers.

Somehow it works. But be cautious when you try for advances. It once backfired on me. Before then, I hadn't heard about asking for advances. But when the Bobby Doyle Trio was asked to work at this club in San Antonio, Texas, it seemed like a good idea. The owner wanted us to play on sheer speculation; that is, by the number of customers. I wasn't willing to do it because it seemed likely that there might be only twenty customers a night. So he offered me $600 for the week. I said we'd need half in advance. He said he couldn't do that, but he would give us 25 percent, $150. He wrote a check and I walked off very proud of myself for having negotiated that. Fine. We played and at the end of the week he paid us the balance in cash. When we returned to Houston and cashed the check, it bounced. The part that burned most was that if I hadn't asked for the advance, we probably would have ended up with the full $600 in cash. Advances are all right. Just beware of checks.

Let's say you've maintained a good relationship with your employers and played well. When the job is done, take the opportunity to lay the groundwork for your future. Ask the owner about later bookings. If you know the club is booked for awhile, tell him you also are booked, but you'd like to discuss the possibility of returning in six weeks. Mention that you enjoyed working there. Whether he books you or not, ask him to write a letter of recommendation for you: "Will you do me a favor? This is one of the first jobs we've played, so would you give me a letter saying we did a good job and were on time every night and that you'll hire us again when you get the chance? It'll help us find work elsewhere." And ask him about other jobs in town.

A portfolio of recommendations is of great value in getting jobs. There will be times when auditioning is inconvenient. When the prospective employer reads that five clubs found you prompt and good at playing danceable Top-40 sets, that you increased attendance by an average of 20 percent, and that you've been offered return bookings, you're bound to get the job. This primitive form of promotion works until your name itself sells the band. Later in your career, when you vie for mass markets, your manager and agents will ply as credentials such things as what chart statistics your records muster (airplay and sales), the number of seats you fill in shows, and the positive comments you receive from music reviewers. They'll use these to land you publishing deals, record contracts, television and tour bookings, feature stories in magazines, financing and musical-equipment sponsorship.

One thing you might eventually do about generating return bookings is insert a return engagement clause in your contracts. Just be careful not to commit yourself too far in advance. You never know what good turns of fortune may lie down the road, and you don't want to be tied to some low-money dates once you've broken into higher circles and developed a prestigious name. What you could do is extend the clause to include a mutual cancellation provision, exercisable by either party thirty days prior to the date. For you, the only drawback is that the club could cancel you. Some shrewd clubs put a clause into their contracts giving them a one-sided option. The important showcase clubs, located mostly in the media centers of Los Angeles and New York, are notorious for this. That's why they'll "risk" booking someone on the verge of breaking big. When the budding artists later bloom into superstars, the clubs bring them back —at the same low price. It has happened to Elton John, Joni Mitchell, and countless others. Some stars, rather than look silly, pay thousands of dollars to get released from these clauses. But new talents continue to sign them because of the possibility the gig holds for a major career breakthrough.

"How Did We Do?"   After your dates, particularly the first few, the band should gather to assess things. However, avoid the temptation to do it *right* after you get offstage. Before tearing down the equipment and loading it into the van—a chore shared by everyone, unless you have roadies—you'll probably gather to change in the dressing rooms (in some clubs this means the bathrooms). Now, exhausted, tense, and still a bit nervous, the most damaging thing anyone can do is pick apart a show that went reasonably well. Most of you will be feeling elated, thinking, "Hey, we had some problems but I think it went all right." You owe it to yourselves to savor, rather than deflate, that little high. For this moment, just say, "If anything bothered anybody, make a note of it and we'll discuss it tomorrow." Sleep on it. For even if the show was a disaster, and everyone is crying, criticism now will only depress you further. The next group meeting is soon enough to iron out the kinks. In this saner atmosphere, sit down and scrutinize the performance objectively. The idea is to improve, not pretend that all was rosy out of fear of offending anyone. Suppose that friends in the audience told you they thought the bass was too loud. Decide to back it down or bring the other instruments up. Suppose one of the numbers was weak because the lead guitarist couldn't sing it well enough. You could determine to beef it up instrumentally, add backing vocals, or have someone else sing it. Suppose there's a list of songs people frequently requested that you couldn't play. Learn them.

This sort of technical improvement only comes through playing before audiences. Another sort of improvement—a sheer reduction of errors—sometimes takes care of itself, but sometimes requires the band's attention. In any case, onstage isn't the place to deal with mistakes. By commenting over the mike, or flashing the offender with angry glares, you make him feel terrible. And you draw attention to the blooper, which very well might have passed by the audience. Even offstage, however, I don't like to criticize members for accidental mistakes. The minute you start attacking someone, he gets paranoid and inhibited, and his playing reflects it. Plus, if he's professional, he'll probably come to the band on his own to apologize for his mistake. (But a pro knows that apologies only work for awhile. After that he has got to have it together on his ax.) Besides, mistakes frequently turn into brilliant ideas. And some screw-ups are merely part of the spontaneity allowed, no, welcomed, in performance.

It's when a goof recurs two or three nights straight that you discuss it with the individual. Find out what the problem is. If he's basically a good musician, he probably misunderstands his part. Explain, "Hey, in the third song that chord after the bridge is a B major, not a minor seventh." If it's not a musical fault, it may be a technical one. Perhaps the drummer, positioned as he is in the rear of the stage, isn't keeping the time because he can't hear the bassist. So solve it. Get an extension speaker by the drums or reposition the bass amp.

A third likelihood is that the musician has a conflicting view of the song. He may feel that what he's doing is right and refuse to play it the way you've worked it out. This is more a personnel problem. As group leader, my first impulse in such a situation is to be diplomatic. If I can, I'll seek a compromise. But in a question of musical judgment that I absolutely can't agree with, I'll be firm. I'll say something like, "I know you'd rather play that figure. But I'm responsible for the sound of this group. So you'll have to do it my way for now. When you put your group together, you can do it that way."

A final possibility is that the musician proves unqualified. This gets touchy, especially where friends are involved. In any case, don't rush out to fire the guy. You apparently cared enough about his playing to add him to the group in the first place. You owe him the benefit of a preliminary talk. "Bob, we really like the way you play ballads. But on the rock things, there's something wrong. Do me a favor. Listen to McCartney's bass playing. Notice where he plays fills and leaves holes." Rather than attacking him, give him a reason to believe he's good but simply has the wrong idea and can change. At First Edition meetings, we often had to caution Mickey to work on more contemporary drum fills. It wasn't that he was incapable. He had just developed a certain feel that he liked and used it and used it until there was little differentiation from one song to the next. I got my knocks, too. The band sometimes sneered at me, "Your bass sounds like 1956." So I sat down once in awhile with Gene Lorenzo, our piano player, and learned bass lines that he suggested.

If the weak musician doesn't heed your advice to take the practice vitamin, either out of stubbornness or denseness, you then owe him the threat of losing his position. Still maintain your tact: "Bob, you've made some improvement. But it still isn't as strong as it has to be. Now if for some reason you don't feel you can cut it, please tell us so we can get another bassist." Now it's more a question of his being honest with himself than of his feeling victimized by an evil conspiracy. He'll either do his homework or decide to leave on his own.

When all attempts fail, the deed must be done. First make sure that you have someone better lined up. To deliver the message, if yours is a group of equal members, you should all visit the about-to-be-severed member; if there's a leader, he should do it. If one of you happens to be his closest friend or the group leader, that person might talk to him privately: "We all love you as friends, but the band has been dissatisfied with your musicianship. We've tried two or three times to make it work, but it doesn't seem like it's going to. So you should find another job over the next two weeks." Also, he could say that it might be better if he (the fired member) went to the others and told them he was leaving.

Hopefully, the ex-member will depart with his head up and enough confidence to go on to improve and be hired by another act—and to remain on reasonably friendly terms with you. In any event, he'll have gained from the experience a firmer sense of reality and of his limitations, and thus be better equipped to direct himself in future ventures.

In the formative stage of the band's life, also move toward eliminating those whose personalities and/or personal problems (e.g., drinking, drug abuse) are as detrimental as someone who can't play well. You'll have enough strains when you develop as performers and individuals and encounter the hard knocks. In this regard, there shouldn't be a situation in which there are backstage, or onstage, fistfights between members of the group. Animosities shouldn't be released this way. You should be able to laugh at things that go awry, as in any other job. My groups have had disagreements, some quite heated. And I've received some dirty looks onstage. But never did things degenerate to the point of out-and-out physical violence. If someone can't get along with those around him, send him to find another job.

Do-It-Yourself Publicity   After you've begun working steadily, and the band's inner workings stabilize somewhat, attend to details that will further establish the band. Print publicity photos, posters, and leaflets, and assemble a portfolio, including a résumé, letters of recommendation, and photographs. If you're like most groups at this stage—on a slight budget—these expenses may seem frivolous. But they *will* pay off. And they can be done cheaply. Find friends, relatives, or neighbors who are good at photography and printing, or who have connections with professional shops and can do you favors. Just be sure that their efforts don't look cheap. My first publicity materials looked ridiculous. The Scholars recorded with a little record label run by Larry Kane and Jimmy Duncan. (Duncan wrote Bobby Helms' hit, "My Special Angel.") They sent us to a photographer. We told him that we wanted just our heads showing. So he punched holes in black backdrop paper and we stuck our heads through. A great idea. Only the pictures revealed the paper folding around our necks and a few of our collars protruding. The Bobby Doyle Trio got a professional photographer. But even in his photos I looked strange. Like the successful singers at the time, I wanted to have wavy hair. Before the session I got a permanent, and in the pictures you could see a little curl hanging in front of my face. It took six months to grow it out.

The background photo props should indicate the type of music you play. If you are an urban-funk group, don't pose for photos sitting on a split-rail fence with horses grazing in the background. Similarly, don't wear fancy suits if you come onstage in street clothes. You've got to solidify an image to allow the band to develop a memorable identity. For the first three years of the First Edition, we were always photographed in black and white outfits, which we also wore onstage. We tried to reinforce the idea of print, its currency and freshness.

Also have printed some placemats or tent cards (a small card folded in the middle) with a picture and the group's name (designed in an artistic but readable logo). For about $50 you can print hundreds to put on tables wherever you work. Make them subtle. Don't blight them with phone numbers and individual names. These cards are strictly to fix the group's name in the public mind. Club patrons often don't bother to find out who is performing. However, if they see the group and like it and find a card that says CATWEASLE, they'll know the name. And you never know who'll be in that audience and how important he'll prove to be. You might even sign a few autographs, now that people have something with your picture to write on.

What the Trio did was put cards on tables of clubs other than the one we worked, the after-hours Show Biz. The other clubs didn't object because our 12:30 to 3:00 A.M. job didn't interfere with their 6:00 to midnight business. Also, we reciprocated by placing cards recommending their nightclubs on the Show Biz's tables.

You can print some big posters, too. Include an enlarged photo, the group's logo, and the words, "Now appearing at . . . ," leaving a space to attach a card saying, "The Duprass Room" or "The Cripple Crutch Inn." Put these in the window or lobby of the places you work. You may be able to get a club owner to pay for all or part of the poster. If you do, just request that the club's name be put on a separate card so you can reuse the poster at other clubs.

Finally, duplicate a bio (or résumé) to include in a portfolio with your photos and letters of recommendation. The bio should catalogue your credentials, sketching the members' credits and the band's more illustrious accomplishments. For example, mention your work on the March of Dimes Telethon and that you worked the Cripple Crutch for four months and increased their business by 30 percent. You might also include a tape or acetate disc of some of your songs—if it's particularly good. The portfolios will not only help you get the jobs you audition for, they'll help you get jobs without auditioning.

For groups at any level, a creative, attractive presentation is valuable. If you present yourself as sloppy and amateurish, that's the kind of money you'll be offered. I've long believed that looking successful helps make you successful. This isn't to say that appearance substitutes for ability, only that, from a business standpoint, people are impressed by how you present yourself. If you look successful, employers figure that you can be successful working for them and, therefore, make them successful. Audiences also like to believe you are successful, and they never want to know it when you're not. They like to think of their entertainers as projections of their fantasies. Watching and listening to winners makes them feel like winners too; it makes them feel that they, too, can rise above the dullness of the workaday world. Another reason for looking successful is that many people are followers, afraid to like something until others like it first. So, a successful image makes you more readily acceptable to them.

I came to believe this when I was with the Trio and had saved my money and bought myself a new Lincoln. Applying for work at a club, I was asked how much the group charged. The owner was blown away by the figure, but he happened to look out the window at my car. "Well, you must be getting it

THE SCHOLARS EXCLUSIVELY ON CUE RECORDS

Samples of my early publicity photos, from the Scholars to solo, as Kenny Rogers "the First," a play on fashionable names like George Hamilton III, that I soon wisely dropped.

KENNY ROGERS
"the First"

somewhere," he said, and hired us. Being poor, my mother used to say, "Son, why don't you get a cheap little Chevrolet and put that money in the bank?" To this day she doesn't understand this psychology.

I'm not advising you to buy Lincolns now. But do play some of these games in soliciting work. Act relaxed but businesslike and dress sharply, if not expensively. Be confident, as if to say, "Your business is running the bar, ours is music. We know what kind of music to play for these people. Give us a chance to prove it to you." You'll be respected—and respect has a distinct tie-in with money. People won't mind paying you. Of course, you have to be able to deliver the goods. But assuming that you can, you'll have that little edge over other acts. There is a place for those who don't care how they dress, or whether anyone else likes their attitude or their music. But they must accept the fact that it will be harder to make it.

Up from the Little Clubs

Before you know it, you'll be thinking of breaking out of the local club scene and giving up long-distance hauls to play little clubs for little money and recognition. You'll want to broaden your horizons—from Peoria to Chicago, from Poughkeepsie to Manhattan, from Hawthorne to Hollywood. The key is to develop original material and incorporate it into your sets. Playing Top-40 material is fine, but people can go to the Next Door Club and hear the same songs. You have to present something that the other bands can't. Writing songs or coming up with original arrangements of obscure or current songs is the way to do it. For the short term, however, this might make life a little difficult. Audiences usually are turned off by unfamiliar songs. For that reason, employers would be reluctant to hire you. So, retain your sets' Top-40 composition, but season the familiar with your new songs, or prepare one set of original songs and staging, and negotiate it with club owners. Say three of four sets will consist of popular songs, but the fourth will be a show of your own stuff, or some other concept, such as a fifties rock-group impersonation or a parody of a sixties English invasion group. This will gradually build a following for you and make performing more fun.

Another way to break into the larger, more prestigious venues is to do local television shows. For instance, volunteer to play on fund-raising telethons. Approach the local March of Dimes people and say, "We'd like to perform on your telethon for free because we think it's a good cause and we have a good group." Offer to audition, if necessary. Before going on, practice in front of a mirror to clean up certain movements you may not like. In the show, don't worry about cameras and all that. Just relax and play. Having had this experience, when an important show comes up and you're asked if you've been on TV, you can tell the producers about the telethons. They don't have to know that you were on at 3:30 A.M.; for all they know, you were on at 8:30 P.M., prime time. I played a lot of telethons in Houston, by myself and with the Trio. They yield tons of work. Although you can't blatantly advertise on telethons, some of the callers may ask how they can book you. With us, they asked how they could hire the group that had the blind piano player.

Getting   Getting a personal manager or booking agency is your next step,
a Manager   actually a leap, considering the number and the value of jobs
                 you'll get. It also will lead you toward becoming recording artists
and an important concert attraction.

The difference between a manager and a booking agent is that an agent brings you job possibilities and a personal manager decides which you should accept. In other words, a manager is career oriented. He says, "Look, they've offered you this job down here for $4,000 a week, but it's in Mule Shoe, Texas, where few people are going to see you. Now I can get you a job over here that pays only $2,500, but a lot of people are going to be there. And a few record executives might even drop in."

Besides helping you get jobs, a manager guides you toward the future. He could arrange, and perhaps pay for, studio time to record demos,* which he would then take to record companies (he probably has friends at some of them), concert promoters, and booking agents. He would screen you from bad deals, negotiate contracts (he should have a good knowledge of music business law), find investors, organize touring schedules, and organize a road crew. A manager also should be creative enough to generate work. For example, after the First Edition had exhausted the regular concert trail, our manager spent $1,800 of my money to make eighteen leather-bound, gold-embossed books personalized for each of eighteen major state-fair promoters. The books itemized "10 reasons why you should hire Kenny Rogers and the First Edition for your fair." The $1,800 yielded us $250,000 in dates that year! For his troubles, the manager generally gets 15 percent of your gross income. An agent gets 10 percent.

The time to take on a personal manager is when you find someone who can bring in enough additional income—and career guidance and potential—to

---

*A demo is a recording made to demonstrate a song or performance. Usually done cheaply, it's not intended for the public's ears.

Choose a manager who will take a personal interest in your career, and whom you'll trust and get along with. Ken Kragen *(right)* fills that bill. Here we're checking a TV script to see that the role is right for me.

justify his expense. On the financial level, think of it this way. If he's charging you 15 percent of the gross, you'd better be sure he can raise your gross by that and more. Judge him by the following: degree of success (how are his other acts doing?), the type of group he's most suited for, his connections with agents, clubs, concert promoters, recording studios and companies, and investors, and, just as importantly, his willingness to use those connections. If he has some major acts, all the better, as long as he doesn't devote himself solely to them at your expense. Other groups and the musicians union could verify his qualifications for you (particularly the union, since it attempts to regulate managers). One species of "manager" that you must avoid is the "flesh peddler." A flesh peddler picks up naïve new talent with no intention of truly managing it; he makes a deal with a record company and leaves the band flat, keeping most of the advance money for himself. As you'll see, getting a record deal is meaningless without the proper guidance and support to produce a good record, get it wide radio play, and bring the act national prominence. In fact, to find a really good manager, look at the artists you think are talentless but remain steadfastly on top—they usually possess good management!

If you want to take a chance on a certain manager but feel a little leery of him, hedge your bet. Negotiate an agreement whereby your commitment to him rises in proportion to his ability to produce. Ask him to take no commission for income up to the level you've been maintaining. If that is, say, $500 a week, tell him that when he brings you in an amount over that, but less than $1,000, he gets 10 percent. When your gross surpasses that, he gets and stays at 15 percent. Also put some time limit on the agreement, perhaps six months, at which time, if you're pleased with things, the contract would renew for the customary three- to five-year period. This protects you and provides the manager with incentive.

When the manager you're approaching is of such high stature that you'd be lucky to have him—perhaps he has two name acts with charted albums—he may make seemingly outrageous demands. He may want 20 percent to 25 percent of the band, 50 percent of your song publishing rights, and the right to produce you himself (which nets him a few more percentage points). Before you scream, consider what he can do for you. Is he planning to invest $2,500 in demoing the band, $15,000 in equipping you, and $5,000 in sprucing up your live act? Perhaps he can make it all happen—get you recorded, land you a record deal with an important company, and book you as an opening act on a prestigious tour. Then, you see, it's worth it. Remember, it often takes a big shot to get through those doors, and in the beginning you'll have to give up pieces of the nonexistent pie to create a pie in the first place. Just don't commit yourself to any deal without adequate escape clauses (such as a time schedule as to when some of these great things are to come to pass) and the careful scrutiny of a top lawyer (yours, not his). And don't give away so large a percentage (over 35 percent) that you come out with no money no matter how successful you become.

Whatever the size of your manager's muscles, retain a CPA (either by the hour or at 2 percent to 6 percent of the gross) to act as your business manager. Accounting for the income and expenditures, the business manager makes sure you receive what you're due in your contracts, budgets your money, pays the salaries, helps you invest, advises you about such things as whether to buy or rent a truck for equipment, and sees that music publishers and record companies pay the right amount of royalties at the right time. In effect, he keeps everyone's hands on the table, which is good, because sooner or later, someone will accuse someone else of cheating.

Finding a Booking Agency   Before you look for a booking agency, be sure you have a manager. Not only will a good manager have his own favorite agency, but a good agency won't handle you *unless* you have a good manager. Agencies don't want five different band members calling daily to hear what work they have. They prefer having a central individual to deal with, one whom they trust so, in turn, they can comfortably entrust important jobs to you. Booking jobs can be one of your manager's functions, but the manager must hold licenses from the state and from the musicians union local in his area to act as an agent. Even with licenses, it's a violation of state business and professional codes for a manager/agent to charge double fees (say 25 percent) for booking jobs. Don't allow it. It's a conflict of interest. How could he exercise a manager's discretion to turn down a lucrative but inappropriate gig if it meant losing a fat agent's commission?

Having a booking agency is a cleaner way of taking work if you can afford that extra 10 percent. The reputable agencies work this way: Once your manager approves of a job and the contracts are signed and filed with the musicians union local, the booking agency collects 50 percent of the wages as a deposit from the employer. This is to assure that all is well with the club or promoter. If the check doesn't clear, they stop you from taking the job. If it clears, you perform. The balance of the money should be collected by your leader, manager, or road manager immediately following your performance. The booking agency pays you the deposit—minus their commission—after the job is completed. Just as they guard against an employer's defaulting, they guard the club against your pulling a no-show.

One thing needs to be said here. Having all these people handling your business and career doesn't mean you can tune out to handle just the music end. Only fools believe that. Let the managers and agents handle things but make sure you understand everything they do. And don't be afraid to question their judgment. Easy things to lose sight of, which you shouldn't, are: One, they work for you. The commissions come out of your money. Two, it's your career. If a manager screws up your career, he can find another artist and start over—while you may be finished. Three, the ultimate responsibility for your act's success lies with you. All the money and grooming in the world can't make a success of a group that audiences simply don't buy.

**Forming
a Partnership**   Once your band has developed a cash flow and played enough to feel there is a future together, you should move to base your existence on more than just a handshake agreement. There are many benefits to be had by defining your obligations to each other in a "general partnership." A partnership formalizes the fact legally that you are, say, five individuals who own equal parts of a company. Promising to each other that you will devote 100 percent of your energies toward making the partnership work, you can do business as a band in the band's name. You can open group bank accounts, hire employees (such as roadies), enter into contracts jointly (rather than as leader/sidemen), share the cost of equipment and other expenses (with it legally binding that each partner owns his share of the assets if the band folds and has to liquidate its property), and save substantially on taxes.

You save on taxes because when you work you are no longer salaried as employees of the club owners and concert promoters. You are now a *company* contracting to do a job. Because companies pay taxes on their net income in one lump sum at the end of the year, the clubs and promoters don't deduct the usual payroll-withholding taxes. Thus, your company will have more cash on hand, more gross income before taxes. By spending that cash on salaries, investments, and expenses, e.g., a truck, P.A. system, or demo recording session, your net, taxable income can be so low that you'll pay very little tax when tax-time comes around. Welcome to tax loopholes. All this will increase your assets far more than possible without a partnership. Extending the principle, when you're making tens of thousands of dollars, the band could buy houses and cars to lease to the partners at a loss, thus bolstering your standard of living. (Without a partnership, individual members couldn't enjoy the same degree of deductions, even if they invested the same amount of money as self-employed people.)

Go to see an experienced entertainment attorney to draw up the partnership papers.* Charging you around $200, he'll tailor the agreement to the group's needs and then file it with your state's secretary of state. In discussing the agreement with the attorney, specify that he limit each partner's liabilities to the extent of their involvement. In other words, should there be a suit against the company (for an unpaid loan or an accident involving band property, for instance), each member should be liable for no more than his share. You also don't want to be liable for other partners' personal debts or want other partners to have rights to someone's personal income.

Originally the First Edition consisted of four equal partners. As a member left, though, the replacement wasn't adopted as a full partner. He was given an employment contract. After we'd established ourselves with two hits, Thelma Camacho left the band. We didn't make Mary Arnold a partner because, for one thing, we didn't know whether or not she was going to be permanent, and, for another, she hadn't suffered through those anxious months before we made it. We added Arnold the same way we added a drummer. (Six months after we formed, we found our music was too high powered to remain drummerless.) We made Mickey Jones an equal *visible* partner. That is, as far as anyone outside of the group knew, Mickey was a partner. He shared the spotlight onstage and off. Monetarily, however, he was equal up to a point. After expenses, hotel and travel bills, commissions, and a $10 allowance per person per day (called a per diem), our earnings averaged about $200 per week each. Mickey received what we did until we reached a point where we were netting $500 per person. Then he stayed at that salary—a very decent living—while we, the partners, divided the balance. The reason for the rising scale was we didn't feel anyone should receive less than the others when there was so little money coming in. Incidentally, when we did make more than $500 per person, we periodically gave our sidemen raises, even if they were only $25 a week. We wanted everyone to feel we were progressing.

The system worked well. For Mickey and Mary (and later Kin Vassy, Gene Lorenzo, and Jimmy Hassell), there was the advantage of being personalities in a group with better earnings than the usual backup musicians and far less risk than the partners. That risk is no idle concern; in the First Edition's early days,

---

*Find a "good" attorney by asking other musicians or people in the business. Or go to a library and look through the Martindale-Hubbell publication listing law firms and many of their clients. Those who represent groups most like yours would be the best bet. *Caveat:* Legal matters discussed here should be taken as general information, not advice. For that, consult an attorney.

even though we had two hit singles, we were almost $60,000 in debt. It wasn't that our management was bad. It's just that we spent large sums on the road to sound and appear successful and it was a long time before that bore fruit. If we had folded then, we would have been in trouble, while Mickey and Mary could have walked away from it.

For the partners, on the other hand, the system was good in that when we made profits, there were fewer slices to cut in the pie. Also, we didn't have to worry about a common, irritating problem: If you make a replacement a full partner and six months later he decides to leave, you have to buy him out. That means financial and legal complications. With our approach, it would have been simple for, say, Mickey, to quit. It would have been a question of how long he could stay until we found another drummer. We would have given him a bonus for being with us so faithfully. And . . . "Mickey, so long. It's been a lot of fun."

Incorporating   The benefits of a partnership are fine when you're playing the club circuit and your income doesn't exceed your expenses and salaries. But when that income begins leaping significantly, such as when a sizable record-company advance is imminent, or when you have to go into heavy debt to launch or maintain the band, it's time to incorporate. As opposed to a partnership, whose collection of individuals shares responsibility for a company's actions, a corporation is like a living individual in the eyes of the business world. Hence, a corporation shields its shareholders (you) from liabilities, so long as its board of directors conducts itself legally. (You assume the roles of chairman, treasurer, secretary, etc.) If the corporation is sued, the suing party can only go after the corporation's assets, not the shareholders'. And if you've paid out, to yourselves, most of the money as it came in, those assets don't have to amount to much.

You also can stockpile money corporately that you can't as a partnership or as individuals. The law permits a corporation to save up to 40 percent of its income as a pension fund, the money from which may be used for other things if the board and shareholders so desire. Another advantage to a corporation is that it can get special medical and accident insurance plans, giving everyone such coverage a lot more economically than they could get individually.

Incorporating involves having your attorney file Articles of Incorporation with the state secretary of state. The Articles detail the corporation's name, the name it will be "doing business as," the names of its officers, the field and scope of its business, how much stock it will issue, when the board of directors meets, etc. Filing costs depend on the complexity of the corporation and attorney and administrative fees. They might be anywhere from $300 to $2,000.

Before you go so far as to form a partnership or incorporate, invest an hour or two with an attorney or a CPA. Let them advise you about tax laws and the best way to set up the business end of the act. An attorney also could help you write a standard club contract to use until you join the union and use theirs. Set the band up with the assumption that you're going to be successful. Otherwise, it'll cost you a lot to rectify things later.

Little Business Practices with Big Long-Term Benefits   A few final recommendations I can make regarding daily business practices involve banking and taxes. First, the bank account should be used. Don't plan on just splitting income; take out a portion, perhaps 10 percent, for cookie-jar savings. If you're paid $1,000 for a week's work and there are five of you, don't count on taking home $200 each. Count on having expenses that come off the top of the gross, such as transportation. Then, count on taking out another $100. Barring other costs, such as manager's or agent's percentages, you'll still be left with about $170 each, and you'll have money for rainy-day emergencies. Inevitably, you'll need to repay loans, buy or repair equipment, instruments, vehicles, or clothing. Later, it'll help you buy studio time to record demos and create promotional materials. The ideal is financial self-sufficiency, sparing you involvements with creditors and their debilitating interest rates or percentages of the gross.

With a healthy cash reserve, you can loan money to members for purchases that help the band. For example, if your broke organist wants an $800 clavinet, the band can buy it with an agreement that he repay the debt. A good reimbursement plan would be one in which the money is deducted regularly from his salary. So, while everyone else receives $170 a week, he'll get $140 until the bank has been repaid. This method is much cleaner than relying on the member to pay a loan back at his own pace. Not that you can't trust people, but reasons tend to crop up why he can't make his payment this week and that. In any case, a cash cushion is essential. For whatever can go wrong, will. Anticipate as many problems, both human and material, as possible.

Taxes are another concern, perhaps not immediately if you're not earning any more than a few thousand dollars a year, but they will be soon. What a CPA can show you, though, is that there are so many deductible expenses in running a group that you won't have to pay much tax until your income is very high.

Nevertheless, get in the habit of keeping tax records, for one of the pitfalls of this business is that if you cannot substantiate your claims when you start making a lot of money, the Internal Revenue Service will come down on your head like a guillotine. The First Edition's CPA kept us in line from the start. He refused to give us our next week's per diem unless we turned in receipts for the money we spent the week before. Since keeping receipts for nickel and dime amounts is impractical, the IRS allows you to claim deductions for items below $15 a day if they are recorded in a ledger book, which you should keep faithfully on the road. Record all expenses that relate to your business: wardrobe, cleaning, equipment, instruments, repairs, food, gas, lodging. For awhile, I kept my own tax records. Wherever I went I carried a briefcase with four envelopes: one for paid invoices, one for accounts payable (bills to pay later), one for cash receipts (for out-of-pocket petty expenses), and one for cash accounted for (receipts that my road manager accounted for). Every time I took a cab, for example, I'd ask for a receipt, including the fare and tip, open my briefcase and stick it into the proper envelope. Then, once a month, when on a plane with nothing else to do, I'd go through all my receipts and fill in the ledger book. In the long run, your financial success depends more on how you manage and account for your money than on how much you gross.

Handling Investors   Once you get something substantial happening with your group, you'll find that some people will offer to invest, hoping to carve out a piece of the action. The idea of outside money coming into the group, though, is one that I dislike intensely. When we put the First Edition together, at one point someone offered us $20,000 for 10 percent of our gross earnings. Twenty grand seemed like an enormous pile of greenbacks, and we needed it. But our manager, Ken Kragen, who has a master's degree in business administration from Harvard, sat us down and had us dissect the idea. He showed us that accepting the offer would effectively mean the group was worth no more than $200,000, that once we made that much, the investor had his money back—and then he got into our money. Which is, of course, the speculator's game. We turned it down and proceeded to make $200,000 in our first year! In the eight years since then we've made millions. Figure what 10 percent of *that* is.

If you do need the capital, tell the financier you'll give him 10 percent until his investment is paid off, plus interest. Twenty-five percent interest wouldn't be a bad compensation for his risk. You might end up paying him back $25,000, but once that's repaid, you won't owe him anything. Also, limit your liability for the loan to the group. You don't want to give him a percentage of the individual's earnings, such as someone's songwriting royalties.

Refrain from giving away percentages because your net is going to be low as it is. With a manager and booking agency, you'll be paying a minimum of 25 percent commissions. Then there are the operating expenses, including travel, car maintenance, equipment repair and purchase, hotel bills, food, union fees, and loan payments. Later there will be two or three roadies, a CPA, and an attorney to pay, and when you start flying, enormous travel costs. If you owed another 10 percent to a financier, that makes half of the pie you'd never taste.

Preferable ways to raise seed capital are those that are more directly involved with the band, such as music publishing and record company deals. The beauty here is they don't take a piece of your overall income. They only profit from sales of your "product," your songs and records. So, it's in their interest to see that you're a success, and they invest in you with money and expertise. They help you develop the songs and make the recordings in exchange for the rights to sell them.

The keys unlocking the company doors that get the music business to work for you are talent, originality, creativity, inspiration, and persistence.

Moving Up

I went down to the library
You know, the big one way downtown
I pulled out my spiral notebook and my Scripto pencil
These are the words that I did put down

I'm a dud firecracker
I ain't got no fuse
I ain't got no inspiration since I lost my muse
I'm a table with two legs
I'm a spider with five
I'm going down slow, muse, when will you arrive?
Oh muse, where are you?

You know, I eat, drink and I smoke stuff
I don't know what to do*
                    LOUDON WAINWRIGHT III, "Muse Blues"

In high school I had a friend who worked at an ice-cream parlor but wanted to be a songwriter. One day he came to me with a song he'd written. It was terrible. I told him to keep the ice-cream-parlor job. A few years later, I was playing with the New Christy Minstrels and he was a struggling songwriter. He played me a new song he'd written. I thought it was great. I asked him to let me record it with the Christies, but he'd already promised the song to Jerry Lee Lewis. A year later, the Christies had dissolved and the First Edition was scrounging around for material to put on its first album. The song kept coming back to me. Finally I got in touch with my high-school buddy. This time he thought it would be all right; Jerry Lee had recorded the song but never released it. So my buddy sent me a tape with a lyric sheet and we took it into the studio. "Just Dropped In (To See What Condition My Condition Was In)" became our first hit, and Mickey Newbury turned out to be one of the most prolific and influential country/folk songwriters of the era.

It seems there are stories behind most of our hits. "But You Know I Love

You" came from within the group. It was written by Mike Settle, but he'd planned to give it to another act until I talked him into letting us cut it. We got Mel Tillis' "Ruby, Don't Take Your Love to Town" when another friend of mine, a radio promotion man for Mercury Records, pointed it out to me on a Roger Miller album. However, we performed it for over a year before it dawned on us it would make a good record. "Good" understates the case; it became our greatest hit and one of the strongest social statements of the Vietnam period.

The story that should win a Grammy, however, is the way the follow-up hit came. In the wake of "Ruby," people from all quarters were approaching us with the "perfect" song. One day the First Edition was playing in a celebrity golf tournament and some guy started running along beside me.

"Kenny, I've got a great song for you."

"Well, I appreciate it," I said. "As soon as this round is over, you can tell me about it."

"No. Let me tell you about it now."

Normally, that sort of pushiness would have me tuned me out so completely I wouldn't have listened to it for a million dollars. But he started singing the lyrics as we walked to the next hole, and it was one of the most beautifully written, catchy songs I'd ever heard. It was "Reuben James." The man running with me wasn't one of the then-undiscovered co-authors, Alex Harvey and Barry Etris. He was a resourceful song-plugger from their music publisher.

●

A universe of elements governs the matter of whether or not your group becomes a hit recording act. You might be distinguished by your good looks, onstage charisma, costumes, theatrics, gimmicky effects, and tremendous musicianship, but the one indispensable element is material. In fact, it's a maxim of the industry that a song makes an act more than an act makes a song. Your originality must be conveyed in the music (theatrics can't be appreciated over the radio). And the songs must be catchy and substantial enough to command and bear repeated listening. Creating or finding such material, however, is easier said than done. It depends on intangibles—creativity, talent, craft, and luck.

It's the Song, Not the Singer   The first criterion in what material you choose to perform is that it in some way be exclusive to you, something other than what is currently being played by radio. This could mean new arrangements of older, almost forgotten hits. Linda Ronstadt,

One source of excellent song material is struggling songwriters. I drew upon many who later became major stars in their own right and who guested on the First Edition's "Rollin'" TV show; Mac Davis *(above)* and Kris Kristofferson *(below)*.

for instance, has had great success with remakes of the Everly Brothers' "When Will I Be Loved" and Smokey Robinson and the Miracles' "Tracks of My Tears." It could mean finding songs on albums that didn't make it. And it could mean new songs, written either by members of the group (the best situation) or by an outside writer or collaborator if the group is weak in songwriting. Elton John, for instance, writes with Bernie Taupin, a nonperforming lyricist.

Another source of material, albeit a tricky one, is the music publisher. Publishers will be reluctant to give you songs unless you're signed to a label or close to a deal because they don't make a dime from live performances. They make money through royalties from record sales and radio airplay. Consequently, they save their best songs for the biggest artist they can find. You can, however, present yourself as having some recording prospects and ask if they can pull some lead sheets and tapes or acetates* from their files that were commercially recorded a year or two ago but didn't make it.

You also might be approached by songwriters who happen to hear you and think you'd be perfect to perform their material. You'll find, though, that there isn't a lot of good, unused original material floating around. This fact should spur you to try writing your own.

Song-   The most frequently asked question about songwriting is, which do
writing you start with first, the lyrics or the melody? The answer is some-
             times music, sometimes words, sometimes both. A song may pop
into your head whole or develop from a fragment months after the initial inspiration. Songs come in unexpected ways if you're always looking for them. The Bee Gees, for example, came up with the hit "Jive Talkin' " when Barry Gibb drove across a bridge in Florida. The rhythm suggested the song. I wrote "Sweet Music Man" when I was having trouble writing a different song for Barbi Benton. I couldn't put out of my mind a story I was told by a lady on a plane—how she left her famous singer/songwriter husband because he was too in love with his music. I wrote about that instead, and it turned out to be one of my best.

Before you can put inspiration to work, you must be practiced in a song-writing technique to recognize a good idea and apply it to good purpose. Probably the best way to get into writing songs is to study those performed by acts you would most like to emulate. Break them down—and practice duplicating them in your own way.

---

*Acetates are glassy discs cut like a record expressly to demo songs. About $10 to $15 each, they're good for only a few plays.

Ignoring the production for now, figure out what catches you about that song. Is it the lyric, melody, music, instrumental break, rhythm, or a combination of these? Think about the subject. Does it have a broad, if not universal, appeal? (Not that everyone necessarily has had the identical experience, but everyone can *relate* to having it by hearing the song.) And see how the writer develops the song through each succeeding verse, unfolding the story (in the case of ballad/story songs) with a description of events and creating an atmosphere to express an idea and feeling.

A good song must have a lyrical hook—a catchphrase that is repeated throughout and often ends up being the song's title. But this isn't to say the lyric is more important than the music. In most cases, the lyrics do inspire the music. The music must fit hand in glove with the lyrics to convey the unstated message, the mood, atmosphere, tone, and spirit. But the music, too, should engage the listener even more immediately than the lyric with an unforgettable melody and a seductive rhythm. Besides noticing how lyrics and melody fit together, see how your favorite song is structured. Most often you'll find that it's a variation on a classic pop scheme—a scheme that evolved because of its proclivity for holding people's attention from start to finish. It usually goes like this: vamp intro (setting the mood and allowing d.j.'s space to introduce the song), verse, chorus, verse, bridge, instrumental break, chorus, verse, chorus.

Avoid the tendency to overwrite. Many novices, trying to seem sophisticated, artful, and articulate, defeat themselves with songs that are musically busy and lyrically involved. The simplest lyrics and melodies make the strongest statements and communicate to more people. Kris Kristofferson, a Rhodes scholar, is among the educated elite. Yet he turns out songs that sound as though they're written by a poor farm boy who dropped out of high school. And some of those songs, such as "Help Me Make It Through the Night" and "Me and Bobby McGee," pack loads of substance and stand as pop classics. Kristofferson's writing isn't illiterate; he draws from his emotions rather than his vocabulary. You need not be esoteric to be profound. The writings of Chuck Berry, Brian Wilson, Bob Dylan, John Lennon, Mick Jagger, and Don Henley testify to that. Just be sure that whatever you say, whether it's about romance, teenage rebellion, or social change, isn't dimensionless or sterile. Good songs breathe life when they appeal to a human emotion, be it joy, hope, love, pain, loneliness, fear, anger, or sorrow.

In songwriting, you can draw on stories you've read, fantasy, the news, things friends tell you, anything. It doesn't have to be about something never written about before to be original. Some of the greatest songs, in fact, are simply fresh approaches to age-old situations.

It might be instructive to dissect one of my songs, "A Stranger in My Place," recorded by both the First Edition and Anne Murray (*Country*, Capitol). I built this on the idea of how our egos refuse to let go of a dissolving relationship. That's where the title came from—I thought I was irreplaceable and now I find I'm not. (I didn't draw the song from personal experience, although two years later I did get a divorce from my second wife.)

To get my idea across, I fabricated a situation. The first verse warms the listener up for a story:

> I see the town where we were born.
> I see the place where we were raised.
> I see all the things you wanted
> That I never gave.
> I see sadness, I see sorrow,
> I see pain upon your face.
> But I just can't see a stranger in my place.*

In this verse, the protagonist reflects on the depth of the relationship and acknowledges, in a regretful tone, responsibility for the problems and their painful effects. But he doesn't explain *why* he failed her. This is realistic; he probably doesn't know himself. Meanwhile, I've established my hook—"a stranger in my place." The story probes deeper levels in the second verse:

> I can see now where we've quarreled.
> I can see now I was wrong.
> I can see where you might weaken
> When I wasn't strong.
> I see memories of a love gone bad
> That time cannot erase.
> But I just can't see a stranger in my place.

Here, the singer catalogues all the reasons for breaking off the relationship; still, he buys them intellectually, not emotionally. His heart and ego refuse to accept what those reasons add up to. Notice I've maintained lyrical consistency with the first verse. The tone, approach, meter, and rhyme scheme remain correct. Also note the simplicity of expression, the absence of confusing abstractions and metaphors, even though I'm describing a difficult situation.

Now, using a bridge, I depart from the path. A good bridge drives a point home while offering a musical relief, a change of pace to prevent monotony.

---

*Words and music by Kenny Rogers and Kin Vassy. TRO— © copyright 1970, 1971 Devon Music, Inc., New York, Flea Show Music Co. and Amos Productions, Inc., Los Angeles, California. Used by permission.

No one seems to know you quite like I.
No one knows the things that make you cry.
Looking back it seems I never showed you,
So now I lay alone and wonder why.

The last line fills in the exterior setting while furthering the story. The small reference to the protagonist lying alone in bed is enough to conjure a sense of his emptiness and loneliness as he meditates on his loss. Appealing to the listeners' emotions, I have the singer explain why it's so painful for him to see a stranger in his place: He and his lover have been especially close. The subsequent and final verse finds the singer reaching something of an emotional catharsis (manifested by his crying) and a new understanding. He recognizes the finality of the affair:

I can see where you might grow tired
Of dreams that don't come true.
I can see where I have fallen short
Of the things I promised you.
I can see now through my tear-filled eyes
No love upon your face.
I must get used to seeing strangers in my place.

This ending, with the singer resolved to accept things, was altered by Anne Murray. Her version has the protagonist refusing to give up; she sings, "But I just can't see a stranger in my place." I resolved it because I believe you can't live in the past, that once a relationship is over you can only do more damage to yourself to stick around. But, the song does work either way.

The emphasis I've placed on a classic song format is based on the fact that it has proven to be a most effective and marketable way to convey a musical statement. If you feel the formula is too rigid to express more "ambitious" concepts, that's all right. Groups like Yes and Pink Floyd continue recording lengthy, almost impressionistic cuts. But they lifted themselves many notches in stature and popularity when they released cuts that were songs in a more traditional sense. Although not one bit less characteristic, Yes' "Roundabout" and Floyd's "Money" appealed to Top-40 AM radio *and* progressive-rock FM audiences. Previously, these groups' airplay and record sales were confined to the smaller FM audiences. In short, more people prefer accessible, succinct pop songs to twelve minutes of instrumental noodling, abstract guitar soloing, or impenetrable lyrics and rambling melodies. And that fact makes the songs commercial; they sell.

Commercial. A decade ago, that word was as dirty as capitalist pig. Today it has regained its respect in pop music. No longer a euphemism for bubble gum, it broadly describes those songs that invite mass appreciation. Anyone who has tried writing good, salable pop songs knows it takes a highly talented and experienced songwriter to create two or three minutes of sensational perfection that can be enjoyed—and bought—by millions. I like to think of the pop-song format as equivalent to a painter's canvas; it challenges you to realize a compelling scene, message, or feeling—profound or silly—in a readily consumable space. The extent of each writer's vision and talent is really the format's only limitation. Listening to a well-done pop song, you don't notice the framework; it falls away as the magic begins to work. Afterward, you won't know quite what the artist did, but you'll want him to do it again.

Of course, there's a more down-to-earth reason why much of your songwriting should aim for the province of Top-40 radio: Record companies and publishers measure performers and songwriters by their potential for scoring hits—selling a lot of records. If you write songs that call for long solos or numerous verses, extending the song beyond the hit single length of 2 to 3½ minutes, do it—if it's good. Though most Top-40 radio stations rarely play longer songs—rapid-fire format seems to keep the average listener's attention best—the song could go long on the album and be edited for single release. A classic case is the Doors' "Light My Fire," which clocks in at 6:50 minutes on the album. The record company halved the length by judiciously removing all but the most interesting part of a long organ and guitar solo in the middle—and it became the best-selling record in the country in the summer of 1967. Today, almost as many hits have been edited for single release as not. Probably the best-known exception to the rule is the Eagles' "Hotel California," all 6½ minutes of it. But then, that's the Eagles.

While no one can tell you just how to write potential hits, songwriting is a discipline, a craft. There are practices you can follow to develop a talent. Mike Settle, for example, honed his lyric writing by applying creative writing exercises. He practiced writing lyrics to one song from different perspectives, a third-person narrator, a first person, and so on. He also maintained a daily work regimen. If you're erratic, he felt, chances are you'll never pen a winner. And if you do, you'll certainly have a hard time waiting for lightning to strike twice. He believed that by sequestering himself in a room for a couple of hours at the same time every day his mind would eventually get in the habit of working. And he'd develop craftsmanship, reducing his dependence on fickle inspiration. Mike similarly believed in carrying a notebook everywhere. Scribbling down those snippets of ideas that occur at odd times and places, he didn't have to rely on memory to recall the promising bits.

Something other writers do is use a cassette recorder as an aural notebook.

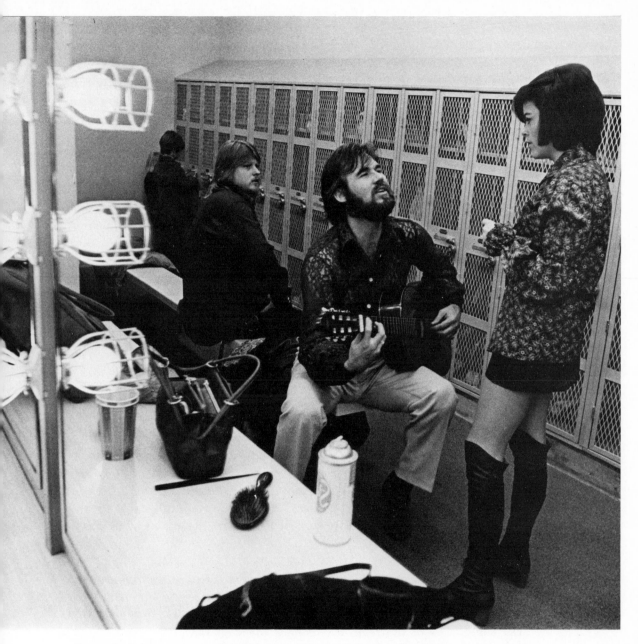

Songs don't happen at predictable times. Here, reflected in the makeup mirror back-stage, I'm seen trying out a just-completed song for Mary Arnold.

Letting the tape go while playing piano or guitar and singing ideas, you can flesh out an inspiration without interrupting the flow to write things down.

Considering myself more a singer than a songwriter, I don't follow a specific method. However, I do adhere to one rule: Once I start a song, I don't leave it until I've taken it as far as I can. It's always easier to improve a mediocre song than complete an unfinished one. It's hard to pick up the train of thought when your mind—pardon the expression—is on another track.

When you feel a song is finished, it's time to give it the acid test. Play it for friends and ask for comments. This is an indispensable stage of the songwriting process, for you're too close to your song to hear it as the world does. Others will relate the song to hits they're familiar with and tell you how yours measures up. And if they're knowledgeable about music, they'll tell you what works and what doesn't and suggest improvements.

Then, if the song suits your group, incorporate it into a set. It's great to be a performing songwriter because you have that built-in sounding board, the audience, which you can watch for reactions. If people lose interest during the third verse, say, you know you have problems. Perhaps the verse should go. Or the song may need a tighter arrangement or a change of color here, an instrumental break there. Whatever, be objective enough to deal with the inevitable prospect that one of your beloved infants may require amputation, internal surgery, or burial. Let the audience be the judge, for if a song is ineffectual, if it fails to provoke people, to communicate, it's a bad song.

By the way, don't be shocked sometime if everyone likes the song but you, the writer. Maybe you stumbled into something others relate to more than you, or it touches too close to home, or it's better than you think. I've written several hard rockers that I regarded as throwaways. One, "Lena Lookie," I felt could have been written by a fourth grader. Yet it became a number one smash in New Zealand and made lots of money for me. Again, the artist isn't always the best judge of his art.

Co-writing Songs   Besides the creative difficulties of songwriting, there are the financial ones, particularly those that arise when writing with collaborators. Co-writing often is a great way to create superior songs—one of the team can bounce ideas off the other, and strengths can be combined. The conflicts arise when contributions are uneven. How, then, to divide the income from the song and by-line it? The answer boils down to this: Only give away a percentage that has been earned. You have to be pragmatic because it's such a nebulous thing—who's to say whose little flourish here and grammatical change there is a song's magic ingredient? So first assign the song two values: 50 percent lyrics and 50 percent music. If someone adds all the music to your lyrics, or vice versa, that's clearly a 50–50 split. Extending the principle, if someone suggests music and lyrics for a bridge, which constitutes ⅓ of the song (the other thirds being the verse and chorus), you owe him 33-⅓ percent. You have to use your judgment to be fair. If someone contributes a mere four lines for a chorus, but the chorus proves a powerful hook, which is repeated throughout and becomes the title, he deserves 50 percent. However, if he just added a lyric to the bridge, there's no reason to give more than 25 percent. It's generally accepted that 25 percent is the least you should give; if someone doesn't deserve 25 percent, he doesn't deserve anything. The figuring of petty amounts is more trouble than it's worth. First, the song would have to be that one in 10,000 to be released as a record, and then it would have to be that one in 100,000 to hit and pay off significantly. Twenty-five percent is fair. For while the person who added a bridge lyric has contributed creatively to the song, he hasn't put as much time and effort into it. Plus, your song inspired his lines more than his lines inspired your song. Consider it as though you've done each other favors. Taking this further, if someone suggests a better word in the lyric or note in the melody, he doesn't deserve a share of the song—just a thank you.

As far as the by-line or name credit goes, if someone contributes enough to merit a financial percentage, 25 percent, his name should go on the song with yours. It's plain he has left a significant personal imprint on the song and deserves to be identified with it. So long as the money is divided proportionately, it's all right to give the contributor equal billing.

Over the years, I've found it's unnecessary to turn to others for minor contributions. But if you do, in the excitement of finishing the song, be careful not to lose your perspective and give away more than is warranted. The fact that you gave something away, and your friend accepted it, could bother you someday and damage the friendship. Despite myself, I've felt mild recriminations from instances of excessive generosity. I came up with the idea for "A Stranger in My Place" while waiting backstage to tape the Mike Douglas Christmas Show in 1971 with the First Edition. I wrote the whole song, words and melody, but Kin Vassy happened to be sitting at the piano. He played some simple country changes for me, and I was so happy with the result that I gave him half of the song. Similarly, I wrote "Momma's Waiting," a minor hit for the First Edition, while sitting in a truck with Terry Williams. Maybe I'm getting senile, but I can't remember a single line he contributed—yet I gave him 50 percent. Now I don't blame anyone. Maybe they did help me through insecure moments and mental blocks, and without their help the songs may not have been successful, if finished at all. Still, I know I could have finished those songs alone had I made the extra effort—and not sacrificed the $10,000 to $20,000 that the songs eventually yielded as their shares. In this light, it's interesting to note that many music publishers don't allow their writers to co-write unless the co-writer is signed to the same publishing company or agrees to assign the songs to that company. Not only do they want to keep their moneymaking talents all to themselves, but they figure two good writers don't need each other—someone must be weaker and it's probably not their writer.

Copyrighting   Having composed some tunes that you feel represent minable gold, see to it that you can't be claim-jumped. Have them copyrighted. Copyrighting is based on the principle that works of the mind are as much the private property of the artist as works of the hands. Thus, songwriters have the right to license and charge users of their songs—record companies, radio and TV stations, clubs, jukebox owners, etc.—for the life of their copyrights. Passed in 1909, the American Copyright Act was revised in 1976. The new law provides that songs copyrighted after January 1, 1978, belong to the author for his lifetime plus fifty years (which the writer's heirs will appreciate). Previously, songs passed into the public domain (PD) after one renewable twenty-eight-year period, or a possible fifty-six years. Public domain exists because it makes no sense to regard a creative work as private property so many years after the artist's death. By law, a PD song can be recorded by anyone. And anyone who records one can collect all the royalties derived from *that* recording just as though he wrote it.

Copyrighting doesn't give you a monopoly on your songs' ideas and titles. It covers the manifestation of those ideas, the words and melodies. To prove your ownership in a case of copyright infringement, you must be able to show that you had the piece first, that the other party had access to it, intentionally stole significant parts of it, and profited at your expense. The action against George Harrison in 1976 for allegedly lifting the music of the Chiffons' 1962 hit, "He's So Fine," for his "My Sweet Lord" in 1970 is an interesting case of "infringement." The judge concluded that in composing "My Sweet Lord" Harrison must have subconsciously used the other song. However, he held that this was still copyright infringement for which the plaintiff could go to trial to recover damages.

The best evidence of your having a song first is an earlier dated Statement of Copyright from the U.S. Copyright Office. To get a copyright, write the Copyright Office, Library of Congress, Washington, D.C. 20559, and request (free) copies of their Form E applications. Return the completed form with a copy of the song's lead sheet and a check for $10, payable to the Registrar of Copyrights. If you have several songs all by the same person(s), you can get a bargain by copyrighting them simultaneously as a "folio." Put up to fifteen songs into a single binder with a table of contents and the name of the book on the outside jacket. Then file it under the name of the folio with one Form E and the $10 fee. Special songs, such as those to be recorded, should be copyrighted individually. Incidentally, your lead sheets must be legible to be accepted. So, if you're anything like me, hire a professional copyist. For about $10 a song, the copyist will transcribe your cassette recordings or rough notations into manuscripts worthy of a true composer. Not only will you need clean copies for copyrighting, but you'll need them to send to publishers you hope will publish them or to artists you want to record them. Amateurish lead sheets won't be taken seriously.

Now song thieves are not waiting behind every bush to rob the treasures of every budding songsmith.* Thieves are more discriminating; they steal from successful songwriters. You don't need to copyright songs formally until they're to be exposed to the public, either published, recorded, or widely performed. Or played for other songwriters. Remember, if you write fifty songs a year, it can cost you $500 for copyrights. Add copyist fees of $500, and you've blown $1,000 on protecting songs, of which only a few might prove salable. In the past you could copyright songs cheaply by simply sending copies to yourself by registered mail, keeping the letters safely sealed; it was proof that you had the songs for at least as long as the postmarked date. Now this is not as widely done, as it's nearly impossible to prove in court that a letter wasn't tampered with or contrived after the fact.

Once your material is about to be published and recorded for commercial release, you'll have to get statutory copyrights, or the songs will be deemed to be offered to the public domain. But by then you shouldn't have to worry about the paper work and expense; securing copyrights is one of the publisher's chief duties.

The Music Publisher   The main concern of music publishers used to be exactly what the name implies: publishing and marketing sheet music. Until the middle of the twentieth century, sheet

---

*Song sharks are a different breed, as you'll see shortly.

music was indeed the largest source of a songwriter's income. That changed when the record became a mass medium. Lead sheets and songbook sales are still significant for classical music, pop standards, and Top-10 hits. But the majority of writers make their money in record sales—"mechanical" royalties —and airplay—"performance royalties." Thus, publishers are now measured by how effectively they get their clients' music recorded or "covered" and by how they promote the records they get (promotion people are employed to try to get radio stations to add the records to their playlists) and then collect the monies due the writers.

Underlying all this is the constant duty of protecting the writers' and their assets—the songs. Publishers keep the copyrights up to date and guard against people damaging the value of their songs. (Anyone can record a song once it has been released for sale as sheet music or a record. But any alterations that affect the song's intent must be approved by the publisher. For instance, when the First Edition did the "Rollin' " TV show, we often did satires of hits of the day and thus had to get approvals from publishers. For some reason, George Harrison's publisher wouldn't let us perform "My Sweet Lord" in a skit about a candy salesman dressed like Jesus.)

Though it isn't as glamorous as recording, publishing should be your concern for two reasons. First, a publisher who believes in your performing talent as much as your songwriting talent would hustle to get you a record deal. (It helps that many major publishing houses are record company affiliates.) Second, it's a major source of financing. Publishers advance groups anywhere from $10,000 to $50,000 for their exclusive publishing rights. Third, it's possible to make a lot more money in publishing than in record sales. Few outsiders realize this. It's impossible to generalize how much a Top-10 hit yields. Some are turntable hits. They're played to death on the radio but sell weakly. Others sell phenomenal numbers of records with little airplay. But simple math illustrates the point: Say you had a Top-5 single that sold a million copies at $1 each. If your record royalty is a fair 7 percent of the full retail price, on sales alone, you'd gross $70,000. Meanwhile, the record company pays the publisher the standard mechanical royalty rate of 2¾ cents per record sold, or $27,500. The publisher keeps half and sends the balance—$13,750—to the song's writer(s).

Now, assume the jocks loved playing the record as much as people loved buying it and it was played an average of ten times a day for three months on more than 5,000 stations in the United States. The songwriters' and publishers' Performance Rights Society—ASCAP or BMI (the writer's publisher must belong to the same one)—would pay (as BMI computes it) about 6 cents per play to the writers and 6 cents to the publisher for the twenty or so large Top-20 stations and 2½ cents per play for the numerous smaller stations. The total exceeds $114,000 to the writers and the same to the publisher. Combining the performance and mechanical royalties, the writer's share comes to $127,750! (Compare this with the $70,000 from record royalties!) This excludes the mechanical royalties as an album track and track on the "Greatest Hits" and "Live" albums, and it excludes the income from performances on TV, sheet-music sales, foreign royalties, and cover versions by other artists (if someone else hits with the same song, the income floods in once again). Then there are residual royalties, perhaps $30,000 on the next quarterly statement, $15,000 on the next, and so on, as its airplay gradually dwindles. If the song is a "publisher's song," a standard, one of those rare across-the-board hits that make it in pop, middle-of-the-road (MOR), country, and even R & B markets, or is repeatedly covered by artists who appeal to those different audiences, then the sky's the limit. The song will pay off royal sums indefinitely. Such is the case with Tony Orlando's "Tie a Yellow Ribbon" and Lennon/McCartney's "Yesterday."

Of course, these are rare exceptions; typical Top-40 fare will yield about $60,000 to the writers. This will keep them living in style for several years but won't make them millionaires. Consistent hits can, though. And in more ways than one. A catalogue of hit songs is immensely valuable as equity. In 1977, for instance, Neil Sedaka purchased back the publishing rights to 116 of his songs from Kirshner Entertainment Corp. to publish them with his own Neil Sedaka Music, Inc. He paid $2 million. A strong catalogue also is a powerful bargaining chip in making record deals. Record companies love having publishing rights because it's another source of income, improving the odds that their risky investment will pay off.

Music Publishers and Record Companies How you approach music publishers also applies in many respects to record companies. While good songs and a talented act burn to be heard, catching the publishers' and record companies' ears requires energy, patience, meticulous planning, and some investment. It also requires tenacity. Waiting blithely to be discovered is more likely to keep you playing nowhere beer joints. You have to pursue success actively and persistently, because the powers-that-be are tied up with those who do. And that's all right. You should be the one who cares most about your career.

The first thing to do is set your sights on the centers of the pop-music industry: Hollywood, New York, and, to a growing degree, Nashville, the heart of country music. While other towns—particularly Austin, Boston, Seattle, Chicago, and San Francisco—have burgeoning music scenes, things ultimately flow through L.A., New York, and Nashville. In these cities there are the heaviest concentrations of professionals and professional facilities, the rehearsal studios, recording studios, night-school courses on everything from songwriting to record contract law, music publishers, lawyers, managers, songwriters, and performers. But don't pack your bags yet. Hollywood, New York City, and Music City can be very intimidating and discouraging places if you land there without plans, specific leads, and a product in hand to sell. They're places swollen with too many people bartending at night and hustling their music during the day. And the publishers and record companies are inundated with so much material from hopefuls from all over the world that the competition for limited new-artist budgets is enormous. These companies can deal with only the most impressive acts. So, before you approach them, you must make yourself desirable.

Most new groups that scored record contracts did it through building themselves into an important regional attraction. People talked about them, and they were able to entice a local but experienced manager or booking agent with well-placed connections in the music capitals to handle them. Then, they found the nearest professional quality recording studio and, with their own or their manager's money, cut a few songs for a carefully thought-out demo. The manager put the demo into a presentation of high-quality posed photos of the band, a printed biography, a selection of impressive newspaper features and reviews, statistics (how regularly the band is booked, the size of halls and crowds it draws, etc.), and lead sheets of all the demoed songs and went to sell it to his contacts in, say, New York. If he interested some A & R people or publishers, they'd go to hear the band.

Speaking strictly of record companies for the moment, the strongest contenders for contracts are those groups that have some members who have been with hit acts. The First Edition members weren't known individually—but we'd been with the New Christy Minstrels. Or, the contenders have some members who've written songs recorded by name artists. For example, the fact that Jack Tempchin co-authored the Eagles' "Already Gone" undoubtedly helped Arista Records make up its mind to sign his group, the Funky Kings. Record companies like to see some handle with which they can promote and publicize an act and entice people into taking a chance on it in the stores.

Without some built-in claim to fame, you must have a damn good demo tape and/or something exciting going in your locality. Aerosmith, who built up a dedicated following in Boston, happened to rehearse in a theater that was owned by a local rock-music promoter. The promoter tipped off his friends, the New York Dolls' managers, Leber and Krebs, and they in turn brought Aero-

TV SCENE

Kenny Rogers, Local Boy, Is on the Way

BY HOWARD STENTZ
Chronicle Staff

A 19-year-old Houston singer, whose tunes have been setting the record circuits on fire, will take the tube Thursday on Dick Clark's American Bandstand.

Fans who watch the rock 'n' roll stint on KTRK-TV (4 p.m. daily) likely will hear Kenny Rogers sing his hit, "That Crazy Feeling."

Rogers, who once sang with the popular Houston-based "Scholars," has ventured out on his own.

Reports are that his hit tune is currently the No. 2 best seller in this area. It has done a landoffice business in other sections of the country, too.

Kenny is a graduate of Jeff Davis High School here, and is currently attending the University of Houston.

* * *

colder in the early 1950s, but he made his comeback, and now is burning up the TV tube.

Currently ┄┄┄
Fra┄┄
TV┄┄
in┄┄
s┄┄
c┄┄

Building credentials is essential for record deals. Collected evidence of local success was also useful in getting me work.

smith down to a showcase in New York at Max's Kansas City. Leber and Krebs had several record company execs in the audience, including Columbia Records' then-president, Clive Davis. The rest is history. In a similar vein, Head East won a deal with A&M Records and broke out of St. Louis by putting out their own album. They received some local radio airplay that got reported in the radio "tip sheets"—"The Confidential," "The Branden Report," the "Gavin Report," "the Friday Morning Quarterback," "the Walrus"—which everyone in the business watches to spot the trends and songs that could break big. When A&M received the promising self-produced album, along with this information, they felt there was a strong enough organization behind the band and sufficient indication that people would like it to gamble.

Record companies are also impressed by bands that the pop-music critics in newspapers and magazines occasionally pick to champion. *The New York Times'* John Rockwell raved repeatedly about the CBGB Club's new-wave groups Television and Talking Heads—and A & R people lumbered in like bears to honey. In other words, it pays to take your recordings to the local radio stations. If you can interest a d.j. in playing it, a chain reaction could develop. Also, be sure to get the local press to review your shows when you open in a town. And, when you do some recording, send copies to a few local and national press outlets. The idea is to draw attention to yourself and build up credentials.

From the music publishing standpoint, working first within a local context also is advisable. It's true that the L.A./N.Y./Nashville publishers are the most desirable, being in the best position to get songs recorded. Still, a strong personal rapport between a writer and publisher is essential to keep the songs actively worked. So if you're not in a position to migrate from Des Moines to L.A., try the publishers in the nearest large city first. They must have some contacts or they wouldn't be in business. So long as they've had some success with your style of music, give them a few songs for a six-month or one-year period. If they can't get the songs on a record released for sale within that time, the contract should stipulate that the rights revert to you. Then you'll have to make your pilgrimage to one of the frenzied music capitals. In the meantime, though, the local publisher may have made approaching the big-city publishers easier. He may have advanced you some money and paid the costs of lead sheets, copyrighting, and demos.

In most cases, you'll find being based in L.A., New York, or Nashville a struggle, but a rewarding struggle. Even if you have to support yourself by emptying ashtrays at a recording studio, as Kristofferson did until his break came along, you'll be where the action is. Your odds on making the right connections are multiplied. And while you're getting a realistic perception of what makes the business tick, the competition and spirit of the scene will excite you to work harder on your music.

Making   As should be plain, an impressive demo is the most elemental key
a Demo   to selling songs and the band. Obviously, you can't just send out
                lead sheets. No one is going to take your music to a piano to dis-
cover if your material is good. Similarly, music publishers and record companies can't chase around auditioning every band that writes to them. But they can turn around and thread a tape machine behind their desks. Furthermore, a demo shows them not only how well you play, but how well you *record*. And it speeds the decision making. If your tape leaps out of the stream of mediocrity, the publisher or A & R person can get opinions from others in the office and basically live with your music a little. (Few executives will see a group if they haven't first heard something promising about them or recorded by them.*) If he likes the tape, he'll go to hear you. If he's still convinced, he'll submit the tape at the next talent acquisition meeting, where decisions are made in committee. (Most talent scouts haven't the authority to sign you on their own.) All this is not to mention that a demo allows the group to present itself in the best light, whereas in live auditions you're handicapped with nervousness and a less-than-controlled environment.

A demo recording can mean anything from simple two-track recordings to lavish sixteen- or twenty-four-track productions. The latter is not only unfeasible for most new groups—big studios charge upwards of $125 an hour—but it's unnecessary and possibly harmful; overproduction can obscure what you're demonstrating and sound awkward. At the opposite extreme, a two-track is only useful for piano-voice demonstrations of songs or solo performances. For a group, something in between is what you need, like a four- or eight-track studio.** I wouldn't use home recording equipment for the demo, unless, again,

---

*For a songwriter trying to get a publishing deal, things are slightly looser. You can more readily make an appointment to sing live at a piano or with a guitar in the office. If the publisher likes what he hears, he might record you in his own small studio or lay out a demo budget to cut piano (or guitar) and voice demos. Still, your percentages are improved by coming in with a tape. Then, if they're interested in signing you, you can ask to be reimbursed for the money you spent demoing the songs, as demoing is one of the publisher's responsibilities.

**Multitrack studios don't just have mixing boards equipped with many channels to record many sources onto one track; they also have tape machines that can record those channels of sound on *separate* tracks. An eight-track recorder is equivalent to having eight tape recorders in one. Multitracking makes it possible for artists to be almost one-person bands, recording the different instruments one at a time on their own tracks and then mixing them together on a normal two-track (stereo) tape recorder. Stevie Wonder is a master of this technique.

you're a solo performer, or the band wants to make test recordings before entering an expensive studio. Though some home equipment is very sophisticated, a studio offers a controlled environment, high-quality equipment in working order, and the services of a trained engineer included in the session rate.

With a medium-sized studio, found in most cities, you get a happy blend of professional quality and economy. There are four- and eight-track studios that charge $25 to $40 an hour. Go with a four-track if the band is small, say a three-piece group; eight-track if it's larger, like a five-piece band using lots of vocal parts. Incidentally, don't disparage four-track equipment; the Beatles cut *Sgt. Pepper's Lonely Hearts Club Band* with it, the biggest available in the mid-sixties. With eight tracks, all the instruments and vocals can be recorded on separate tracks to be mixed later. The chief benefit of this is that the band can concentrate on recording one layer of music and singing at a time, mixing (blending) the perfected parts later. It means the whole band need not wear themselves out replaying a song a dozen times until each soloist gets his part right; the band can record the rhythm track together—bass, drums, piano, and rhythm guitar—and then the engineer can replay it for, say, the lead guitarist until he gets his part down perfectly, too. The difference is, the lead player plays with the tape, not the band. Having eight tracks on hand, you also can reserve a track on which to "double" the voices. By recording the same vocal parts a second time and subsequently mixing the two together, you can make your vocals sound twice as strong and thrilling.

Things, as you can see, are done differently in the studio. So prepare yourselves before you blow your savings learning to record rather than recording. Prepare to multitrack. Rehearse playing the music to the selected songs without singing, and singing the songs without playing the music. You'll find it's quite disorienting, because you're undoubtedly accustomed to working one off the other. I ran into this confusion in my first recording session in the early sixties, when the Trio cut *In a Most Unusual Way*. Some of our numbers were so intricate that I needed to hit the downbeat on my bass to sing on the upbeat and vice versa. Now I might have been able to play parts separately at home, but here I was, an awed twenty-year-old in New York's Columbia Recording Studios with nine famous sidemen to back us, including Doc Severinsen and Plaz Johnson. We tried a few takes with just the instruments, and I kept blowing my part. Finally the producer told me to go ahead and sing—quietly. It was the same story when we later dubbed* in the vocals. I stood at my mike waving my hands in the air as though I were slapping my bass to maintain my timing.

Also, rehearse playing and singing wearing headphones (or "cans," as they're known in studios). Headphones are used to hear what the other musicians are playing or to hear the music when overdubbing vocals. If monitor loudspeakers were used, the already recorded parts would leak into the new parts being recorded and thus destroy the separation that is essential to successful multitracking. What is disorienting about headphones is that you no longer hear sounds directly from your instrument, amplifier, or mouth; you hear the electronic image. In that same Bobby Doyle Trio session, I had trouble singing in tune wearing headphones until one of the seasoned musicians showed me I could remove one side of the phones and hear some of the live sound.

Recording is one of the most satisfying and fun experiences when you have good material and know how to play it well. It's great to start with a concept and build it into a song with a life of its own. But the process is so intense that you could be blown away by the pressures and take twice as long as you should, only to get an inferior product—unless you're confident. Confidence comes with knowing virtually everything you're going to do before entering the studio. Accidents in the making of records sometimes will seem divinely inspired and be left in. But an arrangement and a production—how the songs are developed and put on tape—have to be calculated as deliberately as a movie's scenes, camera shots, and script. Otherwise the result would be a dumb, misspent, and costly exercise.

In planning your repertoire, pick your three best songs, three that are different from each other yet characteristic of your style. Three are enough because if you can't captivate your listeners with those, then ten or a hundred won't help. In fact, too many will hurt you. The busy publisher or A & R person will just not want to get that involved. Also, showing too much at once dilutes the impact of all the songs.

To plan the arrangements and productions of the chosen songs, listen to the records of the groups you want to emulate. Notice how prominent the various instruments are at different points, how the music builds, and how new instru-

---

*Dubbing is a process of recording one part over another already recorded. If the part is on track number one as it's played back, the new part is played with it and the two are joined on a second track. During the days of the Trio's session, recorders hadn't been developed of greater capacity than two tracks. So music was recorded on one track and then "ping-ponged" with the vocals onto a second track. Hence, monaural records. Incidentally, the technique is still used in multitrack studios. For example, it permits the recording of up to ten tracks with a four-track machine by mixing three tracks onto the fourth, freeing the three for other instrumental or vocal parts, and so on. This is how the Beatles made *Sgt. Pepper* so sophisticated.

ments, texture, and background parts are introduced in stages to make the records continually interesting. Also, notice how things *sound*. Be prepared to tell the recording engineer, "Hey, we really want the bass line punchy on this song because it's the key," or, "We're selling the vocals here so we want them out front and sounding crisp. Don't put too much echo on them," or, "The guitar part should sound mystical and dreamy. Can we run it through a phaser with lots of echo on it?" (The engineer will be at your disposal. It's your party. So feel free to explain to him your song's concepts and point out what you like and dislike as you go. But do trust his expertise for details of sound and perhaps production. He has done hundreds of these things.)

Again, keep your songs down to 2½ to 3 minutes. Although it's unlikely you'll be trying to get airplay from demos, make them sound almost as though they could. Airplay sells records. Succinctness also will help by forcing you to delete superfluous parts and concentrate on demonstrating your strengths. If your strengths are your vocals, don't waste time with lengthy instrumental parts; sing and get out. Remember, if those first sixteen bars don't grab the publishers and record companies, most will abruptly move on to the next demo.

A few incidental preparations: First, have lyric sheets (if not complete lead sheets) handy. If someone suddenly is unsure of his part or there's a dispute about a chord or lyric, it'll save time. But don't rely on lead sheets. Reading parts tends to limit the amount of feeling you can pour into your performance. Second, be sure all your equipment and instruments are in perfect repair and that spare parts, especially tubes, guitar strings, and patch cords, are in stock. Third, when you call to book the studio, ask what instruments and equipment they have on hand and whether there are any charges to use them. Studios usually will have an acoustic piano, sometimes a Hammond organ, drums, and extra amplifiers to spare you the trouble of lugging in those unwieldy objects. Inquire if the bassist needs his amplifier or if they plug the bass straight into the board, something frequently done to increase bass presence and clarity. Ask about free setup time. They should allow you at least thirty minutes before the session starts for this. And ask about tape. Every studio requires you to buy your own since the tapes remain your property. Find out what brand and type is best suited to their equipment. You'll need reels of both multitrack tape and regular ¼-inch mastering tape for mix-downs. I recommend you buy the tape at the studio. Sometimes it doesn't sit too well if you don't. It's like bringing parts to a garage and asking the mechanic to attach them to your car. Let them make the 15 percent. It'll cost as much in a store anyway.

Now, determine your budget. Plan how much time you can spend on each song so you can pace yourself and accomplish what you set out to do. A typical demo costs anywhere from $300 to $600, depending on how involved the recording and mixing is. For three songs, you'll need about six hours to lay down the main musical tracks and vocals (longer if you do a lot of overdubs of backing harmonies, solos, percussion, and sound effects); three or four hours for mixing; and one and a half hours to make eight tape copies. With tape costing between $50 to $100, the demo represents a significant investment.

Considering that investment, seek perfection in the studio. Not with the madness of Ahab hunting the white whale, but with the idea that this tape represents your band. Sloppy musicianship or singing captured on tape will haunt you every time it's played. Don't sacrifice feel, but do recut the basic rhythm tracks until you achieve takes without bloopers. On this foundation you'll be building a superstructure of vocals, solos, and simple "sweetening" (adding finishing touches, such as a conga, tambourine, or string synthesizer), so it's crucial that good performances on these up-front parts aren't undercut by a bad drum fill, wrong chord, out-of-tune bass, or accelerating tempo. In mixing you might be able to remove an isolated bad chord, but not pervasive flaws.

Above all, maintain the positive attitude that "this is gonna be a great record." Shoot to make it releasable. What the heck—if you don't aim for it, you won't even come close. I've known groups who've come out of demo sessions with something they were able to sell to a record company. The companies realized the songs wouldn't have the same magical impact even if recut in $6,000 sessions. So they had a producer sweeten the tracks, adding a guitar overdub here, some strings and horns there, and released them. They even gave the groups co-production credit—which is worth a percent or two of the record's retail price. Essentially the same thing happened to Carole King. She had a major hit in the early sixties with "It Might as Well Rain Until September," a demo for Bobby Vee.

Many groups question how far they need to go in producing demos. There are two schools of thought on this. Some publishers and A & R people like demos sparely produced so the bare essentials are clear—the melodies, lyrics, instrumental, and vocal abilities. Old-style music people, they prefer to imagine what *they* can do to enhance the band in terms of sound and production. Others are spoiled. They've been shown so many master-quality demos costing $10,000 that anything less pales by comparison. (Some in this latter group are simply unqualified for their jobs; they lack the imagination and instinct needed to sense raw talent.) The answer isn't to spend ten grand on a demo. Seek a middle ground, keeping the recording full sounding but uncluttered. Season it with just the tastiest of your production ideas, ideas that enhance the songs and add to the band's distinctiveness.

Submitting Your Demo   With the demo finished and more than a half-dozen tape copies made in the studio (save money—duplicate personal copies at home), plot your campaign to get them out there. First, list the key publishers and record companies and the addresses of their head and large branch offices where the creative (as opposed to just sales and promotion) departments are. This information is found in the annual directories published by the record industry trade papers, *Billboard, Record World,* and *Cash Box.* * They list the names and addresses of publishers, record companies, managers, booking agents, concert promoters, recording studios, distributors, and so on. Be selective; narrow your choices to those who handle music like yours successfully. Wherever possible get the names of specific people. Best yet, assemble any direct personal contacts you can muster. Blindly sending a tape in the mail or leaving it with a secretary is fine if the companies you hit happen to have screeners who listen to everything. But even the most conscientious of screeners can grow impervious after listening to two dozen tapes a day, and inadvertently dismiss a promising one along with the junk. And many companies simply don't listen to material from unknown sources. So if you have an aunt who works for a company or knows someone who does, ask her to listen to your tape and—if she likes it—to take it to a decision maker. At least your tape will reach the right person and be considered more seriously.

Whatever contacts you have, just be sure not to short-change yourself on the packaging of the demos and presentation. I cannot overemphasize this because publishers, A & R people, and important managers and lawyers go straight for the most professional-looking packages when presented with a deluge of tapes to listen to. They know that the percentages of finding something worthwhile among them are much greater. So spend a few bucks. Don't use skimpy 2-inch reels; use 7-inch reels wound with the best quality mastering tape. (Enough tape for the songs is fine. You don't need to send full reels.) Buy tape leader to begin the tape and separate the songs by a few seconds. This makes cueing the songs easier. Package the tapes in fresh white boxes. Attach neatly typed labels to the boxes, indicating the song titles, composers, playing times, and the name, address, and phone

---

Billboard: 1 Astor Plaza, New York, NY 10003
     9000 Sunset Blvd., West Hollywood, CA 90046
Record World: 1700 Broadway, New York, NY 10019
     6290 Sunset Blvd., Hollywood, CA 90028
Cash Box: 119 W. 57th St., New York, NY 10019
     6363 Sunset Blvd., Hollywood, CA 90028

number of the person in charge of business or the band's manager. (It makes me scream to think how many tapes I've received with songs I would have liked to record that I ended up throwing away because they carried no clues as to whose they were.) Also, use fresh mailing envelopes addressed with typewritten labels.

The final touch should be a concise cover letter. Supplementing the bio and photo included in the package, the letter should tell what style music you play, what your live show is like, and what your aims are. It should give pertinent information about your business situation, such as who your manager and agent are, whether your publishing rights are available, and what great things are happening with your group. (If writing to a publisher, also name a few artists who would be suitable for each song.) Close the letter by mentioning you'll call in a couple of weeks to get their reactions and perhaps arrange a meeting. (Always leave things on the basis of your calling them. It's unlikely they'll bother calling you—unless you happen to be the Beatles reuniting.)

You might include a stamped, self-addressed envelope to get the package back if it's rejected. However, don't count on having them all returned. First of all, it looks cheap to write, "If you don't like this, please return it. It's the only tape we've got." It's better to say, "We believe in the tape. If you can't help us now, please keep it on file in case things change." Secondly, logistics make it impossible to return everything. For instance, I receive as many as 50 tapes a week from songwriters. I can't possibly prepare each one for mailing and haul them to the post office. I just throw away what I don't like. The problem, obviously, is that much worse for publishers and record companies who receive between 50 and 150 unsolicited tapes a week.

Also, make up your mind not to make a pest of yourself. It's all right to call in a couple of weeks as you promised in the letter, but if this brings no result, back off. If you start getting pushy, you'll turn off the person you want to impress. It could be that he just hasn't gotten to your package yet. I, for one, try to listen to everything I get. But I'll make a point of *not* listening to the tape of someone who becomes obnoxious.

Publishing Deals   Publishing and record deals can be pretty straightforward if you understand them. Basically, you give up the right to sell your work for a limited period of time in exchange for royalties. The companies' problem is finding artists whose works are most salable. Your problem is finding companies who'll exploit your records and songs in the market most effectively and tastefully. Record companies will be discussed in the next chapter.

The publishing house you go with should have these attributes: It must be successful handling songs similar to yours, be accessible to you, be excited about your material, have a staff with whom you feel a strong personal rapport and who can offer you informed songwriting and business guidance, have adequate financial muscle (to cover the costs of administrating copyrights, demos, and copyist fees), be willing to advance you a sizable amount of money upon signing, have people to promote records of your songs, have a reputation for honest royalty accounting, and have solid connections with foreign licensees (publishers who collect overseas royalties).

Publishers vary so widely in strengths and weaknesses that it may take you some time to find the right home for your songs. Shop around. Before binding yourself with an "exclusive term" contract, make a deal with a publisher for an isolated few songs and see how he does with them for six months or a year. Make it clear how you want your songs handled. If you're a nonperforming songwriter, it's essential for the publisher to get the songs covered by good artists. If you're a group that needs to maintain the exclusivity of your material because it constitutes your key selling point, then the important thing is how much dough they can advance you and how well they protect the songs, handle the administrative duties, and promote the songs when released. Don't be surprised if you find that the best isn't necessarily big. Working so hard to please their hit artists, the large houses could lose you in the shuffle.

Music publishing, as most aspects of the business, has its cons, rip-offs, and room for costly errors. Number one, don't agree to involve your manager in your publishing. The manager has no right to a commission on your songwriting because the publisher works the songs, the manager works the act. It's his function to exploit an act's performing abilities, not their creative, i.e., songwriting, abilities. If the manager is the publisher, fine, but then he'd receive the publisher's share. He need not also charge a 15 percent or 20 percent manager's commission.

A second costly error you could make is to try publishing your songs yourself. Technically you could; it only requires nominal fees to BMI or ASCAP (a publisher, like a writer, can only belong to one), the selection of a name (cleared through BMI or ASCAP), and some paper work. But, as should be clear, there's a lot more to publishing than collecting royalties. Unless you're having great chart success and your business organization is ultrasophisticated, you would be hoarding to yourself a large percentage of nothing.

Third, avoid making deals that, innocently or not, threaten to impede your progress or wring you dry. One such trap could be the studio where you record your demo. Many studios also run publishing operations, having access to many new songwriters who don't yet have a publisher and to many artists looking for material. They operate by offering people for whom financing a demo is a problem free studio time in exchange for the rights to "publish" their songs. But they can't possibly protect and service your songs in all the ways a publisher does. Often they'll just sit on your material until your career starts happening through your own devices and then collect the profits! Making a deal with a studio can be all right—but only if it's strictly limited to the songs you demo there and to *half* of the publishing share. (Keeping half leaves you something to barter elsewhere.) Also, as in all publishing deals, their rights to your songs should terminate in a year if they haven't gotten the song commercially recorded and scheduled to be released for sale. (Don't ever merely require a publisher to get a song recorded, for that could mean a simple demo, in which case they'd have the rights to that song indefinitely!) If you sign an exclusive long-term deal without these limiting and safeguarding provisions, you'll have a tough time affiliating with a genuine publishing house. For instance, the studio pseudopublisher could demand that the legitimate publisher buy you out at a high price and thus make you less attractive.

If financing your demo is the problem, the kind of trade-out to make is that of exchanging your talent for recording time. Studios need musicians to demo songs they publish and to back up acts who want to demo songs but aren't "self-contained," that is, don't play all their own instruments. This pays off doubly. You'll be able to record a lot to put together a great demo, and you'll make some valuable contacts by hanging around the studio so much.

Another must-to-avoid trap is the song shark. Under the pretense of listening to your songs in order to consider publishing them, one variety will steal enough of your music to write his own songs but not enough to be liable for plagiarism. Another shark, perhaps the most sinister of all, inhabits matchbook covers and magazine ads. This shark exhorts you to send him your finished or unfinished songs with, say, $100 each. He promises to fill in the missing parts, words, or lyrics, record the songs, and even get them on the radio. To keep a veneer of legitimacy, he might have a combo cut a slew of songs, yours among them, and play the tapes on some station in Mule Shoe, Texas, broadcasting between 3 and 6 A.M. It's more likely, however, that he'll collect your money and change post office boxes. One thing is certain: No one has ever been discovered through these scams.

Above all, steer clear of anyone who asks you to pay them to publish your songs. The performance-rights societies BMI and ASCAP won't even work with publishers caught taking money from songwriters. They know a legit publisher wouldn't deal with a songwriter whose songs can't be promoted profitably in the marketplace. Look at it this way: Publishers keep up to half a song's revenue. Their incentive is to make the song a success. If you pay someone to publish your songs, sure, he'll accept them all, because he won't have to do anything with them. Why should he? He has already made money on them.

To be safe, deal only with people whose credentials you can check—legitimate, reputable people. If *they* won't work with you, take it as a sign something is seriously lacking in your songs.

When you're finally ready to assign your publishing rights on a long-term basis—to sign an "exclusive term" agreement—you'll find that the deals are somewhat standardized. Unless you go in with a record contract in your pocket or a few hits under your belt, you won't have the leverage to insist on more than the normal split, in which you give the publisher 100 percent of the publishing rights to your songs for the life of the copyrights. Understand a song is seen as having two distinct values: publishing and writing. For convenience, it's regarded as being worth 200 percent: 100 percent publishing, 100 percent writing. Initially, an author owns his song completely. He can assign the publishing rights to another party for purposes of commercially exploiting the song, but once he registers the song with BMI or ASCAP, he can never assign or sell his share as the writer. This law was established in the sixties by the performance-rights societies to end the frequent ruthless exploitation of songwriters. Prior to this, song sharks would offer struggling songwriters a pittance for their material—perhaps $100 to $500 for a song. Then, if the song happened to become a smash, the writer would have his few hundred dollars . . . while the shark swam off with $50,000 in royalties.

Ironically, the law backfired on me. A few years after I gave Kin Vassy half credit on "A Stranger in My Place," and after most of the royalties we'd make on the song had already come in, Vassy came to me. He needed some cash and wanted to sell me some songs. Only "Stranger . . ." interested me. So he signed a document assigning his half of the writer's share to me and I gave him $1,000. Only afterward did I learn that the performance-rights societies are intractable about writer's shares. BMI wouldn't acknowledge the deal, so it was a total loss. They continue to send checks to Kin.

In your publishing agreement, then, be sure you're given your lawful 100 percent writer's share, or 50 percent of all mechanical royalties.* Incidentally,

---

*Publishers receive all the mechanical royalties (money from record sales) and send the writers' shares to the writers, whereas ASCAP and BMI split the performance royalties (from airplay, etc.) and send the writers' and publishers' shares to the respective parties.

it's not unusual for a publisher to charge a 15 percent administration fee off the gross income, such that the split is actually 57½ percent to 42½ percent. Be sure the contract gives you no less than half of the royalties received from overseas licensees (this amounts to 25 percent if the licensee takes the normal 50 percent for collecting the royalties, still a very significant source of income because mechanical royalties are much higher overseas), 5 cents per copy of single sheet music sold, 50 percent of income derived from the sale of folios or songbooks (this usually amounts to 5 percent of the wholesale selling price), and 50 percent of "other royalties" such as those received from the song's use in a jingle, movie, or TV show. Also see that the contract gives you the right to audit the publisher's books and approval of any agreement to use a song in a commercial jingle.

A third kind of publishing deal, as opposed to the exclusive and single-song deals, lets you retain 50 percent of your publishing rights, and thus increases your income from your songs by 25 percent. This is a long-term "co-publishing" deal. Usually only those who have a track record of hits or incredible songs and a record deal in the works have enough leverage to swing this. You form your own publishing company and affiliate it with a major, established publisher. The major publisher administrates the copyrights and handles the day-to-day chores.

Whatever sort of agreement you make, a standard contract will have an annual option that allows the publisher to reevaluate whether they want to continue carrying you. The contracts probably won't give you the same option, however. If it doesn't, insert a clause that allows you to reevaluate them in, say, five years.* The First Edition's first publishing experience was a disaster because we didn't know to check this. Signing a co-publishing deal with TRO Music, Inc., a large New York–based company, we felt we were very smart. The deal included a $10,000 advance. Soon after signing, though, we learned we would be held to the same terms indefinitely. In a few years our publishing could be worth ten times what it was then and we wouldn't be able to renegotiate our deal! To rectify this, we went to court and succeeded in breaking the contract on a technicality. An unending personal services contract is illegal; it's tantamount to enforced servitude. Still, the long court fight cost us all our publishing monies, including the $10,000. We couldn't sue to recover damages (the cost of the suit) because our problem arose from our own negligence.

---

*When a publishing contract expires, the publisher retains the music you wrote during the period of that agreement. To get it back from him, as Neil Sedaka did with Kirshner, you or your next publisher would have to buy it for whatever it's worth at the time. A catalogue is figured to be worth five times its average yearly income.

You're supposed to know what you're signing. It was our own fault for relying solely on our attorney.

In both the exclusive and co-publishing agreements, most publishers will subsidize their writers while they write. Anticipating income from the writer's songs in the near future, the publisher will risk thousands of dollars, giving the money in a lump sum or bit by bit, perhaps weekly, for a period of time, like a salary. These advances are "recoupable," that is, before the writer receives a penny of royalties from his songs, the publisher is reimbursed for the advanced monies. Of course, if your songs flop, it's the publisher's loss.

For a single-song publishing deal, a new writer can expect to get an advance of $100 to $200. It could be more, depending on how good your material is, how much leverage you have, and how good a negotiator you are. Maybe *you* can get $500 for a single song.

In any event, publishing advances have made possible the careers of many a struggling talent. Such was the case of Kenny Loggins, who wrote "House at Pooh Corner," a hit for the Nitty Gritty Dirt Band, while he was a "salaried" writer for American Broadcasting Music, Inc., and of a pair of contract writers for the same company, Walter Becker and Donald Fagen, who lived off their periodic checks while they assembled a group—Steely Dan. Though Becker and Fagen submitted a lot of songs under the deal, none were ever recorded. But don't feel sorry for the publisher—Steely Dan's catalogue has since repaid the company's investment in spades.

In accepting advances, take the weekly allowance if you need the sense of security, the lump sum if the band needs the money to buy equipment that will help you get better paying jobs. Just be sure that if only one or a few members write the songs, any advance money is not shared outright by the group. It's not fair. If the group needs the money, the songwriters could loan it the money, but there must be some repayment scheme.

One last point. If you have a good publisher, or you don't have a publisher but you've done a good job of sending your songs to artists or their managers and publishers, the opportunity eventually will arise to have one or several of your songs covered by a hit act. But don't be surprised if the act predicates their recording of it on your assigning their company the publishing rights. They know that they have a good chance of making those rights valuable and may feel they should be compensated for the effort. If the song is one they want badly enough, they may record it even if you or your publisher refuses them. However, if they feel they can take or leave the song, they'll probably find a song that they can get a piece of. Negotiate it. Try to let them have a share, say, 50 percent of the publishing rights, limited to their recording of the song(s) and (perhaps) on the condition that they release it as a single (as opposed to an album track). But if you're an unknown and the opportunity arises for a major name act to cut your song, give up 100 percent of the publishing if necessary. Never mind that you stand to earn a lot as the writer. Having your song covered will boost your fortunes in terms of status and will open doors. It pays to give something away if there's a reasonable chance you can get something worthwhile in return.

Giving away publishing rights also helps you by providing an incentive to the act to invest their own money in promoting the record. A good illustration of this is the First Edition's *Ballad of Calico.* An old high-school friend, Larry Cansler, who directed the music for "Rollin'," approached me in 1971 with an idea that he and then unknown Michael ("Wildfire") Murphey were formulating for a rock opera about the death of a Western mining town. Being knocked out by what they played for me, I told them we'd do it and asked about the publishing. They offered it to my Mar-Ken Music, Inc. Consequently, I invested a lot of extra cash and effort into making the production of the two-record set first class and I put more than $10,000 into the development of a Broadway show based on the music. Unfortunately, the two attempts to get a good script failed . . . and the album sold poorly. Though *Calico* was easily the band's artistic high-water mark, apparently it was a little too radical a departure for our fans to accept and our record company to promote.

Nevertheless, the writers got more support for their project than anyone could reasonably expect. And I got the chance to become a very rich man had my gamble paid off like *Tommy* or *Jesus Christ Superstar.* In any case, the fact that I was a star who promised to record the songs was leverage to gain their publishing rights. It's one of the windfalls of the trade, one you should remember when you're on top.

The Big Break

4

Then it's time to go downtown . . . [and]
sell your soul to the company
who are waiting there
to sell plastic ware. . . .*
    JIM MC GUINN AND CHRIS HILLMAN,
"So You Want to Be a Rock 'n' Roll Star"

It was a classic way to get "discovered." Jimmy Bowen was A & R director at Warner Brothers Records. Bowen's secretary just happened to be Bonnie Williams, the mother of one of the four New Christy Minstrels who secretly plotted splitting to form a contemporary rock band called the First Edition. When Terry Williams and the other co-conspirators—Mike Settle, Thelma Camacho, and I—felt our concept was viable, we went to her. Would she tell Bowen her son was forming a group that was interested in recording?

It's funny, but we weren't frightened going into the audition Bowen subsequently arranged. Filing into his office at Warner Brothers in Burbank with a single guitar in hand, we felt an exciting adrenaline flow. We weren't exactly greenhorns and we knew we were good. To me, it was a question of whether *he* had the taste to recognize how good we were! Our confidence must have been justified, because before we could sing more than two of the eight Settle numbers we'd worked up, he agreed to have us cut a demo at his expense.

"Yes, let's give it a try," Bowen said when he heard the tape. He was impressed with the uniqueness of our sound. He said it was very musical, as opposed to the psychedelic direction rock was taking at the time.

With our immediate acceptance, we didn't consider shopping for other labels. Warner Brothers was about the hottest in the business. Plus, the timing was perfect. We could leave the Christies the day our contracts expired, July 10, 1967, and enter the studio to begin our first album at 9:00 A.M., July 11.

The fairy-tale tone of all this is deceptive—we'd all paid our dues for years.

And leaving our lucrative salaries for the uncertainties of an unestablished act was as frightening as it was exciting. Warner Brothers (actually Reprise, a Warner label begun by Frank Sinatra) didn't make us instantly rich and famous. Cash advances were such a rarity in those days we didn't even think to ask for one. We were content with the $1,500 we each earned as union scale for recording the album.

•

Approaching a Record Company   This wasn't the most common way to land a record contract. But with Mrs. Williams' golden "in," it wasn't the most uncommon, either. Even then, the days of discovering acts singing on street corners were largely gone. And unsolicited demos only occasionally brought results. Today, more than ever, a demo should come from someone respected by the record company executives—an employee, manager, agent, producer, lawyer, or music publisher. This immediately gives the tape a degree of professional credibility, which is essential to making the company's initial big investment—about $100,000 per new act (half for recording advances, half for manufacturing and marketing the product)—seem less risky. The companies know worthwhile acts are those having professional representation, and good representation boosts the odds that an act is stable, well-directed, and able to handle its bit in selling records—getting on the road and working.

One of the better representations you can have is a "production company." Production companies, usually run by successful producers and artists, specialize in signing talent and delivering a finished product to a record company. One disadvantage of this vehicle to record making is that the royalties and advances are smaller than those offered by a record company because the production company takes a healthy cut for its services. Still, if you get an offer from a production company that can tie you in with a good record company, go with it. The First Edition wasn't signed directly to Reprise; it was signed to Jimmy Bowen's Amos Productions, Inc. Amos had its own deal with the record company, the details of which we never knew. Our checks came from Amos. We got a 5 percent royalty rate, standard for that time, and no advance—Amos covered the recording costs with money they got from Reprise, which they recouped when our royalties flowed in. (The artists are responsible for the costs of making the product.) As is typical of most record contracts, we signed for two years with three one-year options, exercisable by Amos and Reprise, and agreed to deliver two albums a year.

When you approach a record or production company for a record deal, let your personal manager or attorney (assuming you have one or both by now) handle the meetings and negotiations. It's easier for someone else to say how great you are than it is for you to say the same thing. A manager can also play the role of the bad guy where necessary. He can hang tough in negotiations without casting aspersions on any future record company–artist relationship. It's quite all right for the record company lawyer and A & R people to think your manager is tough (as long as he's equally capable), whereas it's not all right for them to think you're so tough; they won't want to work with you.

Your attitude when meeting with the company should be businesslike, positive about your career and music, yet empathetic to the company's needs and open to their criticisms and suggestions. Though the business is stuffed with bloated egos, it's not helpful to bare one when you need to seem appealing. If they feel that dealing with you is trouble, they'll end the meeting or return your materials as quickly as it takes to find a "pass" slip. Cooperation is an important ingredient in building success.

If you approach record companies without a heavyweight production company, a manager, or an entertainment lawyer, you're not out of the running for a deal. An impressive presentation, demo, *et al.*, could excite an enterprising artists and repertoire person into packaging you. He could make you attractive by hooking you up with the right manager, producer, or agency. And, by the same token, if he thinks your demo needs more work, he can take you back to the studio on his demo budget. A nonleverage position, in fact, has its benefits. Companies look for credible new talent they can sign at bargain rates because they can make far more money on a Top-10 hit by an act they got cheaply than they can with the same hit by a group of prima donnas with a superstar manager who demands a $150,000 advance, a royalty rate of 15 percent, and outrageous advertising expenditures.

In the event you take it upon yourselves to visit record companies, don't go en masse. Send just a pair of your more business-minded and articulate band members; they can present a coherent point of view and rely on each other for moral support. Being represented by a minority also gives the band a fall-back position. Suppose the company offers a singles deal instead of the album deal you have your hearts set on. If you were all present, you might make a rash decision. Instead, your representatives can tell the A & R person you need to discuss it with the band and will get back to him. Perhaps you'll think of a compromise. For example, you can accept the offer on the condition that the record company guarantees an album if one of your singles reaches the Top 40.

Incidentally, if some personal contact at a company helped get your demo to the A & R person, all subsequent dealings should be done by either your manager or your two-person delegation. This insures that both parties understand each other. An intermediary might not tell you what actually was said in discussions with the company, but what *seemed* to be said. Personally, I enjoy doing business myself, having professionals respond to my work and proposals directly; it keeps me on top of the affairs that determine the course of my career. Being practical, however, I don't recommend that the inexperienced try it. Even I often find it better to participate behind the scenes. The manager manages for a living. Plus, to work with the company as an artist, I have to maintain that good-guy relationship.

What a Record Company Can Do for You

However you contact the record companies, don't blindly sign whatever is placed before you. A record contract usually proves to be one's most important single career move. It can stall you, sometimes insurmountably, or elevate you, like a rocket, to some level of prominence. This is the fulcrum of a musical career, so know what you're looking for in a record company and a contract. (For an extract of terms for a typical new artist's contract, see Appendix III.)

At bottom, a record company serves as a big promoter. It subsidizes the making of a professional recording with an advance—a loan for which you pay no interest and which you repay only if the records sell. (Any advance monies not spent in recording may be used to develop your stage show or to live on until the band gets working.) And, it mass-markets your recorded performances. It puts copies in stores across the country, perhaps the world, and advertises and promotes them. It'll even help subsidize your personal appearances. If these efforts pay off and a grass fire develops, with your record being bought and played on radio stations nationally, everyone stands to make a bundle. Everyone, that is, except you—the group.

In a very real sense this shocking fact is true. Don't look to make money on records, singles or albums, until you've had several major sellers back-to-back. (I'm not talking about the songwriter's income now, just the recording artist's.) As new artists, the royalty rate you get will probably be about 7 percent of the suggested retail price of the records, for instance, $1.25 for a single and $7.98 for an album. This amounts to about 9 cents per single and 56 cents per album. If your album is moderately successful over the several months it's pushed hardest, it might sell 100,000 units (records and tapes).* Your expected royalties: $56,000. Not bad. The problem is that there are certain deductions. If you were advanced $50,000 to make the album, $10,000 for a recoupable promotional budget, and $10,000 in tour shortfall,† that's $70,000 you *owe.* But, there's more. A percentage of sales, perhaps 10 percent of the 100,000 units, isn't counted toward royalties because of the inevitable returns from customers and retailers. Obviously you don't receive royalties from unsold records. Then there are "free goods." To encourage dealers to carry, prominently display, and really push your record, the record company allows a certain quantity free. As much as 16 percent may be given out per album, on which the dealers make a pure profit. (Sometimes a third of single sales are free goods. Record companies give so many singles away to create a hit because a hit single sells albums —on which they make their real money.) This helps you in the long run because the sales in key outlets are monitored by radio stations and the chart departments of the trade magazines. They don't care if early sales were artificially stimulated—the point is people have bought the record. This activity may convince skeptical d.j.'s to give the record a chance and will cause it to appear on the national sales charts. This, in turn, makes other dealers and radio stations across the country take notice. Eventually, the free goods might have spurred the sales of these 100,000 LP's. As with the free promotion copies sent to disc jockeys and reviewers, sales of free goods don't pay royalties.

In addition, you may defray the record company's packaging costs whether or not you insist on an unusually elaborate package (a foldout jacket, posters, die-cut pieces, etc.). This might amount to 10 percent of 60 cents, or 6 cents a record.

Lastly, most record contracts include a reserve clause that permits the company to hold up to half of whatever royalties are left after advances have been repaid. Reserves go toward the *next* album's advances and to offset further returns.

Here's how it looks:

Gross sales:	$100,000	
	− 10,000	free goods
	− 10,000	returns
Real sales:	$ 80,000	

---

*Sales of 500,000 merit a gold record from the Recording Industry Association of America (RIAA); 1 million, platinum. The largest-selling pop albums in history include Fleetwood Mac's *Rumours* (8 million), John Denver's *Greatest Hits Vol. V* (6 million), Peter Frampton's *Frampton Comes Alive* (6 million), and Carole King's *Tapestry* (4 million). An album selling fewer than 10,000 copies, as is the case with most unknown acts who receive little airplay, is considered a "stiff."

†Shortfall refers to a type of tour support that subsidizes the difference between the low amount earned on a promotional tour and the higher costs involved in doing that tour.

	$ 80,000	sales
	×.56	royalty per record
	$44,800	gross royalties
Debits to		
record company:	$ 50,000	advance (mainly for recording costs)
	10,000	extra promotion budget
	10,000	tour shortfall
	6,000	packaging costs
	$ 76,000	owed to record company
Your income:	$ 44,800	gross royalties
	− 76,000	owed to record company
	−$31,200	TOTAL INCOME

A total of 100,000 records were sold, yet you *owe* the record company $31,200! Meanwhile, the record company, making about $1.10 per unit in real sales, has made $88,000. Here's how the income from a $7.98 album breaks down: It's sold to retailers for about half price, or $4 each. From this subtract the costs:

$.50	to the distributors
.60	for packaging
.40	average pressing
.56	artist royalty
.24	3% producer's royalty
.28	mechanical royalty for a hypothetical 10 songs at 2¾ cents each, divided between publisher and songwriter
.12	AFM health and welfare fees (1.5%)
.20	advertising (5% of $4)
$2.90	

$4.00	gross income for each record sold
−2.90	costs
$1.10	remaining for the company (well within the 30% margin they try to maintain of the $3.50 left after paying distributors)

That $1.10 isn't sheer profit, however. The record company might end up with half that to invest in other acts. It has to defray fixed costs such as salaries and office expenses and variable costs such as travel and telephone bills. If your record sells just 100,000 copies, it's safe to say that the company will break even. Their $44,000 profit, plus the $44,800 royalties you've earned, just about cover the $90,000 or so they've spent in advances and in promoting the record. However, the company will have taken you a long way toward the day when you will sell 500,000 or a million albums and a couple million of each single. The money you earn then, though, will go to repay the record company until all past debts are covered. Most artists don't count on seeing more money from their records than their advances, unless they consistently score hits.

You really can make big bucks from records, however. Indirectly. Without laying out a cent of your own money, you'll be given an advance to record your performances on a first-rate album and perhaps buy some equipment to present the group as a first-rate act. Your music will be mass-marketed into thousands of stores throughout the country and advertised and talked about in the public prints and airwaves. The records advertise you. They make you known to a *mass* audience and create a demand for your personal appearances. And here is where the big money enters. Riding your first hit single and newly gold album, you can average $10,000 a night for as many nights of the week as is logistically and humanly possible. Even before the record sells significantly, the fact that you're now "recording artists" gets you into better club and concert bookings and boosts your income.

The quality you should most look for in a record company, then, is the degree to which it can promote you. This means many things: How much it can advance you, promise in advertising and promotion, and offer in terms of personal attention. Most important, though, it means something far more mundane: How well it gets that "product" before the record buyers, how well it distributes the records. All else is in vain if the customer in Podunk, Iowa, can't find your record in a store when he has that $5 in his hand. He'll just pick up the nearest hit and forget about the new group he heard late at night on the FM station or saw as the opening act at the Eagles' concert. He was gonna take a chance, but—and that precious impulse may be forever gone.

Never take it for granted that the records are in the stores. Far too often, even fairly successful acts, let alone tenderfeet, visit stores in towns they're playing and find the racks bereft of their records. The agony of this is that the impact of the live appearance is severely blunted. You do promotional tours at a loss to trigger sales and induce airplay, which in turn is to stimulate mass airplay and sales. If the records are scarce, your efforts are wasted. Perhaps most painful is the thought that the music you put your heart into recording is going unheard and unappreciated.

A powerful distribution is essential when you have hit records. You can get a hit with most of the name companies, but the same hit on a CBS, Warner Communications, or Polygram label—conglomerates of major companies that merged to develop fantastic distribution—might sell two or three times the records. When a chain reaction seems in the making, these giant companies can capitalize on it by mobilizing vast resources. In other words, record companies are one area where *big* is best. While publishers, booking agencies, public-relations firms, production companies, and management firms usually are preferable when small and dedicated to you, a small record company may provide all the personal attention you want but lack the market penetration you need.

There are ways to get the best of both worlds, however. The parent conglomerates with the strong distribution networks have many otherwise independent companies feeding them product. Companies owning branch distribution systems include CBS (Columbia, Epic, Portrait); EMI-Capitol; MCA; Polygram (Polydor, RSO, Casablanca, Phonogram); RCA; and WEA (Warner Brothers/Elektra-Asylum/Atlantic). WEA (a division of Warner Communications) typifies a conglomerate structure:

Major WEA companies:	Small, creatively independent labels bonded to major companies for manufacturing, marketing, and promotion, in addition to distribution:
Warner Brothers:	Bearsville Capricorn Curtom Dark Horse Reprise
Elektra-Asylum:	Nemperer
Atlantic:	Rolling Stones Cotillion Little David Big Tree Swan Song

One might generalize that companies with their own distribution systems are the most desirable. However, there are many that have had significant successes through chains of independent regional distributors. A&M, for example, marketed two of the all-time biggest-selling albums in pop history, *Frampton Comes Alive* and Carole King's *Tapestry.* If asked to order pop-music companies for overall performance, best first, I'd name: Columbia, Warner Brothers, Capitol, RSO, A&M, Atlantic, Elektra-Asylum, Epic, RCA, ABC, MCA, Arista, Polydor Inc., Phonogram, U.A., Casablanca, Chrysalis, Motown, and 20th Century. But it would be a credit to you to be signed to any of these major labels.* Of course, there are many independent labels of varying degrees of smallness but with national scope—Bang, Janus, London, Mushroom, Private Stock, T.K., Vanguard—and hundreds of regional record companies that might be useful as a stepping-stone to a deal with a big-league company.

To satisfy yourself about which labels are preferable, buy a copy of *Billboard, Cash Box,* or *Record World,* and jot down a few albums or singles by groups like yours that are in the 30s and 40s of the charts. Then hunt for these in local stores and see which seem to receive classier treatment with such selling aids as window displays, posters, and mobiles. Get a feel for which companies let you know their records are happening. (How records are stocked when bordering on becoming smashes is most revealing.)

As to choosing a company by size, if distributions seem equivalent, decide whether you'd prefer being a big fish in a small pond or a small fish in a large one. I'd rather be with a label that seems as though it's going to use me as a vehicle for its own growth than be signed to an impersonal giant and be stranded in a traffic jam among a few dozen other new acts crying for attention. I also would be sure to go with a company for the right reasons. Don't just go for the biggest money. Go for the company with a history of handling your kind of music successfully. Motown, for example, the bastion of black pop, R&B, and soul, is notorious for its inability to produce and market white pop acts. Its two grand attempts with the Manticore and Prodigal labels largely failed.

A big part of a company's willingness to "perform" for you isn't just how much cash it can pour into the act, but rather how excited the staff is about you and—more importantly—how enthusiastic they are about their jobs. This forms an accurate barometer of a company's relative health. You can tell if the staff members are going through the motions or jumping straight ahead to help their acts make it—not worried about whether doing this or that will jeopardize their jobs. You also can tell if they are a collection of flunkies or a team of talented record people. Talk to them, watch them in action. Warner Brothers showed this spirit when the First Edition joined the company. Eight gold records later

---

*Addresses can be found in the trades' annual directories or in the Official Talent & Booking Directory. For the latter, send $40 to Specialty Publications, Inc., 7033 Sunset Blvd., Suite 222, Los Angeles, California 90028.

we left for the financially greener pastures of MGM. Sadly, we didn't notice the sickness growing within the company because we were so busy counting the million bucks they advanced First Edition Productions, Inc. We didn't get a hit single during our three years with them and our careers were set back an incalculable distance. On the other hand, U.A., with which I signed as a solo artist after the First Edition disbanded in early 1976, made a personal commitment to me. Artie Mogull, the company's new president, and producer Larry Butler, then president of their Nashville division, vowed to do all they could to catapult me back into the Top 10. Which, by May 1977, happened. "Lucille" was my first pop hit in six years.

Ideally, you want a company that demonstrates it's committed to building your career. Some companies, not really knowing what they're doing, cavalierly sign groups right and left. They release one record and if anything happens, fine. If not, you're dropped. Next? They release from five to twenty-five albums a month, like throwing a handful of darts. If one or two stick on target, reaching the Top 10 and going gold, the companies make enough profits to cover the stiffs and congratulate themselves on how well things are going. Of those that fail, only obviously good groups get picked up for more throws in the game.

The Record Contract— Advance and Royalties

Let's assume the right conditions coalesce and a record company with suitable qualifications calls you.

"We can give you $10,000 up front for an album and 7 percent royalties," the company representative might propose. "We'll pay the producer's fees and cover recording costs, which will come out of the band's royalties when the record sells." This is a basic deal, the company assuming most of the production responsibilities—and control.

"I'm sorry," your manager might respond. "We're interested, but we've got another offer that comes closer to our bottom line. The group needs to buy equipment and wardrobe for their show, and they have to have something to live on while they take time to record. We need at least twenty grand."

This is negotiating. Ten thousand dollars is fine, $15,000 would be great—so try for $20,000. If the record company settles at $15,000, you've upped the deal by 50 percent.

It's very likely, however, that you'll be offered a "production deal," which places the recording responsibilities in your laps. Advancing you $30,000 to $50,000 and giving you a royalty of 10 percent, the record company in effect commissions you to deliver a finished master to them. You pay the recording costs, which include the producer's fees, although the selection of a producer is made in collaboration. An experienced producer commonly charges $5,000 to $10,000 and 3 percent of the project's royalties.

Many labels prefer production deals because they simplify matters. Budgeting is clear-cut, and they keep the manifold creative problems of the artists at arm's length. The record company's main concern, if the finished masters are acceptable, is to manufacture, market, and promote the records. The arrangement obviously is more attractive to the group, too, because it affords greater artistic independence. Whatever species of deal you're offered, make sure you understand the components of the contract. It's impossible to say exactly what the terms will be—they vary from case to case—but the basics remain constant.

Advances to artists are based on the accepted principle that the act pays the recording costs. In a production deal, where the act pays session costs directly, the record company advances a large sum (usually $50,000) to cover those costs, half upon signing, half upon delivery of the master recording tapes. It's an incentive for the group to fulfill its part of the bargain promptly. The record company recoups the advance from the subsequent royalties.*

In deals in which the record company handles the production, it advances you a much smaller amount, perhaps $10,000, because it assumes the studio and musician costs. Here, too, you get half on signing and half when the record is finished. Just specify in the contract that you're to receive payment upon completion of *your* job rather than completion of the producer's job or the release date.

In my U.A. negotiations I insisted on getting the first half of the advance the day I walked into the studio, and the balance the day I walked out. I didn't care to wait for my money if the producer spent an extra two months sweetening and mixing, and the record company delayed the release date.

Since you ultimately pay recording costs in a nonproduction deal, make sure that the contract specifies your right to preapprove expenditures and receive an itemized breakdown of whatever is to be deducted from your royalties. Not only does this insure that you're paid what you should be, but it gives you control over what is done to you. You can stop the producer, say, from adding a fifteen-piece string section to a basic rock and roll number. Not only

---

*Successful artists sometimes bargain for a "nonrecoupable" advance. This increases the value of the deal because the money is theirs to keep. Plus, they receive royalties from the first record sold because they don't have to repay the record company for their initial outlay. As is typical with the business, when you can afford to pay your own recording costs, you don't have to. You have the leverage to make the company pay them.

might the strings be in poor taste, but also they're expensive. Union scale is $100 per musician per three-hour session. That's $1,500—not to mention studio time, $150 an hour for twenty-four-track, and tape costs, about $125. Your producer's string fetish will sap at least $2,075 of your precious advance!

One last word about advances. Though they come out of future royalties, strive to get as much as possible. Now is when you need the money to give yourselves the best shot. Also, an advance is money you know you have. Remember, the odds are your first few albums will have a negligible sale. The advance is risk-free for you. It's speculative money, not a loan to be repaid unless the records sell, in which case you'll make your money in performances. And even then you pay no interest for the time you used it. Banks charge from 12 percent to 18 percent a year!

While a good advance is of immediate importance, your royalty rate is at the heart of your contract. Essentially, a contract promises that in exchange for the record company's right to sell recordings of your performances, you share the proceeds from each copy they sell. It's a partnership.

Whatever royalty rate you settle at, make sure it's figured from 100 percent of the product's suggested retail price, not the 90 percent that was common until the seventies. Previously, a 10 percent allowance compensated for breakages that occurred in normal shipping and handling. Today, records are made of flexible vinyl, not the brittle discs of yore. If a company insists on it, simply bargain for a higher royalty to compensate, e.g., 11 percent of 90 percent—which approaches 10 percent of 100 percent.

If the company offers a low royalty, say 5 percent, it may be all right. Just negotiate an escalating clause so that if they pick up your option after the first year, your royalty goes to 6 percent and 7 percent each succeeding year, working up to a fairer rate. It's terribly unlikely you're going to get a hit the first year of your first record deal. You're settling into a sound, and the company is learning how to promote you. It's very likely, however, that you'll hit in subsequent years. So worry about the rate you get in a year or two and a few albums down the road. The company shouldn't object, because if they pick up your options in future years, it'll mean you're doing well enough to warrant a higher rate. If they reject the sliding scale, perhaps they'll compromise by throwing in a promo budget or bigger advances.

The Term of the Contract   After the advance and royalty, the term of the contract—how long it will run—is its next basic element. The usual agreement is for one or two years, plus four or three one-year options, respectively. Whether you remain with the company is purely the company's prerogative. Sometimes a company will offer a straight five-year long-term contract. This gives you security, but at the same time it locks you into terms based on your current value. Two years from now you should be worth two or three times that. Try to get an option system; tell the company a five-year deal is absurd, that they can't know if they'll be happy with you or if you'll be happy with them a few years later. Also, it's to your advantage to modify the option clause to leave yourselves a loophole. Give them the option to keep you in future years, with the condition that the option is exercisable only if they meet certain sales quotas in the preceding years.

Promotional Budget   If you can weasel that, perhaps you can weasel the real prize: a promotional budget. "Of course we're gonna promote your records," they'll tell you. "We'd be foolish not to after advancing all that dough to you. We have to recoup it." True, but their promotion won't amount to much more than servicing the album with press kits to press and radio, including it in "supermarket" ads featuring a dozen other albums, and "tagging" radio ads in the towns where you perform.

A promo budget of, say, $25,000 could go to flying key journalists and radio program directors to showcase performances, to buying ads in the appropriate publications, to holding debut parties, or to hiring a private publicity firm or independent promotion people to augment the company's efforts.

Try for an amount equal to your advance. If you're lucky, you'll wind up with half that and a qualifier making the budget contingent upon the delivered album's quality. If the budget is recoupable, try to get mutual control over how it is spent with a periodic, detailed accounting.

The First Edition succeeded in landing a promo budget from Reprise to launch our band. We proposed that if they put up $20,000* for debut parties in Hollywood and San Francisco—at which we'd play—we would pay $10,000 of it back out of our royalties. Because we offered to shoulder half and showed them a viable battle plan, Reprise realized we were committed to succeeding and bought it. Generally, the record label isn't going to apportion you things just because you want them—especially if you don't have leverage. But approach the company with ways you can collaborate to increase sales, and you'll find them more receptive.

Yet a company won't make big concessions for a new act unless they feel

---

*Small by today's standards, but considering inflation and the fact that this was rarely done then, it represented a significant amount.

they've discovered a blockbuster. It's up to you to prove yourselves first. Some companies, for instance, don't allocate promo budgets until an act's record makes the Top 40.

The Fine Print While advances and promo budgets affect the band in immediately measurable ways, the bulk of a contract, the fine print *per se,* is equally important. If you don't take care to see that it is fair, it could pare your future earnings to the bone.

The Reserve Clause The reserve clause may bother you most. This allows the company to hold a chunk of your royalties, often up to 50 percent, to apply toward future recording costs and record returns. It's good business from the company's standpoint, but it puts more of the financial burden on you without increasing your profits.

After Reprise's stiff 50 percent reserve clause in the First Edition's deal, I learned to try to keep the reserve down to 20 percent—to get more of what's coming to me sooner—and to specify a limit on how long they can hold the money. It's six months in my U.A. contract. My feeling is, if you sell enough for them to place your money in reserve, then they've profited enough. Plus, if you've become a hit act, your future records are less risky anyway.

The Free-Goods Clause The uninitiated also will be shocked by the allowance for free goods, records given away to stimulate sales. Limit the company to a number that promotes the record well without cutting into the resulting sales—from which you should earn royalties. Free goods of about 10 percent to 15 percent for singles and 5 percent to 10 percent for albums is considered normal. Make your company conform to the "favored nations" concept of not giving away any more of your product than anyone else's. Otherwise, they could conceivably dole out a lot of your records as favors to dealers and distributors. You don't want to sell a million singles and find out that only one third paid royalties!

The Packaging-Costs Clause In the past, recording artists were generally expected to pay a percentage for the record's packaging, that is, the art, design, and materials. Try to avoid a provision asking you to do so. You will have to agree, however, to cover additional costs incurred by your own request for an extraordinarily expensive package.

**The
Assignment
Clauses** Finer points of the record contract, here unencumbered by opaque legalese: The assignment clause allows the company to sell your contract. If one label absorbs another, for example, this clause permits the sold company to include you in the sale without your approval. You can be bought or traded just like a baseball player. To protect yourself, qualify the clause to read that the company can't trade you down to an inferior company. This insures that you can't wind up at impotent and impersonal Penny-Ante Records after signing with another company for its good distribution, promotion department, and personal involvement.

**The
Licensing
Clause** Licensing gives the company the right to permit overseas companies to manufacture and market your records and pay you half your percentage to do it. This is fair when your company licenses unrelated companies, unfair when it licenses other arms of the same multinational corporation that can release the records without investing anything but pressing and distribution costs.

Safeguards Build safeguards into the contract. Attach and initial anything you agree to verbally; specify that financial statements and sales figures be sent to you every six months (which you should *all* read); and make sure the contract allows you the right to audit the books annually at your own expense.

Auditing, incidentally, is best done by a company like the Harry Fox Agency,* which specializes in audits of publishing and record companies. Fox knows where to look for mistakes. The First Edition never audited Warner Brothers; we trusted them. Though I'm sure they were honest, no bookkeeper is infallible. They can forget a zero here or make a 5 a 3 there, and such errors add up quickly. Fox also knows where to find intentionally hidden money. It can determine, for instance, if the company sold records "out the back door," if they somehow pressed and sold 100,000 copies or so off the books. An audit firm is well worth the fee, which is 5 percent of any monies they discover.

See that you have the right to select, or at least approve, your repertoire. Most companies won't take this away because they know you wouldn't perform your best on songs you disliked.

Lastly, be careful about tying your music publishing into the agreement. With publishing a separate business and income source, you'll want to bargain

---

*110 E. 59th St., New York, N.Y. 10022

with publishing houses to make your best deal. If your publishing is available, the record company may tell you that having your publishing would provide them with added incentive to promote you harder. But that point is faulty. Either they believe in you as a recording artist or they don't. If they do, they'll back you 100 percent, publishing or not. If they insist on having the publishing, it means they're signing you for the wrong reasons. U.A. made my publishing a signing condition of my original contract. I told them it was unfair, and why. I wanted to be free to publish writers I discovered and be able to barter publishing rights to get other stars to record the songs I wrote but didn't want to record myself. We compromised. I agreed to give them only the songs that I wrote and recorded first on U.A. Later, when my contract was renegotiated from the position of having several hits, I got back all my rights and sold them to M3 Music Publishing, a company owned by Management III.

You can't always get what you want. In fact, when you're new, all the terms of a record contract will be in the company's favor. But remember that it's a brand-new ball game when you're hot. At that point you can get the company to upgrade your contract because they'll want to keep you happy—and loyal when new contract time comes around and the entire industry starts bidding for you. You can get a larger advance for each album, higher royalties, more promotional guarantees, smaller reserve rates, etc. They'll also want to increase the length of the commitment, to keep a good thing going that much longer. That there may be a an Emerald City down the yellow brick road doesn't mean, however, that you should settle for the wicked witch of the West. Accepting a clearly inferior deal opens you to inferior treatment. Stick to your guns on important reasonable points. They're more likely to be agreeable and they'll respect you. Don't belabor minor points that could cost you the deal.

What Is Fair?   When negotiating with a record company, understand that the bottom line—profits—is the name of their game, most likely yours too. It's a business, a business not much more enlightened than any other. The marketplace dictates conditions—not fairness, morality, kindness, or hipness. Many contractual points that were valid years ago, like the 10 percent breakage allowance, remain in some contracts because the companies figure that for every group shrewd enough to weed them out there are six who aren't. The general balance of terms shifting in the artist's favor occurs not from a new corporate beneficence, but from leveraged artists demanding them. The word filters out about what can be gotten. In fact, many managers believe that once contracts are signed, the most productive relationship with a record company is as adversaries. You scream and yell for what you want. Unfortunately, it's often true. The manager may have to badger the company to get that $10,000 tour support or $7,000 *Rolling Stone* page ad.

My philosophy is far better for your career's sake, if not just for your mental health's: The manager should deal with the record company as a partner. Your goal, success, is, after all, mutually beneficial. Your manager should be tenacious, and tough when appropriate, but Ken Kragen and I have found you get more through having people on your side.

One of the most unfair but still predominating contractual conditions concerns the record company's ownership of your master tapes, even after you've sold enough records to repay all costs incurred by the company. This is more upsetting in light of the fact that to repay the company, you have to sell about four times as many records as it takes for the record company to break even. Their profit is figured into every record sold (except free goods), while they take your royalties and recoup their investment. I believe in a leasing situation. That is, you let the company keep all your masters until they've yielded a certain profit to the company. Then, perhaps five years after you've left the label, your masters revert back to you. You made them and paid for them, the company has profited extensively from them; why shouldn't they ultimately belong to you? Some proven acts manage to do this today, accepting relatively modest advances and royalties for the right to their masters when the deal terminates. Just think how much the Beatles' catalogue means to Capitol Records or Simon and Garfunkel's to Columbia. These companies make some of their biggest profits on old material because the expense of creating the product and the demand for it has already been met. They can sell the music at today's inflated prices, while paying the artists a royalty rate agreed upon in the sixties, when it was 5 percent or 6 percent—about 10 percent less than they'd have to pay those artists today. With some investment in a merchandising campaign, the companies can make gold records gold again, or double platinum—2 million units sold. In negotiating my release from MGM Records, I won the return of my masters in addition to a cash settlement. Some artists seek the return of their masters as an intrinsic part of a contract. Someday the practice may be common.

Despite these questionable habits, it's inaccurate to condemn record companies as music vampires. Their investment in money and service is normally so substantial that risky chances are only worth taking if there's a possibility for high return, either immediately or over many years. One hit, they'll tell you, has to subsidize a dozen misses. Often I think it's unfair that when you're a success you have to support inferior and/or mismanaged acts and pay for the company's bad judgments. (Some companies have incredibly unqualified people signing acts.) But if the companies don't feel they can experiment, funds for new acts—like yourselves—would shrink, yielding a stagnating music scene. Ironically, you also have to help subsidize the record label's superstars who demand so much that companies sign them more for prestige than profits. Prestige helps you and the company by giving the label greater credibility and market penetration. Everyone from the tiny mom and pop stores to the huge department store chains comes out of the woodwork to carry name best sellers. If the record company builds a steady relationship with them, it can enlist their support in carrying new acts.

Whether or not companies exploit artists, remember you're aiming to make the most money possible out of the *business,* not necessarily out of a record company. The bulk of your income will flow from performance. Records are advertisements for your act. The most important thing now is to get a reasonable contract from an effective company—and hits. For hits are the broadest performance advertisements of all—like full-page ads in papers all over the world. I signed with U.A. in 1976 for far less than I swore I ever would, because the intangibles seemed right: the company's potential for growth, personal interest in my career, and, above all, producer.

Producers   The right producer is *that* important. A producer is the one who, to varying degrees, makes the recording. He decides how your musical ideas will be realized on tape and directs the process of achieving that in the studio.* Tailoring your music and sound for distinctiveness, he provides experienced, objective ears, finds and sometimes writes material, determines your instrumentation, selects a studio and engineer to run the equipment, hires whatever side musicians necessary, and plays coach, boss, diplomat, midwife, courtier, mediator, servant, father—whatever—to coax the best performance out of you. Thus, select a producer as much for your personal as for your musical rapport. In a production deal, the record company shares the right of selection, although they sometimes go so far as to make their choice for producer a precondition to signing you. The First Edition's deal with Amos Productions put the production in the hands of Jimmy Bowen, who assigned his partner, Mike

---

*The archetype is Phil Spector, who coined the term "producer," a job in fact more comparable to a film's director. A film producer generally bankrolls the project. Spector created singing acts and paid them scale to perform his material. He was more the artist than his performers, who were just other components in Spector's grand designs. The recording artist in the fullest sense—one who not only composes and performs but who also arranges and produces himself—is a relatively recent innovation.

Post, producer of Mason Williams' "Classical Gas" and later "The Rockford Files," to produce us. At MGM, since our deal was with my Jolly Rogers Records, the label owned by my production company, I produced most of the music myself. With U.A., I have a combination of production terms: If I use a staff producer, or one of whom they approve, U.A. pays the fees. If I use someone of whom they disapprove, I pay the 3 percent and $10,000 fee. (Producers require such a large fee up front because they know that after they've invested their heart, soul, and time in the project, it may not sell. They want to be certain the project is financially worthwhile.)

In agreeing to work with the record company's producer, include in the contract some provision detailing the number of attempts to deliver hits that you'll allow him. Failing to deliver, the contract should read that you'll be free to employ another, albeit company-approved, producer. In the same way, if you resort to an inexperienced producer, let him prove himself before you commit the entire project. Let him do a session. See if he knows what he's doing, that he doesn't waste expensive time, that he gets the most out of you and any (expensive) studio musicians brought in, that he doesn't accept sloppy playing, yet captures the feel and concept you want. Remember, nothing less than your career is at stake. I'd also not give an inexperienced producer top fees; give him union scale, which is probably what you'll end up with for the sessions. Let the opportunity to expand his credentials be his chief compensation.

Making a Record   Making a record involves the same basic methods of demo recording. But it also includes more sophisticated techniques that require greater preparation and precision. Here is where your ideas must reach full expression. Furthermore, if the recording is to be competitive, it must be invested with extraordinary qualities—quite a tall order.

How you get ready to record depends on your producer. Some like to enter a studio relatively unprepared so that they won't feel locked into arrangements. Whereas onstage a guitar might dominate a song, in the studio you might suddenly notice an interesting bass drum part and reconceive the song around it. Most producers, however, prefer extensive preparations. They rehearse you for weeks so you can record your parts in a few takes and save money.

It can take two weeks to two months to record the approximately fifty minutes of music needed for an LP. Also, you should be able to turn out the best album you're capable of for under $50,000. Some groups spend $100,000 an album, but rarely is that much necessary. Usually, half of it is thrown away by good but disorganized producers who end up, say, hiring a string section four times to recut a part because they didn't have the arrangements they liked in the first place, or they were unsure about what they wanted to do, or they just wanted to experiment. Money is also wasted by producers who take as much as one hundred hours of $120-an-hour studio time mixing and remixing when it could be done in ten or twenty hours. The First Edition's debut LP was far overproduced, with great but grandiose string and horn arrangements by Post and Al Capps. It cost $35,000 ($70,000 by modern inflationary standards). Reacting to the musical arrangement's fiscal overkill, we scaled down and reduced our second LP's budget 20 percent.

Post ran the sessions, but we collaborated on various problems. He knew we put a lot of work into our vocal parts, so it concerned him if something bothered us. But we were constrained sometimes by the fact that we had to subjugate our vocal parts to the arrangements. It was easier to change our four parts than rewrite thirty charts of music.

Speaking of hiring musicians for special arrangements, it pays to bring in musicians or vocalists superior at playing particular parts if they help you achieve an outstanding result. The First Edition played few of the instruments on our early albums. Just as the Byrds allowed the music tracks to "Mr. Tambourine Man" to be cut largely by L.A. session pros, we opted for tight, high-quality musicianship over the ego gratification of playing ourselves. We knew that we were too new at electric instruments. For our first sessions at United Recording's Studio A (the scene of many Frank Sinatra sessions), Post had assembled up to thirty musicians, including many of the L.A. rock session clique. Among the $100,000-plus a year pro hit-men were Glen Campbell* (his guitar solo is heard on "Just Dropped In"), bassist Joe Osbourne, drummer Hal Blaine, keyboardist Larry Knechtel (later of Bread), and guitarist James Burton (a sideman with Rick Nelson, Elvis Presley and Emmylou Harris).

Full-scale recording in a fully equipped modern studio not only provides extraordinary sonic quality, but it's so flexible that perfect recordings can be made every time. With computerized mixing boards, precise manipulation of the multitracked parts is possible so that you can enhance, tailor, edit, and insert effects note by note and beat by beat if necessary. A modern studio becomes an instrument in the performance.** We employed the studio extensively on

---

*Campbell often brought in tapes he recorded as an artist. I remember we thought they were good, but we didn't take him seriously as a solo performer!

**Artists like Bob Dylan and Neil Young take a more purist view. They feel a recording studio is meant to record a performance without intruding on it. They record "live," singing and playing simultaneously, getting the song down in one or two takes. They believe frequent retakes and processing refines the life out of the music. But they are a small cabal. There are few who can record live without sounding amateurish, so don't count on this approach. Few hits are made this way. (Live concert recordings are another matter, but even these usually are doctored extensively in the studio.)

musical levels. In "Just Dropped In," Mike Post recorded our voices "dry" (without the effect) and then patched the track through a Leslie speaker (which gives organs their vibrato sound), recording it on another channel. The song also featured a "backwards" guitar, an effect the Beatles used on *Revolver*. We recorded the part normally, then reversed the tape as another recorder took it down. (This is tricky because the part must fit the music track backwards. You have to stay on a single chord or write the segment symmetrically so it reads the same in both directions.) Whatever effects you plan to apply, be it a backwards instrument, echo, phaser, Leslie, etc., record the parts dry first. Trying to work an effect the same time you're trying to play a piece perfectly is like trying to tie your shoes while running. Worse, once you succeed, you won't be able to vary the intensity of the effect—or remove it. If you change your mind about it, you'll have to rerecord the entire part.

The studio also permits you to extend your abilities. On *The Ballad of Calico,* which I produced, we were able to sing notes beyond our range by slowing the recorder down with a variable speed oscillator (VSO). Brought back to normal speed, our harmonies reached the higher register. (If you try this, be careful not to record at too slow a speed. If you do, when you crank it back to normal, your voices will sound more like the Chipmunks.) I also used the VSO to get a regular piano to sound like an old-fashioned tack-hammer model. I recorded it once normally and then again on another track slightly slowed. Combining the two, the hint of dissonance did the trick.

The studio, furthermore, permits you to construct songs—literally. A friend and I wrote "Love Woman" around a previously recorded music track. To make the track fit the song, we edited instrumental sections and spliced them into different places. At one point, we made a sixteen-track tape copy of eight bars of music on a separate machine and spliced it onto the sixteen-track master because the song needed the exact eight-bar section later in the song.

The purpose of effects is to help make your productions unique. This includes dubbing noninstrumental sounds. On "Something's Burning," for instance, we decided to record an actual heartbeat for the percussion, which the song's writer, Mac Davis, had suggested by thumping his guitar between verses when he had originally played it for me. We took recording equipment down to the UCLA Medical Center and recorded the heartbeats of patients! (It wasn't that easy, however. We found a lot of people have some kind of heart murmur. We went through our collection of heartbeat tapes to find and splice together good beats. We also discovered that hearts beat improperly—for our purposes. They beat "bum-Bum, bum-Bum," instead of "Bum-bum, Bum-bum." So we reversed the tape.)

As long as you serve the songs' needs rather than purposelessly fill them with all your gimmicks, use the studio to its fullest capacity. Recording is a separate medium; it's unessential that the songs sound the same in concert as they do on record. Anyway, when you begin getting hits, you'll be able to afford the equipment to reproduce the effects onstage. Queen, for example, employ pretaped music cued to their live performance and echoplexes for vocal and guitar effects.

When the basic rhythm and lead tracks are down, the producer probably will bring in an arranger to write charts to sweeten the tracks, dubbing in horns, strings, voices, or percussion instruments—the subtle colorings that fill out a record. Here, see that your recordings have enough instrumental melodies going on around the lead melody to make the song continually interesting without being cluttered. Also, see that they include the full tonal spectrum, that they're not top or bottom heavy. "But You Know I Love You" sounded a bit mushy, so the producer of the track, Glen D. Hardin (a pianist who backed Elvis and Emmylou Harris), thought of adding a piccolo trumpet, which was the perfect addition to the high end to balance the sound. I've found that the tambourine makes a nice complement to the midrange instruments of piano and guitar, bringing the highs right out. Drums cover a wide range, from the lows of the bass drum to the midrange of the snare and tom-toms to the highs of the cymbals. In sweetening, also see that any holes are patched.

With all the music on multitrack tape, the producer, with or without the band, now mixes the tracks down to two-track master tape. This is a highly critical stage of the recording process as it determines how the record will sound and what the listener hears when. Generally, all the parts should be audible, but those you're selling, the lead vocals, solo guitar or keyboard, must be mixed hottest. The important thing here is not to fool yourselves. Don't mix the music solely on the studio's giant monitor speakers; use the cheap small speakers most studios also provide. Everything sounds like a hit over the monitors, but the entire mix will sound quite altered when played through the type of speakers most people listen to, car radios and cheap stereos. After mixing on the small speakers, check the mix through the large ones to see that there's enough quality for those with sophisticated gear.

The master tape is further improved by equalizing, or "EQing," it. You play the mix through a device that electronically divides the frequency range into sixteen parts so that you can heighten the weaker ones and subdue the overbearing ones. The final tape copy now goes through the record-making process. It's "mastered," that is, cut on a chemically coated aluminum disc or "lacquer." The studio sends this disc to you so you can check for imperfections, pops, skips, distortion, or previously undetected problems in the mix. The lacquer must be perfect because it is from this that another two generations of molds are made —the mother and a stamper. The stamper forms the raw vinyl into records. At this stage, the record company will send you a test pressing. Listen closely to this, too, to see that the stampers aren't flawed.

The Jacket Art   Assuming all is well, it now remains to devise the jacket artwork, something most contracts give you control of (the record company usually retains the right of approval). You'll need photos taken and something designed to make the jacket distinctive, identifiable, and consistent with the music it contains. The art director will devise a logo if you still don't have one, and you'll have to come up with a punchy, catchy, significant title. The only rule of thumb is that the names of the album and the artist should appear across the top of the jacket's front. This is so customers can see them when they flip through the racks and bins in stores. Lastly comes the liner copy. You can include a couple of paragraphs by a writer on the group and its music or at least credit the people who worked on the recording and helped you get this far.

Performance-Rights Societies   With a record scheduled for release, it's time to join a performance-rights society to license your original songs for commercial use. To join Broadcast Music, Inc. (BMI), or the American Society of Composers, Authors, and Publishers (ASCAP)—and have a vehicle to receive airplay royalties—you only need to show that your copyrighted songs are scheduled to go on sale as sheet music or recordings and pay a nominal yearly fee. You may belong to one society only and it must be the same one that your publisher belongs to. This is because the society divides the royalties it collects into writer's and publisher's shares. Consequently, most publishing houses have two divisions to accommodate their writers' preferences. For instance, Polygram's Chappell Music consists of Chappell Music (ASCAP) and Unichappell Music (BMI). Your publisher can arrange appointments for you with managers of both societies.

The pitches they make to you will make two things plain. One, they're archrivals. Two, you're more befuddled than before. Their explanations as to how your earnings potential far surpasses what it would be with Brand X are that arcane. Being associated with both through my two publishing companies (Jolly Rogers Music, ASCAP; and Mar-Ken Music, BMI), I have as good an understanding as any.

ASCAP began in 1914 as a reaction to the plight of Stephen Foster, possibly the first pop composer, who died so poor there wasn't even enough money to bury him. John Philip Sousa and Victor Herbert, so the story goes, discussed this fact in a restaurant when they heard some music and realized that the restaurant improved its business with music. The composers, they decided, should be compensated. With 250 composers in New York, Sousa and Herbert formed ASCAP to monitor broadcasters, clubs, and theaters and charge for the use of their members' works. ASCAP remained the exclusive province of an elite coterie of Tin Pan Alley and Hollywood songwriters such as George Gershwin and Cole Porter until the fifties, when the competition presented by the upstart BMI forced them to open up to the thousands of songwriters and publishers whose music fell into categories previously reviled by ASCAP as "common" and unartistic—country, blues, rock and roll, folk, and jazz.

BMI had been formed by a collection of broadcasters in 1940 after a 1939 strike against ASCAP.* The broadcasters struck because they felt the old society overexploited them. BMI immediately began signing up the unlicensed composers—and the pop-music industry burst wide open.

ASCAP criticizes BMI chiefly for being a privately owned offshoot of radio, the industry from which it collects. Though they're both nonprofit organizations, ASCAP is member-owned and operated and thus believes it can fight harder to win greater benefits for its writers and publishers. BMI counters that ASCAP still seems to benefit an elite group of established members rather than paying by true merit. Whether or not these charges are true, the societies are competitive, each trying to lure good writers to their folds. So they can't be far apart.

Basically, BMI and ASCAP figure performance royalties this way: First they determine how many times a song was played, taking ongoing random samplings from more than 6,000 radio and 700 TV stations in the United States. (Counting actual plays everywhere would be prohibitively expensive.) Each play they catch counts as a "performance credit." Whereas BMI surveys stations by checking their playlists, ASCAP, still distrustful of broadcasters, randomly tapes periods of programming and counts the number of plays. ASCAP determines the value of a performance credit each quarter by dividing the total number of performance credits into their total gross revenue, which, like BMI, comes from percentages of TV and radio stations' advertising income and fees paid by hotels, clubs, theaters, and jukebox owners. In 1977 an ASCAP performance credit was worth 92 cents. A writer's and publisher's royalties are

*That year, ironically enough, the public domain Foster song, "I Dream of Jeannie with the Light Brown Hair," was the most broadcast song. Stations refused to play licensed songwriters' music.

figured, then, by multiplying the number of credits by 92 cents.

BMI also pools its gross income but divides it differently. BMI assigns performance credits fixed values: 6 cents for larger radio stations and 2½ cents for others. BMI multiplies every credit logged by the appropriate value and multiplies that result by a certain ratio—a ratio of the number of stations logged and the number of licensed stations of similar size, audience, and format. (If it finds a song was played thirty times in one week by ten stations, BMI figures it must have been played that many times on the other 500 similar stations. The multiplier here is 50.) Though the 6-cent and 2½-cent base rates seem small, BMI stays competitive by monitoring six times more stations than ASCAP and paying bonuses of two and three times the base rates for songs surpassing certain plateaus of performance credits.

It loses me, too.

If their payment schedules don't help you decide, BMI and ASCAP also are distinguished by their reputations. BMI is known to have better coverage of country, blues, R & B, and rock and roll because it surveys more stations than ASCAP and therefore is apt to check more of the small regional stations that play these styles. ASCAP is noted for paying better for a more standard music —MOR, pop, pop-rock (Top 40), and movie and TV music. BMI also is known to be more liberal in giving advances for songs that show up in their logs and for paying royalties faster; however, you might earn more royalties from ASCAP in the long run.

Grill ASCAP and BMI* yourselves to decide the issue. If that fails, read the record labels of successful artists whose music is similar to yours and go with the society they use. You'll feel in good company when you're sharing the charts with your old idols.

---

*ASCAP: One Lincoln Plaza, New York, NY 10023
     6430 Sunset Blvd., Hollywood, CA 90028
     700 17th Avenue South, Nashville, TN 37203
BMI: 40 W. 57th St., New York, NY 10019
     6255 Sunset Blvd., Hollywood, CA 90028
     710 16th Avenue South, Nashville, TN 37203

Building Success 5

N' you look like a star
But you're still on the dole. . . .*
IAN HUNTER, "All the Way from Memphis"

The First Edition's debut album didn't explode on the world quite like the Beatles' *Sgt. Pepper's Lonely Hearts Club Band*. In fact, it hit more like a snowflake in July. But at least I was prepared for an uphill fight. It hadn't been so long ago that I was disappointed by the fate of the Bobby Doyle Trio's album on Columbia Records, *In a Most Unusual Way*.

I couldn't find the Trio album in record stores. One store manager said they didn't have it, but they'd ordered it. I said, "Oh, great. How many have you ordered?" "Two," he replied. I'd always thought stores bought hundreds of everything that came out!

The Trio's album went so unheralded that the only way I could convince friends we'd really made this alleged album was to give them my promotional copies. Still, at the time, success to me was having done the album; that it didn't sell was virtually beside the point. Besides, if anyone in Houston asked about its sales, I just intimated it was a smash up North. Who knew any differently? There were short-term benefits, however. The prestige helped us book jobs. We told club owners we couldn't audition, but we could give them a copy of our album. "Oh," they'd say. "You have an album!" It doubled our price in Houston. Plus, there was something about being able to tack "Columbia Recording Artists" onto our posters that helped attract audiences. However, we did nothing to make that album happen, and its failure marked the beginning of the end for the Trio.

The First Edition's first album might have gone to the same anonymous vinyl graveyard if our second single, "Just Dropped In," hadn't leaped onto the airwaves. Actually, that we finally got a hit was less a matter of luck than our

---

realistic approach. Unlike the Trio, the First Edition knew we had to do more than record good songs. We had to work them into hits. To that end, we did the most important thing you can do: We hit the road.

●

The twofold purpose of touring is to make a hit and milk it. First, touring exposes you to a large number of people, and assuming your show is special, it encourages them to buy your record. More generally, it forms a hook for record company advertising, publicity, and promotional campaigns, which in turn can sweepingly affect record sales, airplay, and ticket sales. Secondly, touring is your way to exploit your hits. Hits make the concert circuit lucrative. And by working the circuit during this peak, you solidify your success, almost guaranteeing that your subsequent records, if they're good, will do well, if not become automatic hits.

"Breaking" records often is directly related to how frequently you perform. Plant seeds of interest by arranging to have several exposures in a key showcase club or concert hall in a particular city. Such local interest is likely to grow into a following through word of mouth or the crusading of a turned-on disc jockey or music critic. That following can then be cultivated elsewhere. Begin in a place you think would be most receptive to your music and would also be able to support you financially. If you play hard rock à la Bob Seger, Detroit would be a safe starting ground and the Midwest the region in which to build. You spread yourselves like pollen. If you make your record happen in Detroit, you should be able to break it in neighboring Columbus and then Cleveland. If you concentrate on Cleveland and break it there, you can move on to Akron. Eventually you could work Pennsylvania and the Northeast and move around the continent. The First Edition tried to work each area we went to intensely. And we found right away that presence in a market produces results. We managed to score a hit in Columbus, Ohio, with the first single lifted from *The First Edition*, "I Found a Reason," because we played repeatedly at The Bistro, one of the city's most important clubs, and collaborated on some promotional stunts with the local radio stations. Though we failed to transplant the success elsewhere, the fact that something could happen at least proved our viability to ourselves and to Reprise. Had we tried to launch the band in a major market like New York, we would have been overwhelmed by the competition.

Planning a Tour   Launching the band on a promotional tour requires much additional planning and organization. We're no longer talking about lugging your equipment from one local club to another to be background for people to drink or dance to; now you have to present yourselves as recording artists. To develop the appropriate stature and national profile requires a master plan plotted by the band and your management and booking agency, and agreed upon by your record company. The record company won't do it for you, but they can offer their energies and dollars. The plan involves exciting the record company, the industry, and by extension the public. It involves the formulation by the record company of a marketing plan—advertising, merchandising, promotion, and public relations—that suits your music.

Once you sign with the company, the company should invite you, your manager, and your agent to a meet-the-company luncheon. Here the executives fill you in on their procedures and on what they need from you, and you tell them of your status in various markets and your recording plans and touring prospects. Keep it on a sketchy level now, as you are trying to excite the company about your prospects. You can discuss particulars when the release date draws nearer and you have a clearer idea of your needs.

At this preliminary stage, it's time to announce your association to the industry in a news release accompanied by a photo of you and the executives, which can be shot either at the signing ceremony or the luncheon. The record company's publicity department will service this to the record trades and mail it to their press and radio lists.

The rest of your planning picks up after you deliver your album. Now the record company's executives and promotion department—which is responsible for getting records airplay—lift a single off the album. They'll choose the one they feel has the best chance of making it on Top-40 radio. A hit single is the first priority, for a hit commands the widest audience and provides the impetus for album sales—and album sales mean income. Record companies frequently release albums and wait to see if a particular track shows special airplay strength. But albums by new acts seldom arouse that much interest, so a single must be selected and pushed aggressively shortly after the LP's release.

It is while the record company prepares the album and single for release that you should begin mapping tour plans. Though the plans would be altered by any initial action the records achieve in certain markets, you'll have an idea of the type of halls or clubs you'll be playing and the budget within which you'll have to work. You can put together your show and prepare for the road.

Preparing for the road differs from getting ready for small-time beer-bar dates. Here you need the paraphernalia to act, look, and sound like stars (although not too much, or headliners won't take you on their tours, fearing you'll upstage them). And you need a traveling organization that allows you to work night after night, city after city, without taking its toll on your ability to do your best.

The Road Manager   Your first priority is to find a road manager to run the band's day-to-day operations. His (or her) job is to make it easy for the musicians on the road by eliminating virtually all nonmusical concerns. You should be able to walk onstage, pick up your instruments, perform, walk off, and leave. The road manager positions your equipment onstage, tunes instruments, and adjusts, and often operates, the lighting and sound systems (big acts carry sound and lighting men). When equipment fails, he repairs it, allowing as little disruption to your show as possible. To carry out all these functions, he must be as attuned to what you do onstage as if he were a performer.

When you can afford to carry a crew of roadies to divide these jobs, the road manager will oversee their work. In the meantime, he can oversee *your* work, since you'll have to help him set up, tear down, and lug your equipment. The First Edition couldn't hire a full road crew until after our third hit! Because the investment in equipment is huge, its care and maintenance is one of the road manager's most important responsibilities. To protect the gear, he should get custom-built metal and foam cases for the instruments, amplifiers, speakers, electrical kit, and wardrobe. They cost about $150 to $200 each but are well worth it; you wouldn't believe how badly airlines, railroads, and stagehands pummel freight. The road manager should furthermore stencil all the equipment and cases with the band's name and some code indicating what's what. This reduces the risk of theft, which is especially likely to occur at shows with several bands and a profusion of gear.

The second half of the road manager's job is business. Representing the act on the road to promoters and club owners as a sort of surrogate manager, he collects your pay, writes checks, logs all expenditures for accounting and tax purposes, and metes out petty cash. He stays in contact with the manager and booking agent, reporting progress, asking for solutions to special problems, and taking new instructions for you.

If the road manager you find is qualified to handle these chores, also see that he can handle the psychological ones. A road manager must be a diplomat and a front. If there are conflicts with another group working on the bill, the road manager plays the bad guy. He fights to see that you receive fair treatment and are able to perform at your best. A typical conflict occurs when a stage is so small that both acts on a bill can't set up all their equipment. Both bands' road managers will have to figure out how to share equipment so each group has what it needs. This is a touchy situation because there always are a couple of musicians who refuse either to let another person use their equipment or to use someone else's. Of course, if this isn't a co-billing situation, the headliner has preference, since he's responsible for most of the audience's attendance. Still, the headliner's road manager should be as versed in the art of compromise as any other and be willing to make certain concessions to keep everyone happy and the show better overall. (So long, that is, as the alterations don't really detract from his act's show.) Nevertheless, if your road manager has to put his foot down in your behalf, at least the other party (the other band or the promoter) won't hold it against you personally.

The road manager, in addition, might play intragroup mediator. However, I find the best mediating a road manager can do is to stay out of any squabbling. It would be dangerous for him to take sides; it could splinter the group. The band should talk problems out themselves. The First Edition sat down for gripe sessions whenever things felt explosive (and you can sure tell when they do). Talking things out, we'd later feel much closer, perhaps realizing that the problems weren't as bad as they'd seemed.

I'm also against letting a road manager degenerate into a den mother or go-for. Everyone, for instance, should be responsible for waking up on time. You know when payday comes, you should know when to be somewhere to do your job. Although the road manager might prod the slowpokes, he has enough to worry about without that. Also, don't saddle him with annoying demands, such as calls at 4 A.M. to buy you a liter of Jack Daniels. Anyway, having such attentions lavished on you breeds an insidious addiction. Soon you can't lace your own snakeskin boots without a road manager there to do it for you.

Rehearsing   After your road manager has been found and your equipment gathered and prepared and your staging designed, take your next step in preparing for the road. Rehearse in conditions similar to a concert or clubs, trying out your lighting and sound systems. For this, most major cities have rehearsal studios such as Studio Instrument Rentals in L.A. and New York. If this is impossible, find a warehouse for rehearsals. Incidentally, you might be able to get some equipment free or at cost through endorsement deals with manufacturers. Some may help you at this point in exchange for mention on your album jacket or appearance in their advertising. Others won't talk to you until you're famous. Tommy Smothers helped the First Edition get equipment from Fender even before we had a hit. But they eventually got their money's worth. We displayed their equipment in a TV commercial we did for Alcoa, and always had it on camera in our "Rollin' " show because we appreciated their faith in us.

The Tour Proposal   While you get your show together, your manager and booking agent should meet to determine what they need from the record company to make possible an effective promotional tour. Your manager should then draw up a detailed proposal to present to the company. This should include an itinerary, an itemized balance sheet of expected expenses and income, and a shopping list of requests. You may want several thousand dollars a week shortfall and certain guarantees for radio and print advertising, debut parties in New York, Los Angeles, and Chicago, trade ads, advance monies for equipment and wardrobe, etc. As the record company will be cautious about making such a heavy commitment before you've hung gold records on their walls, you must show them they can get a lot of value from investing more. Show them that your plan is austere, that you're making as many sacrifices as possible to hold costs to a minimum. You'll be laughed at if your proposal calls for expensive hotel rooms, one for each person, travel by plane and limousine, and a four-man road crew. They want to see you live two or three to a cheap room, drive from gig to gig in rented station wagons, and carry one road manager and help him with the equipment. Although it can't hurt to try for a little extra, and for the special baubles like record company–paid parties, billboards on Times Square and the Sunset Strip, and a page ad in *Rolling Stone* magazine, you probably won't be able to get them until your first few albums and tours make inroads in popularizing you and you seem on the verge of breaking big. When you do become an established success, the record company won't be needed for tour support, but they'll volunteer these promotional extras to maintain your success and to keep you, their moneymaking stars, happy.

In the meantime, the record company wants to see that you have done everything possible to subsidize your own careers, so that you don't treat their efforts lightly. One of the most popular misconceptions about the record business, in fact, is that the record company does everything for you. They most assuredly do not.

If your band contains members who've established reputations with past successful acts, and your product sounds eminently commercial, the first-class treatment may come sooner. But even this band, as a whole new entity, must endure many of the same sacrifices to make it as a new act.

To get a tour support commitment, show the company some significant dates. The itinerary should include some dates with name talent that promises to draw large audiences, some showcase dates in important clubs, and some radio station–sponsored concerts that promote you as well as the station. Setting up dates like this involves the same secret you'll need to employ at every stage of your career if you are to succeed: Exploit friendships and connections, no matter how seemingly tenuous. The First Edition got a lot of mileage from our friendship with the Smothers Brothers. We taped our first ". . . Comedy Hour" about a month after Reprise released *The First Edition* (which carried Tommy's liner notes). What's more, Ken Kragen, Smothers' co-manager, adopted us and put his contacts to work. A former booker of college folk-music concert tours, Ken knew whom to call to weasel us into gigs all over the country (including that Columbus engagement) and onto other television shows.

Kragen also arranged for Reprise to spring $20,000 for our promo budget (half recoupable), part of which paid for a smashing party at a CBS sound stage in Hollywood. Tommy Smothers got us the free use of the sound stage and hosted the debut party, which proved to be an excellent way to launch our drive to make it (and is something you might consider trying). More than 300 writers, d.j.'s, record-store owners and distributors, booking agents, and Warner Brothers staff partook of cocktails and hors d'oeuvres and then sat down to hear us perform a half-hour set. Our performance was greatly bolstered by our staging, which looked like a TV show's. We used CBS backdrops from which hung large blown-up photos of the band members. Reviving a bit of the old Hollywood extravaganza era, the party set off a buzz in the industry and gave us a degree of legitimacy and respect uncommon for a new group. It looked as though CBS was sponsoring us, Warner Brothers was spending a lot of money on us, and the record industry was endorsing us!

It's very important to excite the industry and the taste-makers (journalists, critics, d.j.'s, program directors, TV talent coordinators), because their opinions influence consumers. However, nothing excites the industry more than customers laying down their cash for records and/or tapes. Again, it boils down to hitting the road to drum up support among the troops. If you play your songs before a thousand people in one town, it's possible that the next day twenty of them will call a local radio station requesting to hear something by you and/or ask for your record at the record shop. If the market has any importance at all, things snowball from there. Sales are monitored by radio stations, trade magazines, and tip sheets, and the stations, assuming they are loosely formatted enough to give unproven records a chance, stick their toes in the water by giving the single or album airplay on a light rotation. (Rotation refers to how frequently a record is programmed. Hits are given heavy, drive-time rotation. Drive time is radio's prime time—the rush hours when most people are in their cars listening to the radio.) Meanwhile, the trades publish the news of this action, and consequently other program directors (p.d.'s determine the playlists of more tightly formatted stations) and d.j.'s give the record a shot, and so on.

The record company also responds. Local promotion people in the field report the action to headquarters, and the company nurtures the spark by making time-buys (radio ads) in the market and by stocking the stores with free goods and merchandising aids (displays, posters, mobiles). The promotion and publicity staffs then fan the flames by trumpeting the news of the action in mailers to writers and radio stations and in trade paper advertisements. And the company makes your record a priority until it either grows into a mass conflagration or burns itself out.

The Booking Agency   Getting you on the road and contracting for concerts is where the booking agency comes in. If you don't have a major agency yet, now is the time to get one. A major agency is vital at this point because the better the agency, the better the opportunities for you. Major agencies have major acts, and major acts do major concert tours. If you're signed with one of these key agencies—American Talent International, International Creative Management, Premier Talent—they can add you to one of their superstar's tours as a "supporting act" (special guest) or as an "opening act." (A supporting act has some marquee value, being somewhat established, while an opening act, paid scale to preoccupy the audience as they settle down and find their seats, is usually unknown and promoting a first record.) If you can ride a superstar's coattails, you can expose yourselves to large audiences rapidly, playing theaters (2,000–3,000 people), hockey rinks (10,000–18,000 people), or stadiums (40,000–60,000 people).

A big agency looks to its own developing acts to couple with the major acts they book because they try to make all the commissions from the tour (unless the headliner specifically requests an act represented by another agency). A concert tour is usually formulated like this: First the main attraction decides with the agency what dates and with which promoters they will work. Then they stipulate how much they can pay the opening and supporting acts and what kind of music those acts should play. They pick acts whose music is compatible but different enough so that it won't steal their thunder, acts that are big enough to add to the tour's prestige without upstaging them. The agent then contracts the prospective acts and negotiates tour conditions, such as how much lighting and effects they can use, the length of the set (usually half the headliner's), and the prominence of their billing. Record companies seldom arrange tours, but they sometimes influence their big acts to take their developing groups on the road by holding out the carrot of extra tour support.

Booking Showcases   Whether or not you have a top agency, you can at least book some dates through your own means by following the regional approach. You might also include a couple of strategically timed appearances at the showcase clubs—New York's Bottom Line, Other End, or Max's Kansas City, or L.A.'s Roxy, Troubadour, or Whiskey. Just be sure you're really ready when you do showcases. The so-called taste-makers tend to be decisive about your fate, either catapulting you or writing your career's death certificate. For all dates, be conscious of your compatibility with the other acts to be booked. A mismatch could prove disastrous. The First Edition was once booked with B. B. King without a predetermination as to who would open or close the show. Backstage, B. B., a most gracious man, said he didn't care—but he did have a plane to catch. "Ah ha. We headline," I thought. Well, B. B. went on and hypnotized the audience for an hour with the most compelling R&B any of us ever heard. No one could have followed him. We felt like a bubble-gum act by comparison and judging by the number of people who walked out on us, the audience agreed.

Shows vary in how their costs break down. You don't need your own sound and light systems to play a showcase club. On a tour of concert halls you might use the headliner's. And even if you're a headliner, the promoter frequently pays the cost of your sound and lights, which might be hired, set up, and run by a company such as Showco, Inc. Nevertheless, the costs and details of contracting for a show are fairly predictable. Let's look at how it might go for a one-nighter at a 10,000-seat basketball stadium. If the average ticket price is $7, the maximum gross for a sold-out show would be $70,000. Of that, the headliner might get $15,000, the supporting act $7,500, and the opening act $3,000. The remaining $44,500 breaks down into the promoter's profit—roughly $12,250—and expenses, as follows:

Rental of room	$7,000	(usually 10%)
Personnel (box office, security, clean-up, etc.)	7,000	
Insurance	500	
Ticket agencies	3,250	(about 5% of gross)
Sales tax (6.5%, for example)	4,550	
Radio time-buys	4,000	(3 stations, 2 weeks)
Newspaper ads	2,000	(2 newspapers, 3 weeks)
Posters	750	
Sound system	1,200	
Lighting system	750	
Miscellaneous	1,250	
SUBTOTAL EXPENSES	$32,250	
Expenses	$32,250	
Artists	$25,500	
Promoter	12,250	
TOTAL	$70,000	

Performance Contracts   After your agent approves of this itemized proposal, he sends the promoter a contract that is amended with a contract "rider." A rider is a list of specific requirements that you need fulfilled to perform most shows (most groups have two, one for concerts and one for club dates). My rider, reproduced in part in Appendix IV, details the stage setup (dimensions, design, size of drum riser) and what facilities and amenities must be provided (stagehands, loading forks, electrical power, sound and light systems,* dressing rooms, refreshments).

My rider also discusses the prominence of my billing on the marquee and in advertisements and gives me the right of approval over the other acts that are added to the show; the right to have my representatives sell posters, souvenir booklets, T-shirts, and other Kenny Rogers merchandise (although the house usually demands 10 percent of the take); the right to adequate setup and rehearsal time before the audience enters; the right to

---

*In cases where the "buyer" (promoter) provides the sound and lighting, the rider specifies exactly what they should include. Incidentally, I often hire a sound company to travel with me for consistently good sound. To defray the cost, my rider requires the promoter to chip in up to $2,000, to be paid in a separate check so commissions won't be deducted from it.

cancel the date with thirty days' notice if an important TV show comes up; the right to see a certified box-office statement and any unsold tickets so we can verify any reduction in our anticipated take from the door; and the right to receive payment before I go onstage. (I only insist on this last provision when I know the promoter is shaky. It's justifiable because the people are inside the building and the cash is collected. If the promoter insists he can't pay you yet, he's probably trying to cheat you. You, in turn, should threaten not to play.)

Our rider furthermore limits a promoter to a certain number of complimentary tickets, perhaps 5 percent. This number serves promotional needs without letting the promoter cheat us. Some disreputable promoters have been known to tell an act that though the house was full, only a fraction of the tickets was actually sold; that they "papered" the house (gave out free tickets) to make the show appear successful. Because there's so much room for fraud in the concert business, I always have a roadie stand at the box office or door counting ticket stubs and the number left on the ticket rolls. Despite such checks, you still can get beaten by counterfeit tickets or a promoter who is dishonest or simply inexperienced. You can sue these crooks, but usually it's futile because they hide behind corporate shields. If a show fails to sell many tickets, they simply bankrupt the corporation and start over elsewhere. Few bands haven't had some experience with this.

Another point to saddle on your rider: Specify that a promoter must clear in advance any press and radio interviews he may set up to promote his show or club. If you have to cancel journalists because you've been on a plane all day —something the promoter might not have counted on or cared about—it'll make you look bad. Control over interviews also prevents you from wasting time with newspapers or radio stations that miss the audience you're trying to reach.

Finally, the rider should disallow dancing. It's a matter of maintaining, or forcing yourselves into, the concert artist stature. The First Edition once played a shoe industry convention (of all things) and people started dancing. We let it continue because we thought it was so hilariously incongruous that they were paying us an incredible salary and yet acted as though we were a $300 dance band. But then this was an exceptional case and happened long after we had become stars. In your developing stage, avoid dance jobs like the plague. In fact, given the choice of headlining a dance for $2,000 and opening a concert for a name act at union scale, take the concert—even if it means subsisting on peanut-butter sandwiches a little longer.

Road   *The Road Goes on Forever* is the pithy title of an Allman Brothers
Life   album. But the monotony it seems to imply does not have to be. Many
            bands play the same set night after night and live an exhausting rou-
tine. They play, carouse, sleep, travel, play, carouse, *ad nauseam.* They live
airport to plane to rent-a-cars to Holiday Inns to limousines to dingy dressing
rooms to junk food to pinball to TV sets. City after city. With this life-style, the
excitement of playing music quickly wears into tedium. But many bands find
they can prevent boredom on stage by mixing things up. For one, I find changing my sets keeps me and my group from falling alseep, especially since I often
call the songs onstage as we go. Mixing things up also keeps club employees
from getting tired of you when you're working a few shows a night for a few
nights in one club. This is important, because the help will sabotage you badly
if they dislike you. They'll drop dishes during your sensitive ballads or take
drink orders in front of you.

Make the road life-style bearable by approaching it as an opportunity to
grow. In music, write and rehearse new material, practice, listen to other music
(bring along a cassette recorder and a selection of tapes). In recreation, do some
sight-seeing on days off or find a park and take a few hours to play some sports.
We carried balls and bats and six bags of golf clubs on the road and played some
of the most beautiful courses in the world. Get into photography, read books,
meet people.

The road also is best taken when you live sensibly. Keep the level of
your band's internal relationships personal as well as professional. For instance, insist on a few private minutes after each show to unwind and talk
things over before opening the dressing room to girl friends, journalists,
business people, groupies, and other outsiders. And don't prohibit members
from bringing boy/girl friends or spouses on the road—as long as the band's
needs continue to be satisfied. Some bands feel having friends on the road
detracts from group spirit. On the contrary, such a belief indicates a dangerous overemphasis on group spirit. Spirit flows from the freedom you
have on the road. If a guy pays the expense of bringing his lady along, he's
obviously happier with her there. It relieves the pressures of loneliness and
homesickness.

The band needs personal freedoms, but within an intelligently planned
context, a context designed to sustain your good health and ability to perform
at your best. Keep regular hours—seven hours' sleep—and eat two, if not three,
meals a day. And be moderate if you indulge yourself at all with drink or drugs.
They both form potential threats to your health, abilities, and existence as a

group. The Bobby Doyle Trio dissolved when the failure of our album turned Doyle to drink and his musicianship deteriorated. Since my father was an alcoholic, I've always been especially against inebriates. It embarrasses me to do my job, for example, and find a member of the band unable to do his. For me, it's always so much fun onstage when I feel in control of things. When I don't, the feeling is nightmarish, like losing control of the steering in a speeding car.

Drugs are particularly insidious because they've become such an integral part of the music scene. I've seen drugs ruin careers. To maintain a grueling pace, some performers succumb to popping uppers to stay awake and downers to sleep, until the drugs destroy their health and talent. Drugs (heroin, cocaine, amphetamines, and depressants) furthermore tend to carry a social milieu that perverts one's business dealings. You might involve yourself, for example, with a manager, agent, or promoter, more for his drug connections than for his business acumen and usefulness to your career. I only use an occasional Valium, which is prescribed for me. I use it because performing sometimes wires me up so much that, without it, I take half a night to fall asleep, and this is especially upsetting when I need to be up early the next morning. (I also tell hotel operators to put a "do not disturb" on my phone. Someone invariably calls me with some dumb question before I want to awaken. And once I'm up, I'm up.)

I include marijuana in my objection to drug use. Raised in a Houston ghetto, I learned early what dope is all about—and saw what the (unfairly) harsh legal consequences of a bust could be. (In Texas, the courts used to throw away the key.) I valued my career and freedom over a few minutes of high. And I know how narcotics convictions hurt many a group. Though the First Edition stayed clean most of the time, we did have one close brush with the law. A policeman met me in the lobby of a Texas hotel and asked for our autographs for his daughter. After giving him mine, I told him which room the rest of the band stayed in. Unknown to me, however, a few group members chose that moment to light a joint. It would have been jail for them had Ken Kragen not happened to leave the room. Noticing a cop heading down the hallway, he ducked into someone else's room and phoned to alert the group to deep-six the dope, which they did a few seconds before the knock came at the door. (They almost fainted when they found that the law merely wanted autographs!) Marijuana laws *are* gradually easing. Still, I find pot ruins one's performance. Other members of the First Edition once talked me into smoking just before a show. They said I'd love it, and I did. In fact, I believed I had given the best performance of my career. But we happened to tape that show, and listening to it later I found that my singing swerved in and out of tune and our pacing was no

The road: Card games on buses . . . sorting luggage at airports . . .

. . . afternoon sound checks (and taking time with your family—my son,
Kenny Rogers II) . . . dressing . . .

. . . more travel . . . and resting your head in unlikely places.

better. But my scintillating between-song raps took the prize. "Yeah, we did this song . . . and, uh, Mike wrote that song. . . ."*

No matter what you want to do to yourselves, remember that you owe it to each other and those who depend on you to preserve your ability to perform. For this reason, I also stay away from dangerous sports, like skiing or car racing. If I'm hospitalized, I put six others out of work. One final health tip: Know the name, phone number, and address of a good doctor and hospital in each town you plan to play. (Warner Brothers' *Book of the Road* and *Billboard*'s annual *On Tour* guide list this information, along with details of club, concert, hotel, restaurant, and other facilities for cities throughout the country.)

As important as caring for yourselves on the road is caring for others you work with, other groups and professionals. Although you must look out for your own best interests, try to work cooperatively rather than competitively with others. You should have no problem if you heed this adage of the business: "Be careful whom you step on going up. You'll pass the same people on your way down." In other words, mistreatment of someone you feel is below you is almost certain to return to haunt you, because the tables have a way of turning in most astonishing ways. And you may not even know the source of the revenge. Some record executive, for instance, might remember your rudeness to him a while ago and blackball your contract renewal if your sales have been marginal. On the road, if a headlining band finds you unreliable or difficult, they could knock you off the tour and their agency could refuse to use you again. In the opposite case, if you mistreat the acts supporting you, they could return the favor when you fall a few notches and need to go out supporting them on tour. I might add that the First Edition was practically supported by The Bistro in Columbus, Ohio, during those first few tough months of our existence. Though they often lost money on us, they booked us because they found us easy to work with—and we repaid them a couple of years later by playing return engagements even when we could have worked other places for ten times the money.

To pinch from Bob Dylan, the rules of the road have been lodged. There is an unwritten code of ethics for bands on the road. For example, though a headliner does claim priority in all aspects of a show, it's understood that they should allow their supporting acts enough lighting, space onstage, time for sound checks, and the like. Unfortunately, such courtesies can't always be taken for granted. I'll never forget one apt illustration of boorishness the First Edition

---

*It's ironic that many of our fans thought I was often stoned. "Just Dropped In" was a blatantly psychedelic song. What convinced them, though, was the glazed look of my nearsighted eyes and my easy manner.

encountered when we were starting out. Preparing to run through a brief, early sound check, we were tuning our instruments when Canned Heat barged onstage and began jamming, their amplifiers cranked up to an obliterating blare. We calmly put our instruments down and walked offstage. This obviously isn't why you don't hear about Canned Heat any more, but it does indicate an attitude that can gradually kill a band.* Remember, success in the entertainment business relies on people liking you. You don't have to be officious, just fair, honest, and respectful.

The guiding principle for a supporting or opening act is, generally, to take care not to step on the headliner's toes. Set up your equipment and do your sound check around the headliner's schedule and don't do anything in your performance to sabotage their act. I remember how mad we felt when a supporting group played one of our hits on our show. Of course we performed it better, but the supporting act's ploy was nonetheless a dirty trick. Rather, try to steal the headliner's audience through the quality and charisma of your performance.

One last remark about road etiquette. While personal habits may be left up to the individual, trashing hotel rooms, backstage areas, and the like is another matter. Even if Keith Moon is your idol, it doesn't give you the right to chuck a color television set eight stories down into a swimming pool. If anyone in my group does anything like this, he'll pay for it or be out of a job. Not only is trashing expensive, but it reflects badly on the group. It could hurt our bookings. While it's true that notoriety sells, as Alice Cooper's history (including the beheadings of baby dolls) attests, the *image* of violence is far different from the actuality of violence. (The latter is destructive, the former possibly constructive, perhaps telling us something about ourselves.) In any case, your stature as recording artists conveys upon you a degree of *noblesse oblige*—the obligation of upper echelon persons to behave nobly toward others.

Promoting Your Show   Having a hit is the greatest possible promotion. However, whether you have a hit or not, promotion can draw audiences and add a special aura to your show. Promotion might mean flying in music journalists to one of your earlier dates so that you can get advance stories. Or, it might mean going to a town a few days before a concert to accompany the record company's local promo man on a tour of

*Some headliners are so afraid a hungry supporting act will blow them off the stage that they all but castrate the acts. My feeling is that every group deserves to sound their best. And if you can't outshine the groups supporting you, your act has deteriorated too much to be camouflaged by petty restrictions on the other acts.

Promotion means doing radio, TV, and press interviews on the road. Photos of these visits can in turn be placed in the trade newspapers to create more energy in the industry. Promotion entails feeding items to trade and consumer publications. Here *(opposite)* is a press release from 1976.

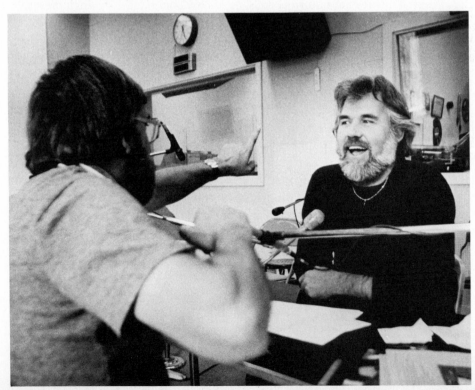

CONTACT: FRANK H. LIEBERMAN
(213) 275-4581

FOR RELEASE: IMMEDIATE

KENNY ROGERS RE-SIGNS WITH ICM:
GETS NEW HARRAH'S HOTEL PACTS

UA recording artist Kenny Rogers has re-signed for three more

years with ICM. The deal was concluded between Dick Gilmore, Rogers'

responsible agent, and Ken Kragen of Management Three. Rogers has

been with ICM since its inception and CMA prior to that.

In addition, Rogers, whose current single "Lucille" is climbing

the national country charts, has been signed for another set of

two week engagements at Harrah's Tahoe and Reno.

Rogers has also been set to appear on "Dinah!" and "The Don Ho

Show."

############

radio stations; you could do live interviews and convince the promo man to arrange for the stations to give away records over the air in call-in contests. Or, promotion might mean pulling some attention-grabbing stunts. Ken Kragen and I once hired a skywriter to write THE FIRST EDITION AT THE AMBASSADOR HOTEL on the first day of a show. It would have been great had it not turned out to be a cloudy day. (We even got beat for the price of the skywriter. You can't cancel them unless the weather is so poor they can't fly.)

Despite that blooper, we've done more visible, if somewhat less lofty, promotions that worked. As the first rock group to play New York's Plaza Hotel, we had several students pass out 10,000 dated balloons that read POP GOES THE PLAZA: KENNY ROGERS AND THE FIRST EDITION PLAY THE PLAZA HOTEL. Consequently, we broke the hotel's show-room attendance record and got bookings in other classy hotels. I ran a similar promotion in Las Vegas at a time when my career was at a low, trying to make it as a solo performer. I had 600 buttons made up reading KENNY ROGERS AT THE GOLDEN NUGGET. We distributed them to taxi drivers in town with invitations to my show. The invitations promised every driver free admission and a free autographed album if he came. In return, many of the drivers not only came to my show, but they spread the word to their riders—and we packed the house three shows a night for all twenty-one nights!

Dynamite promotion can pump your music to the public's ears. Promotion in the record end of the business specifically refers to the department that deals with radio, from the Top-40 AM stations to the FM album-oriented rock (AOR) to the MOR stations. Because radio play is a record company's most powerful selling tool, the promotion department is the company's front line in the battle to make a hit. The promotion staff must be able to coax airplay for their new artists even though most of the stations only play music by familiar artists. And when airplay does crop up, they must react instantaneously if they are to spread it. But promotion is just one facet of a record company's larger marketing campaign, a campaign that also encompasses tour support, press and public relations, advertising, and merchandising.

Merchandising—the creation of selling aids such as mobiles, posters, and window displays—hits the customer at one of his most vulnerable times; when he's in the store. This is the way to tap the compulsive buyer who has $5 to spend but isn't sure what he's going to spend it on. Even more effective than visual aids in swaying customers is in-store play, which the record company attempts to encourage by supplying dealers with sample copies. In-store play is more important than, say, a magazine ad, for if the reader drives to a record store with the advertised record in mind, he's likely to forget about it if he enters the store and hears another record playing, a record that sounds good.

Print advertising in newspapers and magazines is useful, even though it may not have as immediate an impact as in-store play. It lets people know your record exists and induces some of them to check it out. It also contributes to an overall sense that some big guns support you and you're a contender, which triggers d.j.'s, journalists, and so on to give a closer listen to your record. In advertising as in merchandising, your record company may spend some money automatically, but probably not enough to make a real difference. For instance, they might include your album in supermarket ads of ten albums. What you have to do is convince them to do more, since you need it most now to start something happening. (Perhaps you should offer to make half the costs recoupable from your royalties.) This means page ads in national publications with the largest readership of people inclined to buy your record, time-buys on radio stations in key markets with audiences most apt to like you (especially necessary for the few days preceding your appearance in a particular town), newspaper co-op ads with local retail record chains, and ads in the record trade magazines and one of the leading radio trade weeklies, *Radio and Records.* Although trade ads may not sell a single record directly, they do sell records indirectly by demonstrating record company support to the industry and spreading news of breakthroughs in airplay or sales, news that might cause a promoter to chance booking you when you need the break.

The record company takes the active lead in merchandising and advertising (with a bit of prodding from you). You both must collaborate, however, on the other promotional fronts: radio promotion and public relations. For their part, the record company ships promo copies of your records with a press kit to radio stations and music reviewers across the country, and its local promotion people attack stations in their market, doing whatever they can to get your records played. For your part, join the local person to meet the d.j.'s and program directors and do as many on-the-air interviews as possible. Visiting stations, by the way, will show how the culling-out process you experienced in landing a record contract goes brutally on:

"Hey Bob, I've got sixteen great records for you," the promo man said on one such visit I made during my MGM days.

"Well, who've you got?" replied the p.d. They started with the name artists. "Oh, you've got Kenny's record, let me hear that. . . . An Osmonds record, great. . . . Well, I have time for one more."

The promo man rummaged through his pile. "Uh, this is garbage . . . this is pretty good. . . ."

The difficulty is that except for small stations of limited consequence, the

Smashing out of
TEXAS!

HEADING FOR THE
NATION'S
NUMBER ONE SPOT

Kenny Rogers,
The First

SINGS

THAT CRAZY
FEELING

CARLTON 454

Carlton Record
Corporation

157 W. 57th St., N. Y. 19, N. Y.
CI 5-1240

Even in 1958 breaking records nationally required trade ads. Here's one for "That Crazy Feeling," placed in a March 17 issue of *Cash Box*. (Note that I'm Kenneth Rogers on the record, Kenny Rogers The First on the ad—I just couldn't decide what to call myself.)

(Right) A 1958 memo from Carlton directing me to radio contacts on an Eastern promo tour for "That Crazy Feeling."

MEMO

FROM: .... DATE: ....

TO: ....

Dear Kenny —

Just got back from Boston. It wont be long before your record will be moving there.

Hope everything is coming along fine.

In Detroit — give my best to Don McLeod, Clark Reid, Rosemary McGinn Tom Clay (all at WJBK); Bud Davies (CKLW); Bobby Seymour (WKMH); Ed McKenzie, his secy Sunny Pryor and Mickey Shorr (all at WXYZ) and Sammy Kaplan.

When you get to Chicago — Wally Phillips is an old buddy of mine.

Talk to you soon.

— Juggy,

CARLTON
RECORD
CORPORATION
157 W 57 ST
NY 19 NY
CI 5-1240

secondaries or tertiaries, most stations today are so rigidly formatted to reach a mass audience that most unknowns have little, if any, chance of getting programmed on them—until they manage to gain momentum in the outlying radio markets or establish themselves through years on the concert circuit. Commenting on this in a *New York Times* article in May 1977, WABC's vice president of operations, Rick Sklar, admitted that they only play the established hits. "When we can't decide whether or not to add a record, sometimes we even listen to it," he said, essentially.

Not only is there resistance to new, challenging music, the mass taste being so homogenized, but it's even difficult to get a primary station to listen to your record. This is the result of radio's increased reliance on program directors, a wedge forced between the d.j.'s and the record companies and artists. Radio stations give program directors much of the say as to what is played to allay suspicions that many records get play through payoffs to d.j.'s—suspicions grounded in the infamous payola scandals of the late fifties.

The greatest distance between those who spin the discs and those who jockey them exists with radio chains, such as RKO-General, whose many affiliates have been programmed by one individual. Getting that individual to listen to your record, let alone add it to one of his powerful AM stations (WRKO in Boston or KHJ in Los Angeles), required very good connections indeed. It's tough to reach such programming consultants as Lee Abrams in Atlanta, who found great success in turning free-form progressive FM into formulated album-oriented Top 40 and now playlists stations across the nation.

The tight nature of the playlists of the highly competitive big-city radio stations forms the chief reason why the regional approach to promotional touring is so important. As opposed to the primary markets—New York, L.A., San Francisco, Dallas/Fort Worth, Chicago, Boston, Philadelphia/Washington, D.C., Cleveland, and Atlanta—the secondary markets are places where new acts can hope to get their foot in the door. These areas have independently programmed stations and chain affiliates that are more readily swayed. The affiliates may not be able to program your records themselves, but they can suggest to their program director in L.A. or New York or Atlanta that your record be given a shot—a recommendation that carries a lot more weight than a record company promotion man's exhortations.

Promoting your records on radio isn't limited simply to delivering records, visiting stations, and fielding interviews. Even if a station isn't "on" your record, they still may be interested in doing promotional stunts that help keep them one step ahead of their competition and help you build your following. Such a stunt helped make the First Edition's first single, "I Found a Reason," a hit in

Columbus. One station took us out on the ice in tennis shoes at a hockey match to face off against the jocks in a clownish half-time game of broomball. It was great. It exposed us to more than 10,000 people, and for the preceding week, the station had played parts of our album and announced the upcoming battle. It promoted the hockey game, the station, and, of course, us. The only drawback was that we had to play three sets afterward at The Bistro, and I almost passed out from exhaustion.

Perhaps the most effective radio promotion is the radio station–sponsored concert, which the promo department or your manager could arrange. With the record company buying advertising time, paying your expenses (you play for free), and donating albums and/or T-shirts for giveaway contests, the radio station handles the rest. They hire the hall, sell low-priced tickets, and, for several weeks before the date, play your records regularly to promote the show.

Working closely with radio people also yields long-term benefits. People are people. While d.j.'s can't add a record they feel is inferior or wrong for their audience because that would threaten their ratings, they do tend to go on a record by an artist they know faster than an equally suitable record by someone they don't. I found it helpful to develop personal relationships with p.d.'s. For instance, Art Roberts of WLS, Chicago's largest Top-40 station, and I shared a mutual interest in horses, so whenever I was in Chicago, I'd call him and we'd go riding. Consequently, I also could call him whenever we had a new record; though I couldn't ask him to add it to his playlist, my position did give us an edge.

To this end, keep a list of the people you meet. Just remember not to phone or visit the stations without first consulting the record company's local promo person. He or she would know whether or not a call from you would help. Many stations prefer not to deal with artists, being afraid a suggestion of payola might arise, which could cause the station problems with the FCC in renewing their license. The promo person furthermore should accompany you because it strengthens his image and shows a solid artist-company rapport.

And you do want to get in tight with the promo people. They usually work six or twelve or more singles and as many albums at once. It's crucial that they be fully enthused about your record—and you—to inspire confidence in that record to radio. As professionals, promo people should be able to do that regardless of their personal feelings. But this isn't an ideal world and they need coaxing, prodding, and stroking. And incentive. Hence, there is something else you can do to help your radio promotion; offer spiffs. A spiff is a cash award of varying amounts—$50 to $100, for example—that you give to a promo person whenever he succeeds in getting your disc added to a primary or secondary station's playlist. Or, you might put up, say, $1,000 and notify the local promotion staff that the first person to get the record Top 10 in his area wins $500, the second $300, and the third $200. If the money is won, it has been well spent, for it means the record is happening. Some companies prohibit spiffs because they fear once you start it, promotion people won't work a record *unless* there is a spiff involved. It contradicts the philosophy they try to promulgate, that every record of theirs is a potential hit until proven otherwise.

Don't jeopardize your record company relationship, for that relationship constitutes another important element in making your records successful. The first way to keep the staff on your side is to show a willingness to do all you can for yourselves. When we started out, the First Edition appeared for free on dumb TV shows like "Dialing for Dollars" all over the country. The shows may not have sold a single record, but they showed Warner Brothers we were working at it. We made every in-store appearance we could, signing records for customers and meeting employees; did radio and press interviews until we could hardly talk; and attended the parties and industry functions they asked us to. We also did something more subtle but equally smart—we complimented the record company in articles and mentioned them in shows. And they appreciated the pats on the back. In fact, I believe this is where I hammered the nails into the coffin of my subsequent MGM relationship. I told interviewers the way I saw it—that MGM was doing little for the First Edition—and consequently the company made sure they didn't do anything.

Another wise move is to visit the company's offices, not often enough to make pests of yourselves but often enough to keep them on your case. When you visit, have relevant and useful things to say because they're very busy. Discuss new promotional concepts or new information they can publicize or use in the field.

If you want to rely less on company faith—even though you really can't do without it—and more on cash, then you'll need a promotional budget. These aren't as easy to squeeze out of record companies as tour shortfall commitments (which, like promo budgets, are usually all or in part recoupable). But if you succeed in getting some promo budget as did the First Edition, be judicious about when and how you spend it. When you've got a record that you strongly feel could hit if only the right sensation were projected on the street (a time that may not come until your third album), then you go to town throwing parties, etc. Besides timing, think about gearing these parties clearly, but tastefully, toward what you're selling, so that if people like the record, they'll do something with it and take a special interest in you.

The perfect marriage of timing and focus that we achieved in setting up a party in San Francisco several months after our debut party in L.A. helped break our first hit, "Just Dropped In." We took about fifty select d.j.'s and journalists on a large rented boat for a sail around the bay. Hors d'oeuvres and drinks were served and, in mid-cruise, we performed. (Talk about a captive audience!) The party was successful because it was more than a party. It was an event that was talked about for months.

An example of a well-intentioned but ill-conceived promotional event is one U.A. arranged, using about a fourth of the $50,000 promo budget I'd negotiated into my contract. Originally, I had suggested they fly some key journalists to catch one of my first post–First Edition gigs in Las Vegas, a promotion worth about $4,000. U.A. decided later to expand the junket and split the expense with Joey Heatherton's promotional fund, as she was appearing at Caesars Palace. They flew in a flock of press, radio, and sales-account people, wined and dined them, and took them first to Heatherton's show and then to mine. Trouble was that by the time the people saw me they were so drunk and tired they couldn't have cared less who they were seeing, if they could see at all. Anyway, even if they had been sober, the impact of a Kenny Rogers promotion was hopelessly diluted. This is one reason to make sure you share in the control of a promotional fund, which will come, either wholly or in part, out of your royalties.

Every now and then you hear about some new act on whom a record company spends a fortune in promotional dollars but who you find is not worth any of it. In fact, I sometimes think the less talent an erstwhile next-big-thing has, the more excited the executives get. They figure if the group succeeds they can take the credit for it. Usually, however, the big hypes are seen for being just that, and they fall on their contrived faces.

But then there are the genuinely talented whose careers end up singed by a blast of record-company hype, à la Bruce Springsteen. After putting out two critically acclaimed but commercially unsuccessful albums, Springsteen's record company, Columbia, decided in 1975 to muscle him to the top with his third, more commercially appealing album, *Born to Run.* They poured a reported $50,000 into promoting the album and, exploiting critic (cum producer) Jon Landau's old quote, "I've seen the future of rock and roll and his name is Bruce Springsteen," managed to land cover stories on almost every influential pop music and cultural magazine. The coups, of course, were the covers of the mass-circulation newsmagazines, *Time* and *Newsweek, in the same week!* The hype worked; *Born to Run* went gold and the single of the same name became a fair-sized hit. But the follow-up single, "Tenth Avenue Freeze-out," stiffed, largely because many people resented the idea of the eastern media establishment dictating tastes. And even Bruce publicly demonstrated his disgust with the hype. He tore down posters of himself wherever he found them and dissociated himself from it in interviews. Combined with an injunction against his recording, because of a suit against his first manager, which kept him out of the studio until 1977, this reaction evidenced itself in a period of noticeably reduced airplay and press coverage, which proved difficult for even this major talent to surmount. (His songs were heard, but as recorded by other artists such as the Hollies and Manfred Mann.)

Hype, the building up of something into far more than it is, ironically prejudices people against the thing it's meant to draw their attention to: the music. It would have been more productive for the record company to promote him subtly, because the industry, press, and public like to feel they "discovered" a new talent themselves.

Press Coverage   Promotion gets the records played. Promotional events create excitement in the industry and, indirectly, in the public. It's public relations—press—that really reaches the public. While radio promotion has a more immediate impact on sales—people buy what they've heard and liked—press is important in the long-term sense because it builds *careers,* not just one-shot hits. It makes you credible, valid, and established, and it deepens people's sense of you as an artist and personality. In fact, stories in newspapers and magazines on new artists stimulate the consumer *and* the trade, for those d.j.'s, p.d.'s, and record-store owners are greatly influenced by what they find in print. Thus, cooperate in getting as much press coverage as you can (becoming more selective about which journalists you talk to when you can afford to).

As an unestablished performer, getting press will be difficult. Journalists most want to write about the artists they and their readers know and love. Ironically, when you need press the most, it's hardest to get. A good press department, however, can pull strings with writers they're close to. And they can speak and write about your music, sociological importance (if any), credentials, sales activity, and radio play eloquently enough to generate interest. Just remember that even if you get a lot of press, it may not translate into record sales. Many artists who become the favorites of critics challenge the mass audience's sensibilities too much to sell well (as has been the case with Elvis Costello, Graham Parker, and Little Feat). But then, when one of their songs does catch the pop airplay, watch out. Such was the case of Patti Smith.

That a prominent media profile is important is plain, so spend time with

THE FIRST EDITION   KRAGEN/FRITZ,INC.   reprise

THE FIRST EDITION   KRAGEN/FRITZ,INC.   reprise

Publicity stills: The projection of an image. The First Edition pictures in 1967 *(above)* showed us sincere and high purposed and always in (newsprint) black and white, slightly psychedelic garb. We associated ourselves with the socially conscious and realist values of the mid-sixties. To our original quartet configuration *(below)*, with Mike Settle, Terry Williams, Thelma Camacho, and me, we added drummer Mickey Jones. Then our press kit included photos showing more warmth and openness *(opposite)*.

Exit Thelma Camacho in 1969; enter Mary Arnold. Exit Mike Settle in 1970 and enter guitarist Kin Vassy. Now we're Kenny Rogers *and* the First Edition. *(Above, left to right)* Mickey Jones, Kin Vassy, Mary Arnold, Terry Williams, and me. In 1972 we signed with Jolly Rogers Records (on MGM) and created new publicity materials to project the casual but showy Western image we settled on *(left)*. Standing at rear are new members guitarist Jimmy Hassell *(left)*, who replaced Kin Vassy, and keyboardist Gene Lorenzo.

your record company's publicity department to hammer out a sensible strategy for gaining the public's attention. Work out a few hooks that will intrigue the press. Maybe they could build stories around your credentials (have some of you worked with notable stars?), how the group was formed and/or got a record deal, your politics, the uniqueness of your stage show or music, your other talents, philosophy, life-style, and so on.

Before your record's release, the publicists should incorporate the music-oriented information into your bio and assemble a press kit, which is sent with the record to reviewers and d.j.'s. In addition to the bio, the kit should include a posed, professionally shot black and white photo that newspapers can publish with their reviews or features. Eventually, after some impressive reviews have appeared, the kit could include reprints of them.*

The publicity department can make hay out of the other newsy and anecdotal information you supply them. In their frequent mailers to writers, d.j.'s, and dealers, they'll include bits on you to build anticipation for your records and tours and to keep your name out there during the in-between times. As such, make it a habit to feed the publicist stories about the band, no matter how trivial some may seem. You never know which hook will land the major story. Tell how the lead guitarist got busted for shooting fireworks out of your Kansas hotel room, how John Lennon dropped by your rehearsal—anything. Certain items won't reach print; writers usually see a cheap shot for what it is. But if you continually communicate interesting bits, some will stick.

Don't expect to see your record reviewed everywhere; in fact, only the specialized music magazines write about every record fitting their tastes. Whenever you're reviewed, since it's too rare for an artist to receive across-the-board positive reviews, be prepared for a few knocks. Some critics may hate your record (or concert) and say so. Bluntly. A good pop-music critic—such as Lester Bangs, Robert Christgau, Richard Cromelin, Robert Hilburn, Greil Marcus, Dave Marsh, Paul Nelson, John Rockwell, Greg Shaw—will try to find a record's redeeming qualities and pinpoint where an artist has failed, if he has, offering constructive advice grounded in a solid historical perspective and overview of the field. Unfortunately, there are some bad critics who don't really know what they're talking about. For this, and the fact that many artists resent

---

*Once the First Edition was successful, we had custom folders printed for our press kit and inserted press clippings and individual photos of each member along with a group shot and the customary bio. We also published a professional souvenir booklet, which profiled all the members and was filled with pictures of the First Edition onstage, on the road, recording, and on the "Rollin' " set, and introduced our behind-the-scenes people. We gave copies to journalists, hotel employees, promoters, d.j.'s, etc.

nonmusicians judging their work and influencing buyers, you may dislike the idea of critics. Nevertheless, whether you agree or disagree with what they say about you, free public discussion of art is rewarding. It prods artists to come to terms with their limitations and strive to overcome them, and it makes the artists and public conscious of what is being done and what is worth buying. Learn from reviews: Pick the advice that has the ring of truth and think about how you might apply it to improve your future performances, songs, or productions.

A good publicity department should call reviewers to see that your album doesn't get overlooked among the twenty-five or more promo records they receive weekly. They also should call writers in each city—particularly the markets where promotion most needs support—and try to talk them into interviewing you, either over the phone before you play a town, in person on a "rap tour" (the company sends you out for promo purposes), or in town for a concert. A good department also will reprint and proliferate the complimentary press clippings and continually seek to lift you into the more influential publications.

Should your company lack a good press department, you might hire an independent firm for about $1,500 a month. The better firms include Rogers & Cowan, Solters and Roskin, Levinson Associates, and W3. In fact, many acts insist the record company pay for this as a contractual condition. (Similarly, many acts employ independent promotion people to augment the record company's overloaded promotion staff.)

Whoever handles your press, you'll find that it's easier to get space in the specialized music magazines, local underground papers, and small-town newspapers. With some degree of commercial success, you can land modest space in daily newspapers and national music publications. And when you've achieved stardom, you'll be asked for interviews by the large circulation general interest publications, the wire services, news syndicates, and big-city dailies. Even as hit artists much of your press coverage will flow from your publicists' efforts. For instance, they could ask magazines to promise to use your photo on their cover in exchange for more access to you. (Covers affirm your hit stature.)

Interviews   Before you do a single interview with even the most insignificant publication or radio station, preparation is in order. Lack of preparation will very likely have disastrous consequences. You might inadvertently insult others in the band, your friends, or your record company, or leave the wrong impression with the readers. Not only must you decide in committee a policy for interviews, but you must be conscious of the fact that some writers aren't merely interested in what inspires your music and how the band was formed; they're looking for a sensational or controversial hook on which to hang their story, and hence to sell more papers. So plan to discuss only what you know you can live with later. (If you must make a statement you don't want printed, be sure to specify that it's off the record or background only.)

In an interview, it's up to you to see that it serves your purpose. As long as it goes well, follow the questioner. If you realize that he or she is inept or ignorant of your music, however, take the initiative. Volunteer substantive information. Plug what you need plugged. ("Oh, while I think of it, we're on the 'Midnight Special' next week and we hope everyone watches because we're going to introduce our new single.") And plug your record company or the people you work with, tell about the crazy things that happened on the road, and discuss personal interests. I got a lot of press from the fact that I raised horses; it became so well known that fans would ask me about it. Later, I got a lot of press from the fact that I'm a serious photographer and shot some of Glen Campbell's album covers. The more of yourself you make known, the more people identify with you and talk about you. Some artists guard their personal sides as jealously as did Howard Hughes, perhaps for privacy, perhaps fearing their personal image would interfere with people's ability to relate to the music on its purest terms. I see nothing wrong with opening yourself up, so long as you don't go on and on like an egomaniac. Be conscious of your image, but act naturally.

Stock questions to prepare for: How would you classify your music? How did you get started? Who most influenced you? What inspired you to write (your big hit or show stopper)? What made you decide to wear cat-styled make-up and spit fire in your shows? What are your future plans?

The First Edition's favorite question used to be, Where do you go from here? No matter where, we always answered, "Memphis." It became an inside joke. What's the difference, we figured, are the journalists or readers going to follow us?

Generally, be honest in interviews. If you're careless, things can get distorted as they are spread and retold in the press. In the beginning you may not mind distortions as long as they're flattering. But there's a danger that you'll get caught up in the myth of yourself. And if you develop a public persona very unlike your real self, you could regret it later when you want to stop playing games and reveal the "real you." By then no one will want to believe who "you" really are, and you'll alienate your regular followers while failing to win new fans. David Cassidy is a prime example. Cassidy let himself be carved into a teen bubble-gum idol, but when he renounced the image as a masquerade and began trying to establish himself as a serious rock and roller his record company couldn't even give his records away.

One more warning. Journalists generally prefer talking with one member of a band so that they get one clear point of view. It makes writing their stories easier. It also creates a spokesperson for the band, which can breed dissension in a group that is supposed to be democratic. This happened to the First Edition. The press wanted to speak with the singer of the hits whose name was tagged onto the band's, and that individual soon became the band's *de facto* leader by virtue of his prominence in the media: me. You can counter this tendency, however. Rotate who does interviews and insist that press photos treat each of you equally, using individual photos of each member or group shots of the entire band in all your press materials.

Television   If press exposure establishes an act in the public mind and radio makes hits and sells records, television does both. Network television is a great vehicle to overnight mass exposure, with perhaps 30 million viewers in prime time and a little less in the late-night music or variety shows such as the "Midnight Special," "Don Kirshner's Rock Concert," or "Saturday Night Live." Even local shows, depending on the size of the market and broadcast time, hit large audiences and make an act look exciting, what with special lighting, sets, make-up, camera angles, and audience applause. They project what records can't—visual qualities and personality.

Unfortunately, with few exceptions, commercial network shows won't book acts that don't have a current Top-20 hit or haven't had a string of hits in the past. Consequently, on tour, begin by trying to do local or public broadcasting shows and pull any and all strings you might have to get on the major shows. Tommy Smothers got us on their big budget ". . . Comedy Hour" before we had any success with a record. And Kragen, as co-producer of that show, wielded his connections to get us on the "The Tonight Show." I'll never forget the first time we saw ourselves. We taped "The Tonight Show" in New York and then headed for Boston, another leg on our first tour in 1967. Seventy miles out of the city, in the middle of nowhere, the show was about to air, so we pulled into a motel and asked the manager, a little old lady, if we could watch her set. "We're on channel four," we told her. She offered a hesitant yes and, during our segment, kept looking from the screen to us and from us to the screen, as though suspicious that this was some elaborate "Candid Camera" stunt.

Although those first two shows featured "I Found a Reason," our first single, the song stiffed everywhere but in Columbus, where we had performed and promoted extensively. Nevertheless, the shows gave us validity. Booking important concerts became easier. Our agent could say how we'd just done "The Ed Sullivan Show" and were about to do another "Smothers Brothers Comedy Hour"—and more TV followed. We went on to do fifty-six network shows in three years, or one every two and a half weeks. More pointedly, TV helped break records for us. We couldn't get "Something's Burning" played in the United States, but when a "Tom Jones Show" we taped in England was broadcast here, radio seemed to go on the song overnight across the country.

Television today may have lost some of its impact because it's not unusual to see a pop group on any more. Still, one solo appearance I made on "The Tonight Show" in March 1977 is credited with selling more than 10,000 copies of "Lucille" in Atlanta alone!* Of course, we'll never forget the power of seeing Elvis on "The Ed Sullivan Show" in 1956 and then the Beatles in 1964.

While you won't have to worry about doing too much TV until you're supersuccessful, overexposure is a problem to bear in mind. It's possible to create a backlash that will *harm* your record sales. Fans figure, why buy your record (or go to your concert); they'll hear it Sunday night anyway. Plus, they tire of you. For the two and a half years that Glen Campbell had his show, he didn't have a single hit record. The same happened to Cher, the Captain and Tennille, Tony Orlando and Dawn, and Donny and Marie. Elvis, on the other hand, used TV very sparingly and maintained an intensely loyal mass following and high sales.

Some groups reject TV for another reason. They feel the box makes them look smaller than life and the five-inch speaker saps their sonic punch. To counter this, bigger acts like Paul McCartney and Wings and Fleetwood Mac made films of themselves performing—films to be shown on TV. Adding "candid" offstage antics and talk about themselves and producing the sound to their tastes, they made themselves stand apart from other groups on the small screen.

TV or no TV, it may take a few albums, singles, and saturation tours before the world opens up to welcome one of your songs into its heart for a few months and you begin a streak of hits that makes you true pop stars. Suddenly, you're ". . . like a Rhinestone Cowboy . . . with offers comin' over the phone." The damn bursts, and if your accountant is worth his pencil sharpener, you should start making money. You start headlining concerts.

---

*TV has become an important advertising medium for records. But because of the high cost of a thirty-second spot, it's used mainly to make a gold album (500,000 sales), platinum (1 million units sold), or double platinum. Few companies can afford TV to break an unestablished act. Incidentally, "units" refers to both records and tapes.

With a degree of success with records comes TV—a mass promotional device. Here *(above)* is a scene from the set of our show, "Rollin'." Guests were Bo Diddley and Ronnie Hawkins. Upon my reemergence as a solo singer, I hit the talk-show circuit—"The Merv Griffin Show"...

. . . and "The Tonight Show," which I even got to host.

TV talent coordinators who kept finding excuses for not booking you now beg to have you on their shows, and your publicity people find themselves with their hands full, screening floods of requests for interviews.

On the record side of this windfall, the hit single will bring the album along with it, and this means the record company will finally see a return on its investment. The mechanics of selling are interesting. Before you become a hit act, your records are only carried in small quantities in retail record chains like Sam Goody, The Wherehouse, Tower Records, and Music Plus, and in "one stops," wholesale record stores where owners of mom and pop (single unit) record stores, jukeboxes, discos, etc., come to buy their stock. When you have a hit, however, a third vast avenue opens up: the rack jobbers. The rack jobbers serve as a subdistribution service, placing the records in the racks of large department store chains, and account for about 55 percent of all the records sold (retail chains account for 35 percent and one stops 10 percent). But because of the higher prices they charge to cover their costs, they only handle records that promise high sales volume. Thus, after your record has been picked up by the rack jobbers, you can feel assured you've got a seller. Watch it go in sales from 200,000 to 800,-000 or, if a second hit pops off the album, 2 million units.

The thrill of your first hit record ranks right up there with, well—your first lovemaking. With more than 6,000 singles and 3,000 albums released a year, to put it another way, it's the thrill of hitting a grand-slam home run in a World Series. I'll never forget when "Just Dropped In" began skyrocketing up the charts.* We were working a club that was really a glorified pizza parlor in St. Louis, Ruggles Cabaret. The place lacked a phone, but every day for three weeks at 6 o'clock we went to a phone booth and called Terry's mother at Warner Brothers in L.A. to get the latest reports. "Well, you sold 14,000 records today," she started telling us. And then it was 16,000 . . . 18,000. One day we sold 38,000 copies. To Elton John or the Eagles this may seem a modest figure, but when it's your first hit, you identify strongly with it. In fact, we used to sit backstage between sets and speculate about how many records 38,000 really is. Would they fill a room, a house, a warehouse?

"Just Dropped In" never made the crowning number one spot; Paul Mauriat's "Love Is Blue" refused to relinquish the throne. Ours peaked at number

*The record charts reflect the record's action from reports of additions at particular stations. Heavy action on the secondary stations will take it into the Top 60s or 70s; similar action on the primaries will take it into the Top 20s (with a "bullet" if it leaps dramatically). At this point, the trades and stations will survey certain stores: If sales lag, they'll back off the record in favor of those that are selling.

two. To this day I grit my teeth when I hear "Love Is Blue," but it didn't really matter. We'd climbed a stairway to heaven. And from our lofty new vantage point we thought they were all going to hit. There's nothing to it, we thought, as we buried in our minds all the unpleasant memories of our past hard days' nights, and of the often exhausting, frustrating, painful, anxious, rocky, long, and winding road. We felt we'd found the key.

Fame

6

Fame . . . Makes a man take things over
Lets him loose and hard to swallow
Puts you there, where things are hollow . . .

Fame . . . What you like is in the limo
What you get is no tomorrow
What you need you have to borrow . . .

Is it any wonder . . . I reject you first.*
          DAVID BOWIE, JOHN LENNON,
          and CARLOS ALOMAR, "Fame"

It happened before millions of viewers of "The Tonight Show." Sitting on Johnny Carson's panel, a year after "Lucille" renewed my credentials as a celebrity, I was describing a concert I hosted at Detroit's Pontiac stadium—the largest indoor country music concert in history—when I stopped abruptly, reached for my guitar behind the couch, and performed my latest single. My lapse was minor, as it turned out, but it signified something serious: My composure was cracking, the result of a relentless schedule.

The day of "The Tonight Show" taping, a Wednesday, had been filled with interviews—seven over the phone from my house and two in my studio dressing room. And, after weeks of touring, this was one of three days I was supposed to have off! Monday was shot with a doctor's appointment and an early bed, as my biological clock still read eastern time. Tuesday was to be mine—until I learned I had to meet with contractors working on a house I was having built in Beverly Hills as an investment. By Wednesday I was quite out of sorts. And my state of mind wasn't improved by what I had to look forward to after "The Tonight Show" taping: a night flight to New York where I would perform and be interviewed Thursday morning on NBC-TV's "Today Show," and a flight Friday to Sweden to perform Saturday night.

The following weeks offered little relief. While I had Easter Sunday off (whew!), Monday I was in Wembly, England; Tuesday, Rotterdam, Holland; Wednesday through Friday, Russia; Saturday, Helsinki, Finland; Sunday, Oslo, Norway; and Monday, London, doing a BBC-TV show. Tuesday I returned to Los Angeles for a week off before beginning a two-week gig with Olivia Newton-John at the Las Vegas Riviera Hotel. And so on—for 240 dates in 1978. Things had grown so absurd that the night I was awarded a Grammy for "Lucille" I had to catch a flight immediately after the show to perform in Las Vegas, thereby being unable to savor the moment with my wife, Marianne, who attended the post-telecast party with friends.

It's not that I'm ungrateful for this fantastic life, a life of my own making and for which I'm handsomely rewarded. It's just that it's also demanding and draining, and you can put out only so much before you run dry and lose a sense of yourself. Still, it's worth working hard when the long-cultivated fruits are finally there for picking. And this is one reason why the attainment of stardom doesn't guarantee freedom: Stardom compels you to work harder than before, to live up to your success, milk it, and keep it. Stardom, furthermore, institutionalizes you. Now you're responsible for many livelihoods and for the continued careful direction of your *career*.

The intense work and awesome responsibilities—to your art, career, associates, employees, dependents—can get on your nerves. It can also destroy your romantic relationships and marriages. The first of my two divorces occurred during my ascent. My wife couldn't conceive that I'd want to leave "it all"— home and family life (we had one daughter)—to go on the road with the New Christy Minstrels. "Since we don't understand each other's needs," I finally told her, "it's obviously the end of us." The Christies made me their offer on a Thursday. I left Houston with them that Saturday.

Marianne, my third wife, is a television actress and model, and willingly tolerates my schedule, as I do hers. Our relationship is flexible and, besides being based on love and compatibility, places great importance, if not priority, on our vocations. Marianne, moreover, appreciates one of my goals—long-term success and financial independence that would transcend the vicissitudes of the pop roller coaster. This goal stems from a nightmare I had as an impoverished child, in which I saw myself as an old man, abjectly, broke, and lonely. While I no longer feel that this is to be my fate, the memory of this image compels me to accomplish as much as I can, hopefully, within the boundaries of my sanity.

After the First Hit   The riches in the transformation from rags to stardom comes through your live performance income. After "Just Dropped In" became the number two record in the country, the demand for us outstripped club capacities. So, instead of receiving more for club dates, we moved up to the high-paying concert gigs. We went from earning $5,000 a week to $5,000 a night (and in 1968 the dollar was twice as valuable as it is now). As we kept producing hits, our performing income rose; by 1970 we averaged about $10,000 a night.

What you should realize, however, is that all isn't rosy once you have that first smash-hit single. Until the First Edition got a string of hits and lucrative album sales, we almost bankrupted ourselves trying to live up to our new hit stature. We made no money from our first two hits, what with the advances from Reprise to repay. Then we found more money flowed out than in: Our road expenses ate us into a $56,000 debt, which might have sunk us had our income eventually not risen with our consistent chart success. How can you have a hit and go broke? Easy. Look at the balance sheet for the year when we grossed a million dollars:

Agent and manager commissions (25%)	$250,000
Deluxe, individual hotel rooms for five musicians and two-man road crew for 200 nights	50,000
Per diem ($10/day for seven for 200 days)	14,000
Airline tickets	250,000
Airfreight	30,000
New equipment, rent-a-cars, legal and accounting fees, road crew and drummer salaries	166,000
	$760,000

Remaining money to split four ways: $240,000

Sixty thousand dollars each net is not an astronomical amount. True, we did live like royalty for awhile, but what remained to bank did not set anyone up for life.

What you do in the wake of your first hit determines whether or not you remain well known and well off. What this means business-wise I'll discuss shortly. Musically, you have to fine-tune your course with regard to what music

Tangible alloys of success: gold record plaques. *(Above)* Kenny Rogers and the First Edition's first gold record, for our *Greatest Hits* LP, presented to us on the stage of the Las Vegas Hilton. *(Below)* Receiving gold discs in a New Zealand recording studio for one of our several successful albums "down under."

More fruits of success: awards. *(Above)* Here I'm shown flanking "Lucille's" writers, Hal Bynam *(left)* and Roger Bowling, and *(right front)* Ronnie Milsap and Roy Clark, when I won the Country Music Association's Single of the Year award for that song in 1977. *(Right)* I'm holding my Grammy for Best Male Country Vocal, which was voted by members of the National Academy of Recording Arts and Sciences.

of yours you find the public buys. This isn't to say you should define yourself by second-guessing the audience. That could lead you into chasing your tail. It means, rather, that you should focus on whatever magic links you with your audience. The First Edition's first few albums were a hodgepodge of styles and sounds because we began as four lead vocalists with the understanding that everyone would take turns as the soloist. Soon, however, we found the only combination the public bought featured me singing lead. I knew I didn't have a great voice, but it turned out to be a good commercial voice with a readily identifiable character. So though we still let everyone have his moment in our albums and shows, I became the musical focal point. Incidentally, the fact that I didn't sing all the material enhanced my leadership position. Singing lead on the killer songs carried more punch.

Your Next   Fine-tuning your musical course means not only emphasizing
Release   the more successful elements in your arrangements, but also
being careful about what singles you release as follow-ups. Once, the idea was to release a single that sounded very much like the one before it. Now, perhaps because of radio's increased selectivity, it's better to release a song that contains identifiable links to past records but sounds distinctly fresh. The First Edition found success by keeping our songs similar enough to be liked immediately but challengingly different enough to demand the listener's concentration and require some getting into. For example, "Ruby," a war theme about a crippled veteran, featured a two-four shuffle rhythm. We gave the same feel to our next single, "Reuben James," a song also tinged with social consciousness. But "Reuben James" had a faster beat and a different subject matter: the suffering of a black southern sharecropper. So, my advice is, resist the temptation to release a song very close in style and content to your big song. Duplicating the formula probably won't duplicate your success. There must be a reason for your follow-up's existence. It must stand on its own and have something new to make people want to hear from you again. Besides, repeatedly releasing identically styled songs will typecast you.

The best time to release a new record is when your previous one has played itself out and begun heading down the charts. Ideally, the records will pass each other. Don't release a new record while one is still going strong because it'll stop the happening record cold. Confused d.j.'s won't play either record and fans will spend their dollars on one or the other. You may sell as many total records as one big hit but be robbed of the high visibility and far-reaching ramifications that accompany a hit. Also keep an eye to the buying seasons and what is going on around you. Remember, half the business the industry does all year is in the few months before Christmas. Summer is traditionally slow. This explains why "Just Dropped In" only sold 400,000 copies. The same hit in November might have sold a million. On the other hand, had we not released it at that time, we might not have gotten that breakthrough hit. It came out at a moment when none of the superstars had out their latest blockbusters, clogging the charts and reducing the chances for new acts. It didn't matter that the song sold less than a maximum number of copies. To the public, a hit is a hit; they don't know how many copies actually sold.*

Business Considerations   Apart from musical considerations, you'll have much to do in the business department to insure the band's continued growth and longevity on the heels of your first hit. One of your first moves should be to express your appreciation to the people who helped make you a success. Some artists send gifts to the program directors and d.j.'s and record company executives who believed in them first. C. W. McCall gave monogrammed C.B. radio sets to his record company's entire regional promotion staff. Often, I've given custom-made check boxes that cost about $50. On the lid of the box is an engraved brass check made out to the individual for $1,000,000 and signed by me. It's my way of saying, "thanks a million," and as people put them on their desks to stash odds and ends, my way of keeping my name before them daily. I've also given brass Kenny Rogers belt buckles.

Though my check boxes make it seem as though I'm in the habit of writing million-dollar checks, in fact I'm now a model of fiscal responsibility. Once you're successful, you have a dual problem: You have to strive to remain frugal, especially when your income is modest, and you have to learn to invest shrewdly when that income swells into a surplus. You can't spend like there's no tomorrow. The First Edition made so many mistakes in both areas that I'd give anything to have it to do over again. Complacent about money, we didn't pay attention to the monthly computer printout our CPA sent us. It took going to court for my divorce in 1975 to sober me up. I found myself in such bad financial straits that I started keeping the books myself, which proved to be an excellent cure for Spendaholic Fever. The spending germ infects virtually everyone who starts making a lot of money in this business. You want a new amplifier, house, Porsche. You want the biggest suites in the best hotels. You do this, of course, to show your success to yourself and others. But, you're living

---

*Some songs are "turntable hits." They get airplay like a top hit and chart high but don't sell like a hit. Without the concomitant sales, the songs don't chart above the Top 15.

a fantasy if you believe the money will roll in, in such great amounts indefinitely. It won't. In fact, it ends sooner than you think. And if you haven't saved and invested your money in ways that retain and increase its value, you're going to be back playing in clubs for $150 a week with nothing to show for your past success but some memories.

Where you can most nonchalantly charge-card yourself into financial oblivion is on the road. Here is where you must distinguish between necessity and extravagance. Whereas I used to rent two cars to make it easy for everyone when we flew into a town, I found we could be just as comfortable and mobile by renting one car, with a couple of people taking a cab. So, instead of paying $80 a day, or $30,000 a year, for cars, I reduced the bill to $22,000. Such little things make the difference between breaking even and making money. You need not be ascetic, just sensible.

Again, when the days of your mass success are over, you'll find it isn't enough to have memories. When I'm fifty-five, I wouldn't want my wife to ask why we can't afford food and clothes. I couldn't face telling her about the fantastic life I had, about how I traveled all over the world and had such great times making people happy with my music. Assuming that you're like me, while the tide of money is high, get a business manager to invest it for you. I was smarter than most stars; I had the right idea—to invest my money—but I didn't really do it right. Consequently, I wound up near insolvency (bankrupt *with* money) after my divorce. I erred in putting most of my money into nonliquid assets—long-term real-estate deals in Texas. Though those investments eventually will yield a lot of money, they did me no good when my ex-wife took her share of our community property, the cash, house, etc., and left me with my unbankable real estate. I wouldn't have been backed into this scary corner had I had a business manager. A good business manager would have advised me to divide my investments into long- and short-term holdings. In addition, he might have gotten me some income-producing investment so that if my group folded or I became disabled or divorced I wouldn't be caught empty-handed. Heck, I would've been all right if I'd bought, well, a cleaning establishment. If I only made $400 a week from it, that's $400 a week I could have counted on in hard times. In the meantime, I would have enjoyed its fringe benefits: I could have written off the equipment's depreciation on my taxes and gotten my cleaning done free!

If you hired a CPA to manage your business when you were playing the club circuit, now you need a professional business manager (they usually charge 5 percent of the gross profit). Of course, only go with one after verifying his credentials, but no matter whom you hire do NOT give him power of attorney

—the power to spend your money without your signature. This insures that he'll have to explain his decisions to you and get your approval. This is important because it's your money he's gambling with. Also, you should at least have the satisfaction of knowing you've participated in whatever loss or gain accrues. In all investment decisions, be careful, for successful entertainers are easy marks for con artists. They know you have a huge cash flow (bigger than many large businesses!) and must invest the bulk of it or forfeit it to taxes.

While laying the groundwork for your future security, also work on exploiting further the current success you're having. Expand your business interests from simply records and concerts into merchandising, production, publishing. Merchandising is best described by paraphrasing something Ringo Starr once said: "If you put the Beatles name on it and sell it, we get 10 percent." If you've service-marked your name and logo, anyone wanting to sell T-shirts or any other item carrying that name or logo must have your permission and meet your fee. Perhaps better than licensing others to make and sell (at head shops, record stores, concert-hall lobbies) T-shirts, concert programs, buttons, posters, and whatnot is to do it yourselves. Create a merchandising division in your management company.

Being Your Own Publisher   If you are at all into songwriting and have assigned your publishing rights away, regaining them is another significant way to increase your return from your success, for you will be raising your songwriter income by almost 100 percent. (I say almost because you probably should give 7½ percent—15 percent of the publishing share—to an established publishing house to administer the copyrights.) You now undoubtedly have as much access to other artists as any publisher, frequently more. The question is, do you have the time and inclination to do it properly, and do you have some money to invest in it, particularly to hire someone to follow through on leads for you?

As my own publisher, I had some problems. While I got producer Tom Catalano interested in recording "Sweet Music Man" with Anne Murray on the strength of my past work, I almost blew it because I kept putting off bringing him a demo tape of it. It was funny. Three or four weeks after I first called him, I called again. "I can't find that tape I made of it and I keep forgetting to record another one. Do you really think you'd be interested in it?" He answered they were entering the studio the next week. If I could get it to him soon and he liked it, they would do it. A few days and no tape later, I finally told him I'd come down to his office and play it for him. From the way he'd described his office,

I thought it was in some little two-story building. I drove down there and found the address was the high-rise United California Bank Building at Sunset and Vine in Hollywood. Unable to park in the street, I left my car in a garage around the corner. So here I am. I've had nine million-selling records and I'm walking down Sunset in my tennis shorts clutching my Ovation guitar by the neck. I must have looked like some kid off the bus from Mule Shoe. Indeed, Catalano laughed when he saw me. But midway through the song, he stopped me and said, "It's perfect for Anne. Get me a tape and we'll do it." This time I went right out and found a recording studio that could give me ten minutes immediately. If I hadn't cut the demo then and there, Murray might never have gotten the song.

To avoid such hassles, hire someone who knows music and is ambitious to service your catalogue. Keep him hustling by paying a low base salary with bonuses for every cover recording he gets. The value of covers shouldn't be underestimated. It often takes several recordings by different artists for a song to hit; Mel Tillis originally wrote "Ruby" about the *Korean War*. Also, there are few artists whose own performances of songs yield the major portion of their songwriting income. If you sell a million copies of your own song, it's possible to get fifteen covers that sell 100,000 each to the fans of those other artists. That's another *million and a half* in sales and one and a half times the airplay. More than the additional money you make off your own songs, by being a publisher you can attract other songwriters' material and develop the company so that when you're forty-five years old and don't want to travel any more you can fall back on it. And, boy, that's like money in the bank.

Recording   Another area you can cultivate provides not only additional financial remuneration, but artistic satisfaction, too—recording. When your initial production or record contract expires, negotiate a new deal that not only improves the monetary terms but allows you control over your own productions. Then, either hire a producer for a smaller royalty rate or keep the percentage points and produce yourselves. If you choose the latter course, just be sure you know the difference between ego and talent. Nothing seems more thrilling than to be fully self-contained, to boast, "I compose, perform, produce, mix, and master my own records." Trouble is, the next thing you know, you'll want to lick the stamps, too. Again, the smart person isn't necessarily one who knows all the answers but rather one who admits it when he doesn't and finds someone who does. In other words, keep using specialists on the chores you have little aptitude for. Even assuming you're able to handle the performing and production chores and maintain objectivity while working on both sides of the glass, you'll find it is hard, exhausting work, maybe more than you care to shoulder.

Besides reasons of your own limitations, be selective about which tasks you adopt so you won't damage your career by tinkering with the wrong element. The real key to your success often is unclear. It may be your producer, your background singers. I'd experiment when the old scene has played itself out and the sales and applause appear to be waning. Still, experiment first with a young unknown act that needs a break and has less to lose. Signing them to a short-term production deal (with options), you can produce them and try to sell the master to a record company. Just don't take on so many roles that you dilute your strengths and lose the direction you've worked so long to find. I contributed to the cold streak of my career in the early seventies by overextending myself as an artist, TV star, music publisher, producer, and even record executive. Nevertheless, participating in the peripheral aspects of music redefined and renewed my whole relationship with it. For instance, the process of producing *The Ballad of Calico* kept my adrenaline flowing for much of the eight months I worked on it. Every night I lay awake thinking of fresh ways to approach a song or solve a technical or musical problem.

Having hit records opens the door to greater control over your recordings because commercial success supplies you with the leverage to win a better deal with the record company. If you've done well enough, in fact, you may be able to create your own record label, which would be marketed by a major established company. Having your own label—as I did from 1973 to 1975 with Jolly Rogers Records, distributed by MGM Records—not only permits you to control your recordings from start to finish at a maximum royalty rate and advance from the parent company, but permits you to sign and produce other acts. You may be able to negotiate a contract (if not an ambitious label deal) even before the expiration of your current deal. This is because the company will want to be sure you're kept happy and stay with them. It's an opportunity to increase your royalties and "guarantee" (cash advance for each album project) and, possibly, increase your royalties from your past catalogue. In exchange for such better rates, the record company will demand an extension of your contract so that they won't have to worry about losing you or renegotiating things again for awhile. Incidentally, some artists care less about spectacular advance figures that make them look important in the press and more about increasing their actual earnings. They take smaller advances but add hidden benefits that save them taxes and actually increase the deal's value. For example, they might bargain for nonrecoupable advances so they would receive royalties from the first record sold, for salaried independent promotion people and publicists to work their product exclusively, and for rights to the masters.

Renegotiating Your Contract   If you don't open negotiations before the completion of your contract, then of course negotiate for better terms when it does expire. Since you now have the attractiveness of a hit act, you might play the field somewhat to set off some bidding that drives your price many notches higher. This is how I landed a $1 million Jolly Rogers deal from MGM Records in 1972. Dissatisfied with the turn Warner/Reprise took— away from a pop orientation and into the album-oriented hip underground music of the time—we sought a company that could work our singles. So at *Billboard* magazine's annual convention in Acapulco, Ken Kragen and I pitted Buddah Records against MGM, two companies that were having success with pop singles. We got an offer from Buddah's Art Cass and Neil Bogart (now owner of Casablanca Records and FilmWorks) in their hotel room and then visited the room of MGM's then-president, Mike Curb, who topped their proposal. This went back and forth until Curb made us the offer we couldn't refuse: For a million dollars in guaranteed royalties, I would sign my Jolly Rogers Records label to MGM, promising to include the First Edition as the chief act on the label. (I also signed Stanley Steamer, Dean Scott, and others.) It's hard to say if MGM made a bad bargain or if we made a mistake in going with them, for none of our records sold well during the couple of years before they bought me out of that contract. But it's interesting that Columbia Records didn't think we were worth a million dollars. Just before we signed with Curb, my manager met with Clive Davis (now Arista's president). When Kragen told him how high the bidding had reached, Davis said the meeting was over. Clive was only prepared to offer us $200,000, an amount based on our sales histories, which he had before him. (That he does his homework is one reason Davis is among the business's most respected record men.) Though we made more than that in the short term with MGM, the First Edition might have fared far better had we gone with Columbia, with its stronger distribution, promotion, and leadership. Deterioration in your company's promotional abilities notwithstanding, remember that settling for a little less with your present record company has its pluses. For one, staying means having some control over what past catalogue records of yours they reissue. If you go elsewhere, you can bet that as soon as you get something going your former company will take some of the wind out

With hit records to my credit, I negotiated for my own record label with MGM Records.

Longevity on top, the projection of personality, association with other stars, and you're a celebrity. At Dodger Stadium in 1974, "Hollywood Stars Night" with Jack Lemmon and Walter Matthau.

of your sails by dumping on the market a "Greatest Hits" package or some unreleased tracks that really should be forgotten. But there's another, more general reason to stay put: Why toy with a successful record company–artist combination for the uncertainties of another combination?

The Star Syndrome   The first few lines of "Fame" that I quoted at the beginning of this chapter refer to the star syndrome, the result of taking the shower of attention, adulation, and financial success too seriously.

And it's hard to resist it; the figures of fame make the head spin: million-dollar grosses from concert tours, million-selling records, audiences of 20,000 a night. Perhaps because I tasted major success in stages, I kept my balance fairly well. But if 40 percent of the things said about stars is true, there are a lot of people whose heads are severely warped. You know you have a star complex when nothing is good enough for you any more. Room service is late with your food. The satin sheets and pillow cases your road manager got for your hotel bed are the wrong color. The steak is too well done.

Of course you have a perfect right to insist that the Chateaubriand is cooked right if you're paying $30 for it. On the other hand, you can't expect all the comforts of home on the road. The sooner you adjust to that, the more you'll enjoy yourself and the more you'll be liked by those working for you. Remember, acting like a jerk when on top will have its repercussions when you're down. And you will be down. The pop-music business rivals politics for the title of world's biggest roller coaster. When you're on top people will give you anything you want to win your favor. Some do it out of true gratitude for your work; many others do it to seduce you into letting them exploit you. The trick bag is, when you're in a slump, off the charts for a time, many of these "devotees" find greener pastures. Realizing this, feel free to accept the fringe benefits of stardom. If promoters offer chauffeured limousines in a city, or people present you with flowers, or the hotel gives you the presidential suite at no extra cost, accept it graciously. But don't let a superfluous courtesy become a necessity. If you demand it when you start declining, you'll be laughed at—a very disheartening and painful experience. In any case, being down is usually a temporary state if you genuinely have something to offer and stay with it.

Fans   Besides coping with the vicissitudes of fame, you'll have to cope with fans. Usually you can get away with shaking hands and exchanging howdies. But then some real worshipers will approach you and stare.

"How're you doing?" I'd say. I've found that being friendly gets you out of these awkward situations fastest.

"Gosh . . . I just can't believe I'm standing here."

"Well, you are," I answer. "You're standing right here. Now come on over and I'll give you my autograph, and we'll take a picture. . . ."

Things get ugly when fans expect more than you're willing to deliver. I, for one, don't like to get involved with people I really don't have a reason to be with. I might go to dinner with a club owner or promoter, for instance, if we are friends. But when fans ask me to dinner, I excuse myself, tactfully saying I have another appointment. Occasionally, they'll be rude: "Well, we buy all your records." In situations like this, you owe people one chance for them to get gracefully out of the corner they've painted themselves into, to apologize for imposing on you. Explain to them that you appreciate their buying your records, but that doesn't obligate your personal time to them. If that fails, be blunt—they're obviously not the type of people you want to be associated with anyway. Once, in a club, I almost decked a woman who grabbed my arm, spun me around, and said, "Hey, come here." I said, "I'm sorry. I'm with some people and can't leave." She persisted, so I told her again, "I'm busy. Please, let go of my arm or I swear I'll knock you down." She let go and said—I'll never forget this—"*You've* got a lot of nerve."

Groupies   And then there are groupies, women—and men—who make themselves available backstage and at hotels for virtually *anything* you want to do. Common repercussions of partaking of such fruits of fame include venereal disease, hepatitis, and ruptured marriages—problems that have been responsible for canceling many a concert tour. All that aside, most groupies merely regard you as a conquest. I feel people who throw themselves at you probably are not worth having. But—there are exceptions.

Ironically, the genuine fans occasionally become the worst pests because they expect special treatment. There were a couple of ladies in Florida who wrote me three letters a week and often sent me things. They came whenever I played there and even drove to Houston one New Year's Eve to see me perform. Their dedication was nice, but in exchange they expected me to go out with them. In Houston they called my hotel and said so. And here's where I drew the line. True, entertainers depend on the fantasies their audiences build around them, and you have a responsibility to deal gently with those who take their fantasies to heart. But you also have an obligation to keep some of yourself for yourself. When you're very successful, it's easy to lose control over your life.

I've had fan clubs all along. This one was run by my brother, Billy, and certifies my sister, Geraldine, as a member!

THIS IS TO CERTIFY THAT

Jerry Houston

IS A MEMBER IN GOOD STANDING

OF

The Scholars Fan Club

2-19-56
DATE

Billy Rogers
PRESIDENT

But perhaps best of all are the fans. Back in 1974, Kenny Rogers and the First Edition discovered they were superstars in New Zealand.

And losing that control is tantamount to losing the bigger game when you've won the success game. Entertaining is your life, but it's also your business. On the job, you owe people all the friendliness you can muster. But once you're back in your hotel and want to be left alone, you should feel free to rebuff tactfully anyone who calls or visits. You have to draw a line between what is business and what is personal.*

Fan Clubs   I regard fan clubs in a similarly cautious way. A fan club starts when a few zealous fans write your manager asking for a large quantity of photos and information. Then, advertising through fan magazines, they charge members dues and send out pictures, buttons, newsletters, itineraries, stories, etc. The trouble is, again, many club members feel you're obligated to them and insist on special attention. Terry, the First Edition's boyishly handsome, blond lead guitarist frequently got hung up for hours talking to these sweet little girls, whom, in truth, he couldn't have cared less about. This was especially annoying on the road when he really needed to relax or nap in the afternoon before a performance. And it's the performance that counts. A musician's primary concern is to please the 5,000, 10,000, 15,000 ticket buyers, not the eight club members who happened to have driven one hundred miles to see him.

In short, a fan club can be irritating and inconvenient, but it can also prove to be a useful promotional tool. Though a club does little to popularize you (the creation of a club is more a result than a cause of your popularity), it can help you maintain your success. When you've got a new record out, for example, you can inform your membership and ask them to request that their local radio stations play it, which might get that record rolling for you. Of course, it's still what you do musically and what your manager does that govern your future.

Staying   Longevity is a matter of staying in tune with the times, of continu-
Alive   ally managing to sound fresh but not so radically different that you alienate your hard-won audience. It's also a matter of keeping the band excited about the music, for ennui is easily transmitted to audiences. Preventing this requires a regular infusion of new music or staging. However, you'll still have to play many of the same songs night after night at the risk of

---

*The list of brilliant stars who paid dearly for allowing that line to vanish, trying to live up to their projected image of themselves, is tragically long. It includes Janis Joplin, Jimi Hendrix, Jim Morrison, Jan Berry, Duane Allman, and Brian Jones.

growing to hate them because these songs are responsible for much of your audience's presence. If things do become too routine and predictable, one antidote is to make a structural change. The First Edition, originally two guitars, bass, drums, and female vocalist, added a keyboardist three years into the band's life. It helped us stay contemporary and progress musically. Over the subsequent six years, the group went through four other personnel changes (most from attrition), all to good effect. Not that each addition was more talented than the person replaced, but he or she forced us to return to rehearsing and to deal with the unique talents and fresh enthusiasm of the person brought in. The band's character was altered enough to regenerate the sort of excitement found in an entirely new band.

A band also can be rejuvenated through altering its style. But before you dive into something new, test the water so you have some indication that it'll fare well. As I told Terry Williams when he wanted to remake the First Edition into a hard-rock group in its later years, you have to look at the band as if it were a furniture store. If you're doing great selling early American furniture and suddenly decide it would be more hip to sell modern furniture, you'll hurt yourself if you rashly throw out the early American. You have a certain walk-in trade for the early American. You can't expect people to remain your customers and change their tastes just because you changed yours. You also can't expect to develop a clientele for the new line right away, if ever. You may not be capable of competing with the stores that are established and experienced at selling modern furniture. The sensible approach, then, is to open a section of the store for modern. If it catches on, fine. If not, you haven't blown your business.

This became the First Edition's chief internal stress. Terry wanted to do an album that was strictly hard rock, a departure from the pop, rock, and country folk for which we were known. He wanted to appeal to people his age. Eventually I got him to compromise; we added a couple of rock and roll numbers per album. As I suspected, it was a good thing we didn't do entire rock albums, for those few tracks utterly failed to get airplay. We were too unconvincing at rock to compete with groups like Steely Dan. Nevertheless, the conflict worsened, especially as we saw the end in sight. After a two-year run, our "Rollin'" show ended and the hits no longer kept coming. Typical of dissolving groups, the band's members began blaming each other for the troubles and coming up with diverse solutions—solutions revolving around everyone's self-interests rather than the group's. Thus, things got ugly onstage. Every time I called "Reuben James," which had been a very big hit for us, I got a look from Terry that said, *Oh my God. We're not going to do that song again.* I had the conflict of trying to please our audience and keeping my partner happy.* One solution for this was for Terry to do a solo album. I renegotiated our MGM contract to include one. Unfortunately, this too failed.

Breaking Up (Is Hard to Do)   When this sort of division develops in your group, and it remains unresolved with changes in personnel or style, breaking up is imminent. Like a marriage, a group is beautiful when the members strive to make it work and all gain from it. The time to find somewhere else to sleep is when you cease moving up any of the ladders—professional, artistic, or personal. Though the First Edition still made good money, we were divided not only about direction but had reached a stagnation bordering on rigor mortis. We did no new material because everyone said, "Well, the people in Omaha haven't seen this show, so why change it? We're going to Omaha." True, Omaha wouldn't know the difference. But *we* did. Consequently, we did too many shows on automatic pilot. And you know your band is in trouble when you catch yourself thinking about your tennis backhand in the middle of your biggest hit.

When this happens, you owe it to yourself to join another group or strike out on your own. You have a responsibility to exercise the talents you spent so many years developing. Terry asked to leave the First Edition first. So, after seeing that the deterioration of our affairs was irreversible, I negotiated the release of Jolly Rogers Records from MGM in 1975 and we decided there was no point in negotiating a new group deal. We disbanded the First Edition in January 1976 after eight and a half fantastic years.

Going Solo   Losing your group, if it has meant anything at all to you, is like losing your family. No matter how famous or talented, you're left naked, lonely, insecure. How much of your success, you wonder, was due to the group? This state affects various ex-members differently. Some run to form or join another group, some become plumbers, some move into another facet of the business, and others—who feel they have the charisma and distinctive talent to front an act—try a solo career. As I did. I regarded it as an opportunity to become more of my own man. I wouldn't have to answer to anyone, worry about massaging egos, or depend on others to make my music. It seemed

---

*Offstage, things were just as bad. The band divided into cliques. Terry dated Mary Arnold and it evolved that Jimmy Hassell and Gene Lorenzo stuck with them, while Mickey Jones stuck with me. A resentment built between the two camps. Terry felt I held him back from playing rock and roll; I was disturbed with his heavy-metal approach to the show, with a commensurate volume level.

simpler and more promising to hire backup musicians and set about establishing myself for what I do, which could ultimately leave me more secure than I felt with a group.

Going out on my own quickly proved to be a tonic experience. Even before I hit with "Lucille" in 1977, it reinvigorated my relationship with music. I was under fire out there alone. I couldn't fall asleep onstage any more. If I didn't go over, I would be the one people would think was awful. It would have affirmed my insecurities and left me permanently scarred. I also had to consider my direction thoroughly, to map a strategy for working my way back to the top. Now, more than ever, I realized, you need a game plan because, paradoxically, it's frequently more difficult for a person who has had a string of hits to get hits again than it is for a new artist. D.j.'s (as well as the public) stand to gain little by being the first to play an "established" artist's record, while they can put a big notch in their turntables by debuting a smash new act. A solid game plan is necessary now, moreover, because everyone is watching you. Sure you should be able to land a record deal on the strength of your past. But if you blow this shot, the record industry and the public will be disinclined to give you a second.

I decided that I would adjust my ambitions to a more readily attainable goal than the pop market, that I would try to conquer the limited country-music market first, and use that base to work my way across the charts and up into the general pop market. I went to country not only because my music had always been rooted in it ("Just Dropped In" is by Mickey Newbury and "Ruby" is by Mel Tillis), but because country fans are less fickle toward their stars than pop fans are toward theirs. In pop, you can have five hits in a row and five years later be passé because a whole new generation of kids is listening. In country, you can have one hit and be established for life. I aimed to become a cross-over country artist à la Glen Campbell and Charlie Rich and gain the best of both worlds. The plan was complete when I was able to make a deal with United Artists to be produced by the then-president of their Nashville division, Larry Butler.

The transition wasn't that simple, however. In the first place, I came into the U.A. negotiations with far less leverage than ever, for though I had a certain amount of prestige, in this business you're only as good as your last hit—and my last hit was in 1971, five years before. I signed for far less than I swore I ever would. Second, the setback, which I attribute to my days with MGM, forced me to start over again, to play places I felt I was above playing.

In going solo, be careful about the image you establish. Cut off your identification with your old group so you don't have to compete with it. For instance, I found a backing group and resisted the temptation to add a woman vocalist because I didn't want it to resemble the First Edition's configuration too closely.

Second, I made sure my billing stuck as Kenny Rogers, not Kenny Rogers and Vocal Point, the name of the group I found in Nashville to back me.* I didn't want to become tied once again to a group image, so that if Vocal Point didn't work out I wouldn't have to establish myself as a solo artist a second time. I sought to cross that fine line separating Kenny Rogers "of the First Edition" and Kenny Rogers "who was once backed by the First Edition." One thing that helped me take on the latter identification was the inclusion of Len Epand's liner notes on the inner sleeve of my first U.A. solo album, *Love Lifted Me.* The notes gave d.j.'s and journalists a sense of me as an individual, while reminding them of my artistic and commercial credentials.

Going solo also requires some rearranging of your material. With the First Edition, it was fine for me to step back during a three-minute guitar break. Now, people get itchy if an instrumental passage is too long. They talk among themselves or look bored because they've come to hear me sing, not to hear my guitarist solo. Assuming you've not had hits for awhile, you'll probably have to suffer similar indignities, reverting to playing toilets again and going out as a supporting act for currently popular groups that have far fewer hits under their belts. You'll also notice that the professional courtesies will be fewer and farther between. The concert promoters don't send limos to meet you at the airport or fill the dressing rooms with flowers, food, and drink. Even though you may not really care about these things and may have prepared yourself for the change, you miss the attention nonetheless.

One incident that really brought home how things had changed for me occurred on a promo tour I did as a supporting act for the Captain and Tennille in the fall of 1976. Having had some minor country success, I found I had no leverage when it turned out their elaborate lighting and sound equipment was situated solely to suit their needs and worked at a fraction of its capacity for my segment. I went to their representatives and asked for some adjustments so my show would look and sound at least moderately professional. I wasn't an unknown warm-up act, I explained. I was responsible for drawing some of the audience. The Captain and Tennille people weren't disrespectful, but they made no effort to please me, using weak excuses to keep things as they were. It was especially disheartening because it happened on my first solo tour when I was unsure about getting out from behind my bass to walk on stage holding only a microphone and tambourine, which isn't easy under even the best of circumstances.

---

*Bobby Daniels, drums; Rick Harper, guitar (replacing T. G. Engel); Steve Glassmeyer, pianos; Gene Golden, organ and key bass; Randy Dorman, guitar; and Edgar Struble, clavinet and synthesizer.

THE COUNTRY SINGLES CHART

APR. 2	MAR. 26	TITLE, ARTIST, Label, Number	WKS. ON CHART
1	3	LUCILLE KENNY ROGERS United Artists XW929 Y	10
2	1	SOUTHERN NIGHTS GLEN CAMPBELL/Capitol 4376	10
3	6	IT COULDN'T HAVE BEEN ANY BETTER JOHNNY DUNCAN/ Columbia 3 10474	9
4	2	SHE'S JUST AN OLD LOVE TURNED MEMORY CHARLEY PRIDE/RCA PB 10875	10
5	7	ADIOS AMIGO MARTY ROBBINS/Columbia 3 10472	9
6	8	PAPER ROSIE GENE WATSON/Capitol 4378	10
7	10	DON'T THROW IT ALL AWAY DAVE & SUGAR/ RCA PB 10876	8
8	4	TORN BETWEEN TWO LOVERS MARY MacGREGOR/ Ariola America 7638	13
9	14	SHE'S GOT YOU Loretta Lynn/MCA 40679	6
10	17	SLIDE OFF OF YOUR SATIN SHEETS JOHNNY PAYCHECK/ Epic 8 50334	8
11	12	EASY LOOK CHARLIE RICH/Epic 8 50329	9
12	13	MOCKINGBIRD HILL DONNA	
13	18	SHE'S PULLING ME BACK AG	
14	19	(YOU NEVER CAN TELL) C'ES	
15	15	I'M NOT EASY BILLIE JO SPE	
16	9	YOU'RE FREE TO GO SONN'	
17	22	PLAY GUITAR PLAY CONWA	
18	5	DESPERADO JOHNNY RODRI	
19	21	LOVIN' ARMS SAMMI SMITI	
20	24	ANYTHING BUT LEAVING LAI	
21	30	SOME BROKEN HEARTS NEVI	
22	28	YESTERDAY'S GONE VERN G	
23	11	SAY YOU'LL STAY UNTIL TO	
24	20	WRAP YOUR LOVE ALL AROU LYNN AI	
25	33	THE FEELING'S RIGHT NARVE	
26	31	LOVIN' ON T. G. SHEPPARD'	
27	29	TEXAS ANGEL JACKY WARD	
28	16	I JUST CAME HOME TO COU	
29	23	HEART HEALER MEL TILLIS/M	
30	37	I'M SORRY FOR YOU MY FRI	
31	43	LOVE'S EXPLOSION MARGO S	
32	39	SEMOLITA JERRY REED/RCA	
33	40	RIGHT TIME OF THE NIGHT J	
34	36	I'M LIVING A LIE JEANNE P	
35	42	I'VE GOT YOU (TO COME HC	
36	50	(LET'S GET TOGETHER) ONE L	
37	25	YOUR PRETTY ROSES CAME	
38	26	HE'LL PLAY THE MUSIC LITTLE	
39	47	JUST A LITTLE THING BILLY	
40	48	I NEED YOU ALL THE TIME	
41	52	THE RAINS CAME/SUGAR COATED LOVE FREDDY FENDER/ ABC Dot DO 17686	3
42	49	LIVING NEXT DOOR TO ALICE JOHNNY CARVER/ ABC Dot DO 17685	4
43	27	MOODY BLUE ELVIS PRESLEY/RCA PB 10857	15
44	32	I'M GONNA LOVE YOU RIGHT OUT OF THIS WORLD DAVID ROGERS/Republic IRDA 343	13
45	55	LOOK WHO I'M CHEATING ON TONIGHT BOBBY BARE/ RCA PB 10902	

			WKS. ON CHART
49	62	IF YOU GOTTA MAKE A FOOL OF SOMEBODY DICKEY LEE/ RCA PB 10914	3
50	68	I'D DO IT ALL OVER AGAIN CRYSTAL GAYLE/ United Artists XW948 Y	2
51	58	TRYING TO FORGET ABOUT YOU CRISTY LANE/LS 110	6
52	54	AUDOBON C. W. McCALL/Polydor PD 14377	6
53	60	I LEFT MY HEART IN SAN FRANCISCO RED STEAGALL/ ABC Dot DO 17684	4
54	63	LET LOVE YOU ONCE BEFORE YOU GO BARBARA FAIRCHILD/Columbia 3 10495	4
55	34	THERE SHE GOES AGAIN JOE STAMPLEY/Epic 8 50316	15
56	67	FAN THE FLAME, FEED THE FIRE DON GIBSON/ABC Hickory AH 54010	3
57	35	THE MOVIES STATLER BROTHERS/Mercury 73877	12

CHARTMAKER OF THE WEEK

58	—	IF WE'RE NOT BACK IN LOVE BY MONDAY MERLE HAGGARD MCA 40700	1

59	38	ME AND THE ELEPHANTS KENNY STARR/MCA 40672	9

FOR WEEK ENDING JUNE 18, 1977

Billboard HOT 100

Copyright 1977, Billboard Publications, Inc. No part of this publication may be reproduced, stored in a retrieval system, or transmitted, in any form or by any means, electronic, mechanical, photocopying, recording, or otherwise, without the prior written permission of the publisher.

THIS WEEK	LAST WEEK	WKS. ON CHART	TITLE—Artist (Producer) Writer, Label & Number (Distributing Label)		THIS WEEK	LAST WEEK	WKS. ON CHART	TITLE—Artist (Producer) Writer, Label & Number (Distributing Label)		THIS WEEK	LAST WEEK	WKS. ON CHART
☆	2	10	DREAMS—Fleetwood Mac (Fleetwood Mac), Richard Dashut, Ken Caillat), S. Nicks, Warner Bros. 8371	CPP	☆	39	10	WHATCHA GONNA DO?—Pablo Cruise (Bill Schnee), Lerios, Jenkins, A&M 1920	ALM	☆	80	
☆	3	10	GOT TO GIVE IT UP Pt. 1—Marvin Gaye (Art Stewart), M. Gaye, Tamla 54280 (Motown)	CPP	☆	38	7	LUCKENBACH, TEXAS (Back To The Basics Of Love)—Waylon Jennings (Chips Moman), B. Emmons, C. Moman, RCA 10924	CPP	☆	82	
☆	4	9	GONNA FLY NOW (Theme From "Rocky")—Bill Conti (Bill Conti), B. Conti, C. Connors, A. Robbins, United Artists 940	B-3		40	8	YOU AND ME—Alice Cooper (Bob Ezrin), A. Cooper, D. Wagner, Warner Bros. 8349	WBM	71	75	
			SHE'S GONE/THE FIRST TIME—Foreigner (John Sinclair, Gary Lyons), M. Jones, Atlantic 3394	WBM		42	6	PEACE OF MIND—Boston (John Boylan, Tom Scholz), T. Scholz, Epic 8-50381	CPP	72	58	
☆	6	13	LUCILLE—Kenny Rogers (Larry Butler), R. Bowling, H. Bynum, United Artists 929	B-3	☆	41	7	IT'S SAD TO BELONG—England Dan & John Ford Coley (Kyle Lehning), R. Goodrum, Big Tree 16088 (Atlantic)	HAN		84	
☆	8	12	UNDERCOVER ANGEL—Alan O'Day (Steve Barri, Michael Omartian), A. O'Day, Pacific 001 (Warner/Curb)	WBM	☆	44	5	ALL YOU GET FROM LOVE IS A LOVE SONG—Carpenters (Richard Carpenter), S. Eaton, A&M 1940	WBM	74	63	
☆	7	14	LONELY BOY—Andrew Gold (Peter Asher), A. Gold, Asylum 45384	WBM		53	5	PEOPLE IN LOVE—10cc (10cc), E. Stewart, G. Gouldman, Mercury 73917 (Phonogram)	WBM	☆	85	
8	1	17	I'M YOUR BOOGIE MAN—K.C. & The Sunshine Band (H.W. Casey, Richard Finch for Sunshine Sound Ent.), H.W. Casey, R. Finch, TK 1022	CPP	☆	57		YOU MADE ME BELIEVE IN MAGIC—Bay City Rollers (Harry Maslin), L. Boone, Arista 0256	ALM	☆	87	
9	9	12	SIR DUKE—Stevie Wonder (Stevie Wonder), S. Wonder, Tamla 54281 (Motown)	CPP	43	47	11	YOU'RE MOVIN' OUT TODAY—Bette Midler (Tom Dowd), B. Midler, C. Sager, B. Roberts, Atlantic 3379	CHA/WBM	77	77	
☆	11	18	ANGEL IN YOUR ARMS—Hot (Clayton Ivey, Terry Woodford), T. Woodford, C. Ivey, T. Brasfield, Big Tree 16085 (Atlantic)	CPP	44	34	13	SLOWDOWN—John Miles (Rupert Holmes), J. Miles, D. Marshall, London 20092	MCA	☆	90	
☆	13	8	JET AIRLINER—Steve Miller Band (Steve Miller), P. Pena, Capitol 4424	WBM	45	45	15	UPTOWN FESTIVAL—Shalamar (Simon Soussan), Holland, Dozier, Holland, Soul Train 10885 (RCA)	CPP	79	79	
12	12	12	AIN'T GONNA BUMP NO MORE (With No Big Fat Woman)—Joe Tex (Buddy Killen), B.L. McGinty, B. Killen, Epic 8-50313	B-3	46	46	15	DO WHAT YOU WANNA DO—T Connection (Cory Wade, Alex Sadkin), T. Caokley, Dash 5032 (TK)	CPP			
☆	15	6	LIFE IN THE FAST LANE—Eagles (Bill Szymczyk), J. Walsh, D. Henley, G. Frey, Asylum 45403	WBM	☆	64		EASY—Commodores (James Carmichael, Commodores), L. Richie, Motown 1418		☆	92	
14	14	15	HEARD IT IN A LOVE SONG—Marshall Tucker Band (Paul Hornsby), T. Caldwell, Capricorn 0270 (Warner Bros.)	WBM	☆	60		BARRACUDA—Heart (Mike Flicker), A. Wilson, R. Fisher, N. Wilson, Portrait/CBS 6-70004		☆		
☆	18	7	LOOKS LIKE WE MADE IT—Barry Manilow (Ron Dante, Barry Manilow), R. Kerr, W. Jennings, Arista 0244	ALM	49	29	14	HELLO STRANGER—Yvonne Elliman (Freddie Perren for Grand Slam Prod.), B. Lewis, RSO 871 (Polydor)	WBM	☆		NEW ENTRY
☆	20	6	DA DOO RON RON—Shaun Cassidy (Michael Lloyd), J. Barry, P. Spector, E. Greenwich, Warner/Curb 8365	CPP	☆	62	4	AMARILLO—Neil Sedaka (George Martin), N. Sedaka, H. Greenfield, Elektra 45406	WBM	☆		NEW ENTRY
			MARGARITAVILLE—Jimmy Buffett ... ABC 12254					JUST A SONG BEFORE I GO—... & Nash		☆		NEW ENTRY
					91	92		I CAN GIVE YOU LOVE MUNDO EARWOOD/True 101				2
					92	—		PLEASE JAMES NAT STUCKEY/MCA 40693				1
					93	95		FOOL JOHN WESLEY RYLES/ABC Dot DOA 17679				2
					94	—		VITAMIN L MARY KAY PLACE AS LORETTA HAGGERS/ Columbia 3 10510				1
					95	87		WORLD FAMOUS PARADISE INN BUCK OWENS/ Warner Bros. WBS 8316				7
					96	97		THE REASON WHY I'M HERE JONI LEE/MCA 40687				

Here "Lucille" tops the Country Singles Chart in *Record World* and two months later takes a high place in *Billboard*'s Hot 100 pop chart.

Back on Top   Whether you're solo or still with a group, you should be able to return to the top of the roller coaster if you have the talent and persistence and treat the down times with business savvy. I recovered from my slump not only because I formulated a good game plan, but because I continued to spend dollars on independent publicity people to keep my name alive in the newspapers and trades. The mistake most artists make when they see their careers slipping is to cut out the expense of publicity and promotion, thinking it superfluous. On the contrary, it's most important to maintain your profile, even if it's at the expense of your life-style. Fly coach. Rent one car, not two. Carry two changes of costume, not six, but make them as stunning as the clothes you wore when you were on top. Looking successful provides some of the thrust that will help carry you back to the top.

To deal with the dynamics of the music business, you must understand that if a pop artist's fortune is like a roller coaster, the coaster mutates every few years. The record buyers are largely teenagers. As they grow up their concerns change until they get their careers organized and go back to the music they liked when they were younger. A good example is the return to the early sixties street rock in the Phil Spector-meets-Bob Dylan-ish music of Bruce Springsteen and Graham Parker, which emerged in the mid-seventies, or the return in the late seventies to the mid-sixties Mersey beat sound with new-wave rock. For you, this means you can trade on the nostalgia element of your past hits when you're making a comeback with new music. This bolstered my emergence as a solo artist. People wanted to hear all the old First Edition hits. Fortunately, there's another aspect in your favor in climbing back to the top. That is, people don't remember the stiffs, the releases that flopped. They only remember the hits. Such was the case when I began hitting again. It was as though I'd just returned from a vacation, not a slump. People didn't ask about all the records released since the First Edition's "Heed the Call." They asked, "Why haven't you been recording? We missed you. . . ." They knew nothing of the dozen stiffs I had had during my "hiatus."

Retiring   Eventually, after riding the undulations and permutations of the music scene, the time will come when you decide to retire from active performing. You may continue recording but drop touring out of a desire to stay home with your family or pursue other interests. Or, you may tire of playing music. Hopefully, you'll be able to quit when you want to rather than when the business and the audiences tell you you're through; that is, when your records and concert tickets don't sell. Like an athlete, a pop star has a certain few peak years. If you've planned for it, by developing avenues off the road that keep you in the same income bracket, it won't be a tragic experience. Peter Asher used to be half of Peter and Gordon, for instance. Now he produces James Taylor and Linda Ronstadt. Similarly, Spencer ("Gimme Some Lovin' ") Davis became Island Records' director of artist relations.

If you don't care to find a job within the industry, you may still trade on your name, for success in one field gives you validity in others. This means you wouldn't have to struggle with bit parts if you went into acting; you could contend for leading roles.

No matter how long you stay in the limelight, one of the most satisfying aspects of stardom is being in a position to help other talents up. Behind every success lie innumerable nameless people who devote themselves to cultivating talent that only they may recognize. They understand the importance of getting that talent heard. For them, it's a sort of rebirth and affirmation of their own lives' validity. Their reward is the pleasure they experience every time they hear that talent. I learned a lot from Kirby Stone ("Baubles, Bangles, and Beads," etc.) when the Bobby Doyle Trio toured with him. For instance, Stone taught me that jokes that exclude the audience aren't funny. And he bothered to explain things. "You don't get up, do fourteen songs, and say 'Good night,' " he once said. "The show has to have some kind of pace to it and take people somewhere if it is to satisfy them." I, in turn, often sit down with younger musicians I work with, such as Vocal Point. I explain my reasons for doing certain things in my show and elaborate on my ideas about the music business.

I sometimes offer more than philosophy, however. In 1969, I discovered a country-rock group in Linden, Texas, which was originally called Felicity ("happiness" in Spanish) and then Shiloh. After paying their way to L.A., I put them up at my ranch while I produced an album for them on my Jolly Rogers Records. Unfortunately—or fortunately—Shiloh disbanded before the record's release. Some of the members joined Linda Ronstadt's backing band, while steel guitarist Al Perkins joined Steven Stills' Manassas. As it happened, Ronstadt's band coalesced and Shiloh's ex-drummer, Don Henley, came to me. Would I, he wanted to know, give up the rights to his music publishing? He was forming a group called the Eagles and needed his publishing as a part of the band's record deal and partnership agreement. Never one to exploit people, to sit with the rights to their work in hopes that I'd eventually profit from their good fortune, I gave him a full release. Furthermore, I went to ASCAP at the Eagles' behest and helped win them a $10,000 advance on performance royalties.

If I ever felt a twinge of sickness over giving away such a gold mine—and

Tommy Smothers, seen *(above)* rehearsing with me for an appearance on "Rollin'," was one of several friends behind my success. Another was John Davidson, *(left, below)* who used his leverage with "The Tonight Show" in December 1976 to get me on as his guest. Other friends in this photo taken after my marriage to Marianne Gordon are Glen Campbell and John Denver.

I never have—then I would only have to recall all that Tommy Smothers did for me and the First Edition.

I won't take credit for the Eagles' success. But I will say that I get a profoundly good feeling when I sing Henley's "Desperado" in my show. The lasting thrill of being a success in the music business lies in knowing you have been at least partly responsible for the creation of great music, music that gives so many people pleasure, inspiration, meaning. It matters little in the end whether that music is your own or someone else's. It's everyone's.

A union performance contract form used primarily for club, dance and party work.

UNION COPY

Contract Blank

AMERICAN FEDERATION OF MUSICIANS
OF THE UNITED STATES AND CANADA
MUSICIANS UNION LOCAL 47, LOS ANGELES, CALIFORNIA
817 VINE STREET, LOS ANGELES, CALIFORNIA, 90038

THIS CONTRACT for the personal services of musicians, made this_____day of_____, 19____.
between the undersigned employer (hereinafter called the "employer") and_____musicians
(hereinafter called "employees").
                                                    (number of musicians, including the Leader)

The employer engages the employees as musicians severally on the terms and conditions below, **and as further specified on the reverse side.** The leader represents that the musicians already designated have agreed to be bound by said terms and conditions. The employer agrees that musicians may be selected by the leader. Each employee yet to be chosen shall be so bound by said terms and conditions upon agreeing to accept his employment. Each musician may enforce this agreement.

The employees severally agree to render collectively to the employer services as musicians in the orchestra under the leadership of (Please Print)_____as follows:

Print Name of Place of Engagement_____

Print Address of Place of Engagement_____

DURATION OF ENGAGEMENT
(Mark "X" in ONE box only.)

INDEFINITE: Commencing_____
                                        (date)

TERM: Commencing_____ To and including_____
                        (date)   (date)

No. of Days per week_____, Specify each day_____

Hours (Specify starting and ending time)_____

Print Type of Engagement_____
                (specify whether night club, theatrical, hotel, lounge, ballroom, etc.)

WAGES* AGREED UPON PER WEEK...................... $ _____
made payable by separate check(s) to the musician(s) in accordance with the
schedule of wages indicated below and Paragraph 9 on the reverse side hereof.

TOTAL WEEKLY AFM & EPW PENSION FUND CONTRIBUTIONS.......... $ _____
made payable by separate check to AFM & EPW Fund each time wages are paid.

TOTAL WEEKLY HEALTH AND WELFARE CONTRIBUTIONS .... $ _____
made payable by separate check to the Musicians and Employers H & W Fund each
time wages are paid.

* This wage includes expenses agreed to be reimbursed by the employer in accordance with the attached schedule, or a schedule to be furnished to the employer on or before the date of engagement.

To be paid_____
                (Specify when Wages, Pensions and H & W Fund payments are to be made)

Upon request by the Musicians' Union Local 47, or the American Federation of Musicians, the employer shall make a security cash deposit with the Treasurer of Musicians' Union Local 47 in the amount of $_____, in accordance with Paragraph 14 on the reverse side hereof.

Print Employee's Name (As on Social Security Card)			Local Union No.	Social Security No.	Wages	E.P.W. Fund	H & W Fund
Last	First	Initial					
1 :(Leader)							
2							
3							
4							
5							
6							
7							
8							

(Continue on Reverse Side)

Print Employer's Name (Title)	Print Leader's Name Local No.
X	X
Authorized Signature Date	Leader's Signature Date
Print Street Address	Print Street Address
City State Phone	City State Phone

X

Approved A.F. of M. Booking Agent   Authorized Signature   Phone

Note—Additional Terms on Reverse Side

FORM B-28 Cal. (47)   (OVER)   11

NEW YEAR'S EVE DOUBLE SCALE

A sample publishing contract for one or several song(s).

<u>ROYALTY AGREEMENT</u>

AGREEMENT made and entered into the day and year indicated on the last page hereof by and between the undersigned lyricist(s) and/or composer(s) and/or arranger(s) (hereinafter referred to jointly and/or severally as "Writer"), and the undersigned publisher (hereinafter referred to as "Publisher").

<u>W I T N E S S E T H :</u>

WHEREAS, Writer has written and/or composed and/or arranged the composition(s) set forth on schedule A annexed hereto and made part hereof (each is hereinafter referred to as "the composition").

NOW, therefore, in consideration of the sum of One ($1.00) dollar and other good and valuable consideration, in hand paid to each of the undersigned at or before the ensealing and delivery of these presents, receipt whereof is hereby mutually acknowledged, it is agreed:

1. Writer represents and warrants that he is the sole lyricist and/or composer and/or arranger of the composition; that said composition and/or arrangement is his own original work and creation (except such part thereof as is taken from the public domain) and is not a copy of any other copyrighted work; that he has not sold, assigned, leased, licensed or in any manner disposed of or encumbered the rights herein granted to Publisher; and that he has the right to enter into this agreement. Writer agrees to indemnify and hold Publisher harmless from all loss, liability, damages and expenses by reason of breach of said representations and warranties.

2. Writer hereby sells, assigns, transfers and sets over unto Publisher the composition and each and every arrangement, adaptation and version thereof, together with the universe-wide copyright thereof, and the right to secure copyright therein throughout the entire universe, and all rights of whatsoever nature, both legal and equitable therein thereto and thereunder, including but not limited to the sole and exclusive universe-wide publication, mechanical instrument, electrical transcription, video cassette and recording, and motion picture, television and CATV synchronization rights, commercial rights, and the right of public performance for profit by any and all means, and through any and all media, and the right to arrange and adapt and all other rights now known or here-after to become known.

3. In consideration for and in full payment of the aforesaid sale, Publisher hereby agrees to pay to Writer the royalties set forth on the royalty schedule annexed hereto and made part hereof with respect to the composition.

4. The term "Writer" used herein is deemed to mean all of the undersigned persons and any and all royalties herein provided to be paid to the Writer shall be paid jointly to the said persons if there be more than one, and shall be divided equally among them unless otherwise indicated on schedule A. The term "Publisher" used herein is deemed to mean only the signatory Publisher excluding all affiliates and subpublishers.

5. Publisher agrees that within sixty (60) days after the last days of June and December in each year it will prepare and furnish state-ments showing any royalties which may become payable hereunder, and each such statement shall be accompanied by a check or checks in payment of any and all sums shown to be due thereby. Payments shall not be furnished until at least ten ($10.00) dollars shall become payable. Publisher may combine accounts with Writer.

6.   Writer shall deliver a lead sheet of the composition to the Publisher promptly after the execution and delivery of this agreement. If Writer fails to do so, the cost to Publisher of notating the composition shall be deducted from royalties payable to Writer hereunder.

7.   Writer grants Publisher the right to use his name, photograph, likeness, facsimile signature and biographical material in, on and in connection with publications, recordings and advertisements of, containing or relating to the composition.

8.   Publisher may destroy excess inventory of the composition.

9.   Writer hereby assigns to Publisher the United States renewal copyright and all extensions and longer or different terms of copyright which may be provided by law in and to the composition and Writer hereby authorizes and empowers Publisher to renew such copyright, pursuant to law in the name of Writer and to execute and deliver to Publisher such formal written assignment thereof, as may be required by Publisher, subject to the terms of this agreement.

10.   Writer hereby consents to the assignment of this agreement and/or the composition and/or the copyright thereof, or any and all of the rights therein by Publisher, subject, however to the terms hereof and payment of the royalties herein specified.

11.   This agreement is binding upon the parties hereto and their respective personal representatives, successors and assigns.

IN WITNESS WHEREOF, Writer has hereunto set his hand and seal and Publisher has caused these presents to be signed by its duly authorized officer, the   day of   197 .

_____(L.S.)
Writer

Publisher _____

_____
Address

By_____

_____
Social Security Number

_____(L.S.)
Writer

_____
Address

_____
Social Security Number

Form #73-2/74   -2-

SCHEDULE A

Title of Composition(s):

Share of royalties:

WRITER: SHARE:

_____   _____

_____   _____

_____   _____

_____   _____

ROYALTY SCHEDULE

(a) Five (5¢) cents per copy for each and every
    regular pianoforte copy published and sold
    by and paid for to Publisher in the United
    States and Canada.

(b) Ten (10%) percent of all net sums actually
    received upon each and every printed copy
    of each and every arrangement and edition
    other than the regular pianoforte edition,
    published and sold and paid for to Publisher
    in the United States and Canada, except that
    in the event that the composition shall be
    used or caused to be used in whole or in part
    in conjunction with one or more other musical
    compositions in a folio or album, Writer shall
    be entitled to receive that proportion of ten
    (10%) percent of all net sums actually received
    from such publication which the composition
    shall bear to the total number of copyrighted
    or royalty-bearing works contained in such
    folio or album.

(c) Publisher shall not be required to pay royalties on
    professional and complimentary copies and records
    or copies and records which are distributed for
    exploitation purposes.

(d) Fifty (50%) percent of all net sums actually
    received by Publisher from the licensing of
    mechanical instrument, electrical transcription,
    motion picture and television synchronization
    rights and all other rights (including the use
    thereof in song lyric folios or magazines) now
    known or hereafter to become known in the United
    States and Canada, except that Writer shall not
    be entitled to receive or share in any sum or sums
    which Publisher may receive from ASCAP or BMI, (as
    the case may be) or from any other performance
    right society throughout the world which pays a
    share of performance fees directly to authors and
    composers.

(e) If the respective performance right society shall
    cease to operate, Publisher shall administer the
    performance rights in the composition and shall
    pay Writer the percentage thereof indicated in
    (d) above.

(f) If and when publication or use of the composition
    is made outside of the United States and Canada,
    Publisher shall pay to Writer fifty (50%) percent
    of all net sums actually received by Publisher
    from sales and uses (except performance fees re-
    ferred to in (d) above), all subject to deduction
    for foreign income and other taxes required to be
    withheld.

An extract of terms for a typical new artists' record contract.

———————————————————————————

MASTER PURCHASE DATA BRIEF

ARTIST:____The Raw Talents_____

1. PARTIES

Company Notice Address: Notice and Payments To:

Major Records   Formidable Management
800 6th Ave   6511 Sunset Boulevard
New York, New York 10019   Hollywood, California 90028

                                    cc: Johnson & Johnson, Esqs.
                                           Beverly Hills, California 90069

2. DATE OF CONTRACT:____March 3, 1977_____

    a. Commencement of Initial Period____March 3, 1977_____

    b. Term____one year + 4 one-year options_____

    c. Exercise of Options:

      _____Notice to Termination   XX___Notice to Extend
    Time for Notice:__30__ days prior to expiration of current period.

3. TERRITORY:____World_____

4. RECORDING OBLIGATIONS/COSTS: Costs recoupable:____yes_

    a. *Record Company Commitment*   *Artist Maximum Obligation*

Initial Period: 1 LP   2 lp's or 22 masters per contract
                                           year

Option Years: 1 LP per option year

b. Master Purchase Price (Recoupable)

	SINGLE	ALBUM	MASTER*

Initial Period:

First Option:

Second Option: see "ADVANCES"

Third Option:

Fourth Option:

* Purchase price reduced by stated amount for each master previously purchased by Company and embodied in a newly delivered album or single.

c. Union scale may be paid in lieu of *requesting* minimum masters for any period (in the event there is no release obligation):

XX   yes   _____no   _____not expressly stated

d. Payment:_____50% on commencement of recording and 50% within 10 days of receipt of tapes

                              -OR-

_____100% within 10 days of receipt of tapes

Includes all recording costs (without limitation, studios, musicians, individual producers fees, etc.)

5. Release Obligations: All LP's recorded shall be released within 150 days after our request for same.

6. Advances, Guarantees, Lumpsum payments, etc.

Minimum scale and recording costs per session.

Individual producer's fees are subject to mutual agreement regarding producer and Company's approval of fee. N.B. No more than 50% of individual producer's fee shall be payable prior to delivery of any master.

_____100%_____recoupable

7. Tour Shortfall: NONE

7a. Promotion Obligation: NONE

_____recoupable

8. Recording Budget: Approval shall not be unreasonable withheld on a budget of $50,000.- per LP or $5,000.- per master maximum.

9. Free Goods: singles: 3 for 10 purchased

    lp's and tapes: 2 for 10 purchased

10. Label Designation: In U.S. during Term initial release on "top pop"

11. Royalties:

    Singles: Producer:__10__ % of____retail____price of_90_ % of records sold.

    Albums: Producer:__10__ % of____retail____price of_100_ % of records sold.

    Company Tape:_____full album rate_____

    Step Up Provision:

    Step Up Trigger_175,000_ ,__1__ % increase above ___175,000___ lps and

    __75,000__ tapes.

    Second Trigger_350,000_ ,__1__ % increase above___350,000___ lps and

    _150,000_ tapes.

    Budget____50% net_____   Foreign____7% on 100% retail_____

    Record Club____50% net_____   Premiums____50% net_____

    Direct Mail____50% net_____   Key Outlet Marketing____50% net___

    Other____flat fee licenses: 50% net - see Sp. Provs._____

12. Container Charge (Packaging Deduction):

    10%_ Single fold   15%_ Double fold   25%_ Tape

    XX___ Foreign (Standard)

13. Mechanical Rates:

    statutory_____per controlled composition   _____maximum per master

    statutory X_2___ maximum per single   _____current Harry Fox rates

    statutory X_10__ maximum per album

    a. Right to deduct excess rates from royalties: XX___ yes _____no

14. Artist union affiliation:

John Guitar	Bob Piano	Sam Singer
AFM/Local 402	AFM/Local 202	AFTRA membership
074–37–2876	376–89–7654	applied for/786–23–4325

Mary Bass	Tommy Drums	
AFM/local 402	AFM/local 802	
543–56–3478	876–56–3456	

15.   Special Provisions:

a)   If, at our option, a 2nd LP is requested in Initial Period, the Initial Period shall be deemed to be extended to June 2, 1977 for a total Initial Period of 15 months.

b)   In the event a "quad" mix is requested for any recording a reasonable cost therefor, not to exceed $2000.- per LP, may be charged against Producer's royalty account as a recording cost.

c)   Producer has right of first refusal for post-production work on all masters for 3 years after date of delivery. Producer shall receive FULL ROYALTY on all masters embodying post-production work.

d)   In U.S. during Term no more than 3 masters may be coupled without Producer's prior written consent. Additionally, no one master may be coupled more than 3 times during any Contract Year in U.S. during Term.

e)   No BUDGET release in U.S. during Term until 1 year after initial full price release.

f)   *Reserves* shall be liquidated within 2 years after date first withheld.

g)   Flat fee license uses limited to 3 per Contract Year in U.S. during Term without Producer's consent.

h) Individual producer shall be engaged by Producer subject to Company's approval.

i)   Re: CONTROLLED COMPOSITIONS Deduction of excess rates on Controlled Compositions allowed *provided* that Company notifies Producer in writing of any failure* to comply with the above rates and that Producer has 30 days after receipt of notice to cure such failure.

j)   Artwork - Consultation with Producer for album artwork during Term in U.S. Company's approval of Producer's artwork concept proposals that would entail extraordinary initial or manufacturing costs will be conditional upon Producer's agreement that all or part of the excess costs shall be an advance against royalties and recoupable and/or deductible from same. Company's decision on artwork shall be final and binding.

---

*or refusal

An extract from a performance contract rider.

Rider to agreement between KENNY ROGERS PRODUCTIONS f/s/o KENNY ROGERS, herein referred to as ARTIST, and_____, (herein referred to as BUYER) dated_____for a performance on_____.

A. BUYER understands that ARTIST <u>cannot perform</u> without all of the following items, and that the failure to provide any of these could result in BUYER being in default of this contract.

Furthermore, the items requested below are necessary in order that ARTIST can provide the best possible show for the BUYER. If BUYER has any questions, or cannot for some reason provide any of the following, he should contact the Personal Manager of KENNY ROGERS IMMEDIATELY:

> Ken Kragen, Personal Manager
> Gary A. Shaw (Garth) Road Manager
> Management Three
> 9744 Wilshire Blvd.
> Beverly Hills, California 90212
> (213) 550-7100

B. BUYER agrees to furnish the following:

1. A raised performance area (stage) which is a minimum of twenty (20') feet deep and thirty (30') feet wide. In any room where there is no stage, a platform which is at least four (4') feet high and of the dimensions given above shall be provided.

2. One eight (8') foot by eight (8') foot riser platform for the drummer to be two (2') feet in height. Riser must be of solid construction, reinforced underneath. Top of riser must be covered with carpet.

Drum riser should be assembled and positioned at center stage, approximately ten (10') feet from stage front prior to arrival of ARTIST'S equipment.

3. Two kitchen type bar stools with rungs which are thirty
    (30") inches high, and with no back.

4. A concert or Baby Grand piano (Steinway, Yamaha, or
    Baldwin are preferable) tuned on the day of the show to
    A-440 pitch.

5. A Hammond B-3 organ with Leslie Type 122 speaker. In
    the event that a B-3 is not available, the only
    substitutes which will be accepted are a C-3, an A-100,
    or an A-105. Organ and leslie must have proper connect-
    ing cables. Music stand MUST be removed from organ.

6. A truck for the transportation of ARTIST'S equipment to
    and from airport (a twelve (12') foot U-Haul or Ryder
    type truck with loading ramp is best suited) at time
    most convenient to road manager. Two men will be needed
    with the truck. Also, there should be direct access to
    the stage for unloading and reloading of said truck.

7. ARTIST'S road manager will need the assistance of not
    less than three (3) stage hands upon arrival to assist
    in unloading and set-up of equipment. Three (3) men
    will also be needed at the end of the engagement for
    breakdown and reloading. Set-up and breakdown will each
    take about three (3) hours. The BUYER'S electrician,
    sound and light technicians, should be available through-
    out set-up.

8. BUYER agrees that auditorium, hall, theatre, or club in
    which show is held shall not be open to the public prior
    to one (1) hour before show time. Further, said hall,
    club, etc. shall be available to ARTIST'S road manager
    for technical set-up at least five (5) hours prior to
    show time.

9. Two separate dressing rooms with mirrors, soap, sinks,
    and twelve (12) towels. Dressing rooms should be stocked
    with ice, Cokes, and beer at no cost to ARTIST. Keys
    shall be provided and/or a security guard will watch the
    dressing rooms at all times. ARTIST shall not be required
    to share these rooms with any other performers.

10. BUYER recognizes that ARTIST presents a show, not a
    dance set, and there will be NO DANCING DURING THE
    PERFORMANCE.

PAGE 2

C. LIGHTS

1. Two (2) follow spot lights and two (2) expierenced oper-
    ators. The spots should be Super-Trouper or Trouper,
    arc-type lights (incandescent spot lights are not accept-
    able). A five or six color boom shall be fitted to the
    light for color changes. A working iris and doser must
    also be mounted onto the light. The lamps shall be
    coloured with Roscolene color media or equivalent as
    follows:

    Frame #1 819 (very light red)
          2   817 (amber)
          3   857 (blue)
          4   842 (lavender)
          5   826 (pink)
          6   838 (magenta) optional

2. A professionally complete lighting system shall be pro-
    vided at the sole cost of BUYER. A crew to focus and
    operate same shall be available at load-in to assist in
    focus, as well as run show.

    a. In clubs or permanent theatre situations the follow-
        ing is considered minimimly acceptable, but not
        limited to:

        22 back lights
        16 side lights (8 per side)
        18 channels of dimming
        (see light plot enclosed for color and circuits required.)

    b. In arena, concert hall, and fair concerts, the follow-
        ing portable lighting system is considered miniumly
        acceptable, but not limited to:

        24 back lights
        24 side lights (12 per side)
        24 channels of dimming
        (see light plot enclosed for color and circuits required.)

        BUYER is to provide at his sole cost, all colour media
        herein specified or indicated on the enclosed light plots.

3. A double muff headset and noise cancelling microphone
    intercom system shall be provided. A minimum of five (5)
    stations which are 2 followspots, 1 house lights, 1 board
    operator, and 1 for road manager.

4. It is to be expressly understood that any stock lighting,
    stage or sound equipment at the facility is available to the
    ARTIST, if he deems it applicable to his needs, even beyond
    the requirements herein specified, at sole cost of BUYER.

D.   SOUND

This sound specification is for the express purpose of providing ARTIST with neccessary technical support and is <u>essential</u>
to the performance.

1.   MICROPHONES: Professional quality microphones <u>without</u>
     switches shall be provided. Microphones with switches,
     shiny finish, or other than recognized professional stage
     microphones shall not be acceptable. Vocal mics should
     be equal to or consist of Shure SM57, SM58, SM54, etc.

     Instrument mics shall fall under the same qualifications
     as vocal mics, and can be expanded to include SM56,
     AKG D-1000E, etc. If direct boxes are used on amps.,
     they should be equiped with ground lift switches, and the
     amplifiers should be powered from the same outlet which
     powers the sound system to avoid shock and hum loops.

2.   MONITERS: Shall be units which are designed for use as
     stage moniters. Stereo speakers are not acceptable, as
     well as' semi-professional equipment such as Peavey, Kustom,
     Acoustic, or similar units. Acceptable types are Altec
     1221, etc., or cabinets with known quality components
     such as JBL or Altec. In addition, two (2) side-fill
     moniters shall be provided.

     The moniter mixer shall be in sight of ARTIST to either
     side of the stage, out of view of the audience. The
     moniter mix board shall be of professional quality and
     accept low impedance mic inputs. Shure SR101, Yamaha
     PM400, PM430, PM700, etc. consoles are acceptable.

3.   HOUSE SYSTEM: The house system shall consist of professional
     horns, drivers, bass cabinets, and woofers, utilizing JBL,
     Altec, etc. The characteristics of the house system shall
     be such that there is smooth, even distribution of the pro-
     gram to all paying seats. Semi-professional equipment such
     as Peavey, Kustom, Acoustic, Sunn, etc. is not acceptable.

     The house system shall be powered by "laboratory-grade"
     power amplifiers such as Phase Linear, Crown, Yamaha, SAE,
     etc. in sufficient quantity to achieve the required sound
     level for the room or arena being played.

     House console shall be a professional live mixdown console
     designed for this use and accepting low impedance mic
     inputs.   Each input channel shall have at least low and
     high frequency EQ controls, input pad, and reverb or an
     effects or echo buss. Acceptable types are Yamaha PM1000
     or similar. Talkback facilities from the house console to
     the moniter system are desireable.

E. ARTIST is to be afforded sole star billing in not less than 100% size type, and prominence in all advertising, lights, displays, and programs, and in general, all forms of advertising and publicity under control of local promoter.

F. Where applicable, BUYER agrees to furnish ARTIST or ARTIST'S representative, by intermission, with a certified box office statement, together with all unsold tickets for count and verification of gross box office receipts.

G. ARTIST shall have the right to cancel the engagement without liability, upon written notice to the BUYER, not less than thirty (30) days prior to the date of the performance, in the event ARTIST'S services are needed in a motion picture, a television series, or a television special.

H. ARTIST will have approval over opening or supporting acts.

I. BUYER warrants that he or she is of legal age and has the right to enter into this contract.

J. Artist shall not be available for any interviews, promotional or public appearances unless these have been cleared in advance through the artist's manager or press representative (Guy Thomas/Rogers and Cowan, Inc./213-275-4581/9665 Wilshire Blvd. Beverly Hills, California 90210).

K. Exhibits 1 and 2 attached are incorporated as part of this rider. Exhibit 3 is a checklist which Buyer should utilize.

ACCEPTED AND AGREED BY:

_____   _____
BUYER   ARTIST

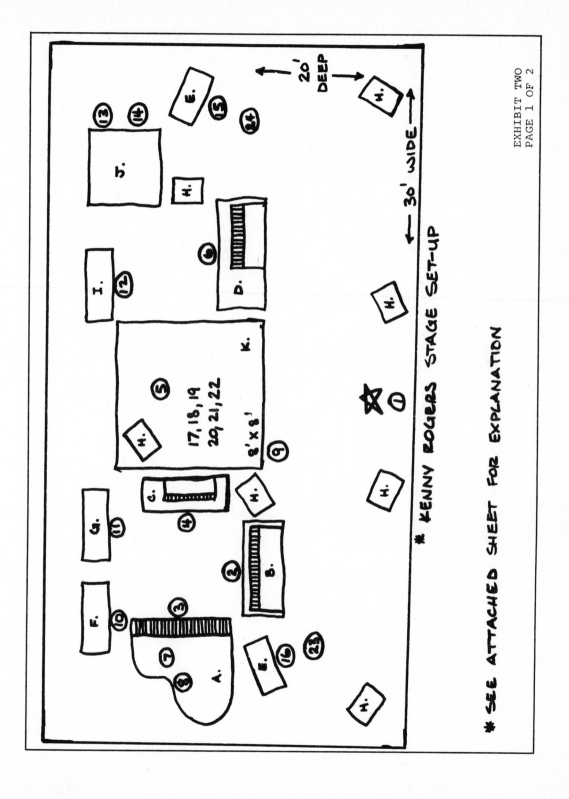

* KENNY ROGERS STAGE SET-UP

* SEE ATTACHED SHEET FOR EXPLANATION

MICROPHONES:

1. Kenny/vocal/straight stand
2. Vocal/boom ⎫
3. Vocal/boom ⎬ may be y'd
4. Vocal/boom ⎭
5. Vocal/boom
6. Vocal/boom
7. Piano ⎫
8. Piano ⎭ may be y'd
9. Acoustic guitar/straight stand
10. Electric piano/string ensemble
11. Clavinet/arp oddessy
12. Bass
13. Leslie ⎫ high
14. Leslie ⎭ low   may be y'd
15. Guitar
16. Guitar
17. Kick drum
18. Snare/hi-hat
19. Overhead ⎫
20. Overhead ⎭ may be y'd
21. Rack toms (optional)
22. Floor toms (optional)
23. Vocal
24. Vocal

STAGE SET-UP:

A. Grand piano
B. Electric piano/string ensemble*
C. Clavinet/Arp oddessy*
D. Hammond B-3/Rhodes keyboard bass
E. Guitar amps.
F. Electric piano/string amp.
G. Clavinet/oddessy amp.
H. Stage moniters (minimum of FIVE)
I. Bass amp.
J. Leslie
K. Drum riser (8' by 8')

*Where amps. are not mic'd,
string ensemble & Arp oddessy
MUST run direct.

A twenty-four (24) channel board is desireable, but a sixteen (16)
channel board is the MINIMUM that will be accepted for large concerts.
In clubs of 500 seats or less, the microphone complement can be reduced to include Grand piano, electric piano, *string ensemble, *Arp
oddessy, acoustic guitar, keyboard bass, kick drum, and vocals (this
is also what must be heard in the moniters). All mics which are y'd
must be of the same kind.

POWER REQUIREMENTS:

Band: Will need three (3) 20amp, 110v circuits or two (2) 30amp,
       110v circuits with eight (8) outlets on each side of the
       stage, with a voltage drop of no more than 5%.

Sound: The power drop of the sound system should be capable of
        delivering a total of 100amps of 110 volt power.

Lights: Will need two (2) 30amp, 110v circuits for spotlights,
         and a 200amp, 220v circuit for stage lighting.

Index

221